UNDERSTANDING THE POLICY PROCESS

Analysing welfare policy and practice

John Hudson and Stuart Lowe

First published in Great Britain in June 2004 by

The Policy Press
University of Bristol
Fourth Floor, Beacon House
Queen's Road
Bristol BS8 1QU
UK

Tel +44 (0)117 331 4054
Fax +44 (0)117 331 4093
e-mail tpp-info@bristol.ac.uk
www.policypress.org.uk

British Library Cataloguing in Publication Data
A catalogue record for this book is available from the British Library.

Library of Congress Cataloging-in-Publication Data
A catalog record for this book has been requested.

ISBN 1 86134 540 2 paperback

A hardcover version of this book is also available

John Hudson is Lecturer in Social Policy and **Stuart Lowe** is Senior Lecturer in Social Policy, both in the Department of Social Policy and Social Work, University of York, UK.

The right of John Hudson and Stuart Lowe to be identified as authors of this work has been asserted by them in accordance with the 1988 Copyright, Designs and Patents Act.

The statements and opinions contained within this publication are solely those of the authors and not of The University of Bristol, The Policy Press or the Social Policy Association. The University of Bristol, The Policy Press and the Social Policy Association disclaim responsibility for any injury to persons or property resulting from any material published in this publication.

The Policy Press works to counter discrimination on grounds of gender, race, disability, age and sexuality.

Cover design by Qube Design Associates, Bristol.
Front cover: photograph kindly supplied by Associated Press Ltd.
Printed and bound in Great Britain by Hobbs the Printers Ltd, Southampton.

UNDERSTANDING THE POLICY PROCESS

Other titles in the series

Contents

Detailed contents

List of tables, figures and boxes

Tables

Figures

Boxes

Preface

This book arose from a number of modules we jointly teach in the Department of Social Policy and Social Work at the University of York: two undergraduate modules (Analysing Welfare Policy and Advanced Policy Analysis) and a postgraduate module (Policy Analysis). Teaching as we do in a social policy department, we felt there was a gap in the literature in terms of a single text that brings to life the difficult and complex world of policy making while also concerning itself with the subject matter of the welfare state.

The end product here is unlikely to satisfy everyone and is by no means comprehensive (some schools of thought have necessarily been overlooked or given scant attention), but we hope that what we have lost in breadth of coverage we have made up for in terms of bringing this material to life. Often the policy process material is presented in a very dry and abstract manner and can make teaching in this area a challenge. Much of the material in the book has been tried out in our lecture programmes and feedback from successive student groups has helped us to think creatively about how to present the literature in an accessible way without sacrificing the analytic insight of the key theoretical and conceptual tools in the policy analysis armoury.

Our thanks go to the students who have offered useful feedback on our teaching in this field and challenged us towards greater clarity. Special thanks also go to a number of colleagues who have provided support and inspiration in this area, notably Mark Evans (Department of Politics, University of York), Gyu-Jin Hwang (School of Public Policy, University of Birmingham), Lisa O'Malley (Centre for Housing Policy, University of York) and Michael Hill (Department of Politics, Goldsmiths College, University of London). Thanks also to the three anonymous referees who gave very helpful comments on the first draft of the text and helped us to clarify our thoughts and approach in key areas. Any mistakes, omissions or errors, however, remain our own.

We would also like to take this opportunity to thank our commissioning editor, Dawn Rushen of The Policy Press, for being so supportive and accommodating. We are very grateful to our family and friends for their forbearance because writing a book of this type inevitably spills over into weekends, evenings and even holidays. Most of all we wish to thank our respective partners Louise and Sue who have offered constant support despite their own hectic careers.

Introduction: what is policy analysis?

Introduction

The attacks on the World Trade Centre and the Pentagon on September 11th 2001 proved beyond a shadow of a doubt that we live in a truly interconnected global era. Small cells of terrorists dotted around the world and connected to each other through the Internet and mobile phones killed 3,000 people and plunged the most powerful nation in the world – and its economy – into crisis. Within moments of the first plane hitting the World Trade Centre, news of the tragedy was being reported around the globe, and by the time the first tower fell millions of people from all around Earth were watching events unfolding on their television screens. More recently, the SARS outbreak – which appeared to originate from only a few carriers of the virus, possibly even just one person – also demonstrated the fragility and vulnerability of the modern worldwide economic order. Power supplies have been cut in American cities as networks falter and the whole of Italy lost its electricity supply in a recent incident involving one tree falling on a power cable! Electronic viruses like MyDoom spread at the speed of light through the Internet, halting communication and crashing computer systems. The watchwords of all these events are **speed**, **communication**, **networks**, **interdependency** and **risk**.

These examples are only the dark side of a much larger story, a story with a narrative encompassing literally the whole world and everyone in it. **Globalisation** is now such a commonplace part of everyday life that, to use sociological jargon, it is 'embedded' in society. Our shirts and trainers are made in Vietnam and Bangladesh; our supermarket flowers are grown in Kenya; our telephone queries are answered from call centres in Delhi; we see live broadcasts of solo yachtswomen from the South Atlantic (and can e-mail them personally). Who can doubt any longer that we live on a planet in which we interact on a daily basis, even hourly, as part of our normal routine, with people we have never seen, know next to nothing about, and who live thousands of miles away? These types of interaction were unimaginable even a few years ago.

The consequences of globalisation do not stop at what Giddens (1999) calls 'the personal pole', but impact on every aspect of society including the political system and how it is organised and managed. 'Politics' sometimes seems to be overwhelmed by the velocity of the global economy, with huge corporations straddling the world and billions of dollars hurtling around the globe at the speed of light. Against this awesome economic power, the old-fashioned nation state might seem almost to be a relic from the 19th and 20th centuries. We, however, think that this is not the case. Indeed, most of this book is based around explaining how and why politics and political institutions matter. Paradoxically, global governance seems very weak – it does not match the power of the economic level – and, we argue, the role of the nation state, although very different from the past, is if anything *more* important now than it has ever been. Within this agenda, we focus particularly on how **welfare policy** is being compelled to change in the face of the new world order.

We believe these issues to be vital for our day-to-day lives, more so than where our clothes are made or the identities of people from far-flung places that we might meet in Internet chat rooms! Those things are symptoms (or, more correctly, *products*) of a deeper story. The British state has been compelled to change under the impact of globalisation in ways that are equally as dramatic as the shifts in the centres of manufacturing, and the range of new technologies are part and parcel of what has happened. Witness the new mayors and cabinets running local government, the privatised public utilities and telecommunications companies, the reformed House of Lords, the revolution in the management of the civil service, devolution of significant parts of government to Scotland and to a lesser extent Wales and London – the list is long and growing. It all adds up to the fact that the way British politics is organised and managed, how policy is made and delivered down to us, and the very nature of our society as a democratic state has radically changed since the 1980s. Gone is the unitary, centralised state managed from Whitehall; in has come a much more fragmented and more 'networked' system of governance. Indeed, we no longer talk so much of 'government' as *governance* – a much broader concept implying that the centres of power reside as much outside as inside Westminster and have been dispersed to new assemblies, new agencies, supranational organisations such as the EU and into the private and 'quasi-private' sector (Rhodes, 1996).

Policy analysis

Policy analysis is a sub-field of political science that tries to understand and build up knowledge of the whole process of public policy beginning from the big picture of the global economy through the complex issues of which policies are chosen for inclusion on the political agenda (and which are excluded), who designs them and how, finally, they are delivered in the classroom, the hospital, the homeless hostels, the prisons of Britain. The policy analysis approach was developed in its modern form in circumstances not unlike our own in the aftermath of the Second World War when the so-called 'Cold War' was just beginning. Britain's wartime leader, Winston Churchill, talked about the 'Iron Curtain' that already separated western capitalism from the communist Soviet Republic. It was a dangerous and tense era that threatened to engulf the world in the horrific consequences of nuclear war. It was a time of crisis, and policy analysis was part of the response to preparing for war and trying to understand what was going on. The person who was most responsible for thinking through the political response, indeed for inventing what he called the 'policy orientation', was an American political scientist Harold Lasswell. An indication of what was on his mind is evident in the opening words of one of his post-war books:

> The continuing crisis of national security in which we live calls for the most efficient use of manpower, facilities and resources of the American people. (Lasswell, 1951, p 3)

He goes on to say that there is a need to overcome divisions between the disciplines such as philosophy, natural science, biology and social science in this effort. He suggested that there was a growing awareness of the "policy process as a suitable object of study in its own right, primarily in the hope of improving the rationality of the flow of decisions" (1951, p 3). A number of key themes in policy analysis are thus immediately apparent:

- it is not a social science discipline in its own right but is inherently interdisciplinary;
- it has a problem-centred orientation;
- it aims to improve the rationality of decision making.

As Wildavsky (1979, p 15) defines it:

> Policy analysis is an applied sub-field whose content cannot be determined by disciplinary boundaries but by whatever appears appropriate to the circumstances of the time and the nature of the problem.

As we have seen above, Lasswell's motivation for creating a policy 'orientation' was the intelligent application of different disciplines to improve society and to defend democracy, "the special emphasis is upon the policy sciences of democracy, in which the ultimate goal is the realisation of human dignity in theory and practice" (1951, pp 14-15). His main contribution was to see public policy as a form of public education in which citizens learn how to be active in society for their own improvement and the betterment of society as a whole. In later papers, Lasswell showed that the policy sciences had an increasingly indispensable role in mediating and bringing rationality to complex

---

Box 1.1: The disciplinary focus

The physical and social sciences are divided up into different subject areas or dimensions. They are conceptual abstractions of reality that have developed in universities and help us make sense of a complex world. Disciplines provide an epistemological basis for understanding the physical and social world. The major social sciences are:

Economics	– analyses financial and economic structures
Geography	– deals with spatial structures and consequences
Political science	– focuses on the dimension of power and political institutions
Psychology	– deals with the individual psyche
Sociology	– abstracts out social relationships and structures

It is worth noting that:

- each discipline has different characteristics;
- each provides a body of literature to stop researchers and students from continually reinventing the wheel;
- these divisions should **not** be exaggerated ('reified'); they are to a large extent the product of power struggles in universities and are not theoretically pure;
- each discipline divides itself up into different specialisms. In political science we find, among others, political philosophy, international relations, public administration, comparative political systems, political history and **policy analysis**.

This book is mainly written from inside the knowledge base of political science but it also draws on the other disciplines, especially sociology. We repeat the point that it is important not to exaggerate the boundaries between them.

Note that Social Policy is **not** a discipline – the failure to recognise this is one of its main weaknesses because the findings of its research tends to be isolated, unable to feed back into the disciplinary knowledge bank. Social Policy is an interdisciplinary field of study – it draws on all the main social science disciplines – with a special focus on social problems.

decision making. He developed the idea of 'think tanks' for this purpose and set up Masters-level degree courses to train a new generation of policy analysts.

The policy cycle

In looking to develop a more systematic approach to the analysis of policies, Lasswell suggested that the policy process could be broken down into a series of consecutive stages and functions. Policy generation begins with 'intelligence' about a problem, 'promotion' of the issue, 'prescription' of what should be done, 'innovation' of a policy, 'application' of the policy in practice, 'termination' when the problem has been solved, and 'appraisal' of the impact (Lasswell, 1956). However, Lasswell did not consider these stages as 'real', in the sense that they encompassed a beginning and end point, their function being merely analytic – to help us explore different dimensions of the policy process. Rather, he was concerned with the value systems, institutions and wider social processes that shaped policy in the real world.

The policy cycle – or stages approach as this is called – should not, therefore, be thought of as a 'real-world' description but as a model or metaphor for developing knowledge about the policy process. It is a common image of how policy systems work and is useful in the evaluation of case studies. The danger, however, is that it implies a 'top-down' view of policy making in which there is a high degree of rationality. As a result, it fails to take into account the impact of front-line workers (or street-level bureaucrats); does not adequately explain how policy moves from one stage to the next; and does not easily account for the myriad and complex sets of policy networks that are at the heart of real-world politics. There is also a subtle danger that, by creating a discourse around rationality, cycles and stages, policy analysts forget the interdisciplinary foundations of the subject.

Given this danger, we have decided to largely abandon the conventional 'policy-cycle' approach in this text. There are alternative metaphors to the policy cycle that have been developed for explaining or thinking about policy and many (such as the idea that policy is made and delivered by networks) that capture more readily the complexity of the policy process and so are used throughout this book. More extreme metaphors (such as the 'garbage can' model) dispute that there are any rational boundaries on the policy process. Instead of policies leading to solutions, this explanation argues that there are a limited number of solutions, which are mixed up with problems and, moreover, the nature of this garbage changes from time to time so that there are no settled contents. Policy, it is claimed, thus emerges as solutions and problems more or less randomly collide inside the garbage can (Cohen, 1972).

The policy process as 'mess'

The most widely read and significant critique of rationality and 'stage-ism' in the policy process was made by another American political scientist, Charles Lindblom. Rejecting the notion of policy as a series of stages he saw policy as essentially *incremental*. Lindblom's (1959) famous article on the 'science of muddling through' is probably the single most widely read policy analysis paper and a key contribution to the literature. He argued that policy cannot be understood as a series of packaged stages but is essentially a process of gradual change and accretion. This early version was criticised for being a defence of the status quo, "a champion of market systems and dedicated opponent of planning" (Hogwood and Gunn, 1984, p 57). But in later work, Lindblom elaborated his ideas claiming that problems such as unemployment or damage to the natural environment were the fault of structural problems in the American constitution, its system of government and the threat posed by corporate and business interests (Lindblom, 1979). Later still he warned of 'deeper forces' at work in US politics and the growth of political inequalities (Lindblom and Woodhouse, 1993). It is thus clear that Lindblom's incrementalist approach is not reactionary, but he has maintained consistently that the essence of policy making is 'muddle'.

Our approach is eclectic: it draws on a range of different theoretical approaches, in part because we have a great deal of sympathy with perspectives that view policy making as a messy process. We think of the policy analysis literature as a tool kit with a rich repertory of concepts, which should be taken out and used depending on the issues under the microscope. To begin with, however, it is useful to have a conceptual map in order to make sense of this very diverse field of inquiry. Policy mapping is a commonly used metaphor and is intended to help steer a pathway that brings clarity to often very complex situations. There are of course different types of map and they are drawn at different scales. The gas companies have very detailed maps of where all the gas pipes are, down to individual properties. On the other hand, we can see day-by-day on the TV weather maps of whole continents, even the globe as a whole showing patterns of weather. So: different maps for different purposes. This book has an inner map based around three layers of the policy process: *macro-*, *meso-* and *micro-*levels.

Macro-level analysis

Macro-level analysis deals with the broad issues that shape the wide context in which policy is made. Parsons (1995) refers to these as 'boundary' issues. One obvious case of this is **globalisation**, particularly the impact of the worldwide economy on nation states, on the environment and weather, and on animal habitats. These are the broad parameters within which all policy is shaped and managed. Of crucial importance here is the radically changed structure of the worldwide economy which over the course of two or three decades has been transformed. The question that arises from this for students of social policy is to find out how and to what extent the post-Fordist networked global economy has impacted on welfare states.

There are a number of questions that have to be levelled at this type of analysis and some dangers in using *only* this wide level of analysis and relying on it for answers. One of the main dangers is that scholars who adopt what is sometimes called a 'universalistic' approach are rather deterministic. In other words, the outcome of their analysis is already predicted in the way they ask the questions. For example, one of the dominant explanations in the 20th century of how welfare states evolved concerned a school of authors who adopted a **logic of industrialism** stance. These scholars assumed that all advanced industrial societies were more or less moving in the same direction, the main difference simply being the pace at which different countries moved – what Wilensky (1975) famously called 'leaders' and 'laggards'. So-called *hyperglobalists* (such as Ohmae, 1990) believe that the modern world has been overwhelmed by worldwide economic forces that make the nation state redundant and strongly imply that history as we have previously known it – that is, a history of battles between nations – has largely been superseded by global 'superhighways' and transnational networks. The idea that **global capitalism** was a unified force was, of course, the essence of Marx's plea for the 'workers of the world to unite'. The point about this way of thinking about social change is that it is based on the premise that all the nations of the world are moving or being pushed inexorably to a particular conclusion from which there is no escape and very little real choice. Macro-level theorists tend unwittingly to adopt a **convergence approach**. This is not to say that macro-analysis is flawed or unimportant. It means that in using concepts drawn from this level it is necessary to be aware of the dangers that are implicit within such concepts.

Indeed, in terms of the policy analysis agenda, the big picture is a key dimension that has to be accounted for. As we will show in Chapter Two, 'globalisation' is a vital context in which the policy process has to be read and understood in the 21st century. In particular, the global economic order operating through high-speed communications networks has restructured the global political economy, dramatically changed the world's labour markets since the 1980s, and has caused nation states to respond to these new competitive pressures by reinventing governance. These issues are discussed in detail in the first cluster of chapters in this book. The key question posed by the globalisation agenda for students of the policy process is to determine to what extent these new forces – new information technologies, new forms of economic structure, new patterns of national and global governance – shape the outcome of policy.

Micro-level analysis

Micro-level analysis operates at the opposite extreme to macro-level analysis – it is the level that deals with the most basic unit of society: *individual people*. This involves consideration of the impact that particular people (such as politicians, civil servants, trade union leaders) have in designing policy and in its final outcome. It asks questions about all ends of the policy process: politicians, consumers and 'street-level' bureaucrats. Prime Minister Tony Blair has helped design and promote the idea of 'Foundation Hospitals' – but will the doctors and nurses engaged in the delivery of health care be committed to making such a system a success? If the staff decide to oppose the scheme, can it be implemented against their wishes? The question principally posed by micro-analysis is: *What happens to policy at the point in time when it is finally delivered?*

Micro-level analysis deals with key issues concerning the role of individuals in the policy process. It has two main purposes. The first is to account for one of the deep-theory issues in the social sciences: the question of **structure** and **agency**. In other words, to what extent are individuals constrained in what they do by the institutions (social and political) in which they live – to what extent does 'structure' predetermine outcomes? And, on the other hand, how much influence can individuals have in shaping their own destiny autonomously, outside the limits of structures? This applies to every one of us; however, in policy analysis this deals especially with key actors in the decision-making process from the prime minister down to the individual citizen or consumer. Tony Blair decided to take Britain into the 2003 war against Iraq, a decision that was against the vast majority of the wishes of his own ministers, the Labour Party membership and the public at large. Despite widespread condemnation of the decision, British forces went to war. Would the same events have occurred if Gordon Brown or Charles Kennedy had been Prime Minister rather than Tony Blair? Although we cannot know the answer to this question, that it sows doubt in the mind illustrates that *agency* – in this case, the actions of Tony Blair – matters greatly in the policy process.

Micro-level analysis is also concerned with that stage of the policy process when the 'policy' is finally delivered at the street level. For many years it was assumed that 'street-level bureaucrats' more or less were doing what they were told by policy makers. It became apparent that this was not so and, at its most extreme, policy completely failed to be delivered as intended. Indeed, the title of one of the first major texts that concerned itself with implementation issues says it all: *Implementation: How great expectations in Washington are dashed in Oakland; or why it's amazing that federal programs work at all, this being a saga of the economic development administration as told by two sympathetic observers who seek to build morals on a foundation ruined by hopes*[!]. In this study, Pressman and Wildavsky (1973) suggested that many policies fail to meet their goals because of factors such as *poor communication* within government agencies, the *lack of a clear direction* and *weak control over resources*. Their solution was to advocate stronger central control of policy implementation: the so-called **top-down approach**. What all this suggests is that micro-level activity is a crucial part of the policy process, for it is through the actions of individual housing officers, nurses, teachers and civil servants – and in the offices, classrooms and hospitals in which they work – that policy is ultimately delivered. To use a 'housing' example, it is well known that the treatment of homeless people by local authorities varies considerably from place to place despite the fact that there is strong national legislation (currently enshrined in the 2002 Homelessness Act) and centrally issued codes of practice. In one famous case, a south coast local authority was eventually told by the courts to house a pregnant woman who had been living in a beach hut. They had claimed that she *was* adequately housed! This is the sharp end of the policy process and where 'policy' is in reality being delivered, whatever officials in Whitehall or MPs in parliament might think or hope. Moreover, looked at in this way, from the 'bottom end' of the process, not only is the policy maker's 'policy' not being delivered, but also a different policy made up by street-level bureaucrats becomes de facto the *real* policy.

Finally, as with the macro-level, there are methodological issues that need to be addressed. Here the potential problem is one of not being able to see the wood for the trees. In other words, by focusing on the smallest unit of analysis, the investigation is boiled down to its lowest common denominator where it is impossible to discern patterns or interconnections between different cases. In this sense, all trees and no wood is the converse problem to the universalistic tendencies of the macro-level studies. This is one of the reasons why our approach to policy analysis is strongly shaped by meso-level research methods. The meso-level also contains the core subject matter of the policy process, for it is here that the literature attempts to explain how and, crucially, why policy is made, and in whose interest.

Meso-level analysis

Meso-level analysis is the **middle part** of the policy process. It deals with *how* policies come to be made, *who* puts them on the policy agenda, and the *structure* of the institutional arrangements in which policy is defined and eventually implemented. It plays a key role in **bridging** the macro- and micro-levels of analysis and, in practical terms, meso-level institutions and networks are crucial in that they *filter* the impact of macro-trends.

Meso-analysis has its theoretical roots in a school of thought that was overshadowed for many decades by the big-issue explanations. It can be traced particularly to a group of American sociologists, the founding father of which was Robert Merton. Merton (1957) recognised the necessity of broad conceptual horizons but preferred to contribute to the creation of what he called 'theories of the middle range'. Together with Lazarsfeld, he was a pioneer of policy-related research using empirical research methodologies, such as (what he called) 'focused groups', the precursor of market research and modern focus groups.

In its most obvious sense, the meso-level is the middle of the policy process sandwich, sitting between the broad parameters of macro-analysis and the detailed focus of micro-level studies. In this way, meso-level analysis is not just the middle layer but, crucially, acts as a bridge between the other two levels. It contains a rich seam of social science concepts and analytical approaches. Significantly, meso-level analysis focuses on the institutions that are working to design and deliver policy. This is, as it were, the engine room of the policy process where ideas are tried and tested and through which political interests are filtered. A key meso-level concept here is the idea of policy networks. We argue later in the book that the old-fashioned 'unitary' state governed from Whitehall has largely been superseded by a much more fragmented system of governance which operates very largely through networks and policy communities acting as filters (see Rhodes, 1997). A principal feature of this is the separation of central government's role in designing policy and delivering it, the latter of which is now very largely in the hands of quasi-governmental agencies, public–private partnerships, and to an increasing extent the private sector controlled only by regulatory authorities. What this means in terms of policy making is that the state is increasingly dependent on a network of other organisations in order to meet its goals. Indeed, this was always the case to a degree, but these networks now play a more prominent role in shaping, constraining or even determining social policies.

The influence of the 'new institutionalism' literature is also very strong in the way we think about the policy process. What happens inside the institutions of government and the subtle ways in which they influence policy in setting agendas is crucial. As theorists such as Castles (1998), Skocpol and Amenta (1986) and Pierson (1994) have shown, *politics matters*, and how the state operates to deliver policy really does make a significant difference. (These ideas are discussed in detail in Chapter Nine.) Of special importance in this discussion is the influence of 'historical institutionalists', scholars whose work is built up from thinking about and evaluating previous policies and the impact of great events, such as the 20th century's world wars, on the development of welfare policies (for example, Baldwin, 1990; Skocpol, 1992). Theories of the middle range are sensitive to cultural and historical factors that underlie the differences between countries. There is no attempt to impose an overarching theory, rather the aim is to discern the factors that lead to the creation of 'types' or clusters of nations. The implication of such theory is not the convergence logic of universalistic studies but one of *divergence*. This is not to say that every country is unique (which, as we saw above, would make comparison meaningless), but that there may be underlying patterns that influence how groups of countries cluster.

Meso-level analysis is thus characterised by two distinct features: the use of *middle-range theory* to explain the policy process from the moment a social problem is identified – following the various stages of design and implementation – and the emphasis on the *cultural/historical explanation* for how the welfare states of countries differ. As we will see, these two facets are in reality closely connected because the institutional structures are part and parcel of *why* nations have different approaches to welfare policy.

The structure of this book

The main reason why we have talked at length here about these different levels of analysis is that the design of this book is based around them. We begin by introducing some of the broad macro-concepts: globalisation (Chapter Two) and related issues such as the changing political economies that underpin state action and the shift from an industrial to a post-industrial labour market (Chapters Three and Four). We look too at the crucial role played by new technologies in facilitating these changes (Chapter Five) and the ways in which the structures of the state and the way it governs have changed in response to the pressures of globalisation and economic change (Chapter Six).

In the second part of the book, we move on to explore some key examples of the meso-level approach, examining the role of policy networks (Chapter Eight), political institutions (Chapter Nine) and policy transfer (Chapter Ten) in shaping policy. We also consider arguments about how political agendas are set and in whose interests (Chapter Seven).

The third part of the book looks at some important micro-level issues, considering who makes decisions and how (Chapter Eleven), what happens to policies at the implementation stage (Chapter Twelve) and how the effectiveness of policies is monitored and judged and how evidence informs policy making (Chapter Thirteen).

In the Conclusion, we round off the book with some thoughts on how the various theories and concepts examined in the book can be applied to real-world policy scenarios and consider the value of utilising a policy analysis approach when examining social policy problems. One of the arguments we emphasise here, and something which we feel it is important to make clear from the outset of this book, is that each layer offers only a partial picture of the policy process. Therefore, to understand the policy process as a whole, a **multi-level perspective** is required. So, for instance, in the chapters on globalisation and new technologies, we explore some of the many social and political changes – in some cases transformations – that have been brought about by these significant macro-forces. A reader who stops there without proceeding further could, perhaps, be left with the impression that the detailed attention we give to these forces suggests we subscribe to a position which sees them as being of such a magnitude and ferocity that they undermine the autonomy of national governments. The truth, however, is far from it: reading further they would see, for instance, that we ascribe great analytic importance at the meso-level to institutions and networks and, at the micro-level, street-level bureaucrats, in muting and shaping the impact of globalisation or technological change. Likewise, someone beginning with the meso-level chapters might feel we believe that all the answers can be found there, but these perspectives are at their strongest when combined with a macro-level theory of change.

In other words, the individual layers must be viewed as parts of a meal rather than the meal in themselves. Rather like a Big Mac™, our meal has three layers and simply eating the bun, the burger or the relish does not give a true impression of the full flavour of the offering: although it can be broken down into constituent components, for analytic purposes this is no way to eat it!

Part 1: Macro-level analysis

two   **Globalisation**

three   **Political economy**

four   **Changes in the world of work**

five   **Technological change**

six   **The changing nature of governance**

Globalisation

Overview

Globalisation is a key macro-level concept and has changed the way we need to think about our world. Time and distance have been radically altered. Globalisation has impacted on the nature of the state and the welfare state. This chapter outlines three schools of thought about what impact it is having, ranging from hyperglobalists to those who argue that there is nothing really new here. Globalisation has enabled economic and political power to be more easily redistributed than ever before.

Key concepts

Network society; economic stretching; individualisation; reflexivity; hyperglobalism.

Introduction

When Marx famously exhorted the workers of the world to unite in the face of international capitalism he was giving expression to what people knew to be a fundamental truth. Indeed, the worldwide nature of political and economic processes is by no means a new phenomenon. The British Empire once spanned the whole of planet Earth. More recently, one of the founding fathers of 'policy analysis', the American political scientist Harold Lasswell, persistently wrote about the global character of the political process and how nation states were having to adapt to new transnational realities. At this time, after the Second World War, the Cold War threatened Armageddon, the wholesale destruction of the world in a nuclear holocaust. More recently, this threat having receded, new global forces unleashed their terrible consequences – the AIDS pandemic has ravaged Africa, global warming threatens fundamental climate change with unknown consequences, 'September 11th' sent shudders through the Western world as global terrorism tore at the very heart of modern capitalism and its way of life. Who any longer can doubt the truly global nature of human society? These events, however, suggest that something rather new has happened to the world in recent decades. This is because they arise not from great empires but from a variety of sources – new viruses spread by human contact, small cells of mobile terrorists linked by mass communication technologies, transnational companies operating across the globe.

There is something very distinctive about all this compared to the past, much of which arises from the fact that the world is connected in ways that were unimaginable even a few decades ago. In our time, the invention of the Internet has unleashed a tool of awesome power with information and communication networks operating at the speed of light. The globe has been wrapped in an electronic 'virtual reality' web. Against such a backdrop, few

---

Box 2.1: SARS and globalisation

Severe Acute Respiratory Syndrome first emerged in the Guandong Province of China in 2002. Its deadly flu-like symptoms spread rapidly into other parts of Asia and jumped across the globe, appearing in Toronto in the spring of 2003.

It was very contagious and was spread by a few mobile individuals. The outbreak in Hong Kong was traced to one man. One hundred and twenty people died.

Key features of this incident were:
- a drug which helped control the virus was available within six months of the outbreak;
- governments in the countries affected took draconian measures to stamp out the disease but the World Health Organisation found it very difficult to coordinate the worldwide campaign;
- the threat of the spread of SARS created panic in some industries; Cathy Pacific airline based in Hong Kong cut its flights by 45%, hotels all over Asia saw trade decrease dramatically, the stock market in Taiwan slumped, and its currency weakened considerably.

The lessons of SARS
Global governance is weak in the face of new and rapidly developing problems: relatively few people, even just individuals, can move viruses across the planet very quickly with increasing risks of global pandemics; scientists connected via the Internet quickly found drugs that combated the virus; a relatively small-scale outbreak of a new virus caused massive damage to the Asian economy and threatened to spill over into the whole global economy.

Globalisation means increased velocity of action, a high-risk society, a networked planet (greater 'extensity') and 'deepening' through which we connect to people across the world we have never met and do not know.

serious social scientists dispute the significance of this end-of-millennium phenomenon, even if they do not agree on the precise nature of globalisation and its consequences. At stake here is something quite extraordinary; that we may have to rethink our understanding of the nature of 'society' with its relatively fixed social structures and geographical boundaries. As Giddens has pointed out, we need "a starting point that concentrates upon analysing how social life is ordered across time and space" (Giddens in Held and McGrew, 2000, p 76).

In other words, knowingly or not, we are daily connected to people across the world who we may never meet and know little about but whose products we buy and whose websites we can view from anywhere and at any time. This is really the essence of the idea to which the word 'globalisation' has been attached; that more than ever before, time and distance have broken down, have been stretched so that very local issues and ways of life connect to people and economic forces that are sourced a great distance away (or possibly close by, but whether near or far no longer matters). Globalisation is essentially about the networking of the planet – through the Internet, satellite telecommunications and rapid transport – by new forms of local, regional and transnational social connections, economic markets and political structures. Even the very notion of globalisation is an example of this. Little more than a decade ago it was unknown as a word let alone as a social science concept, and yet now there is never a day when it is not on the lips of politicians, social commentators and academics. Its sudden appearance is highly symbolic of one of its main messages: that the *velocity* of worldwide communication has increased dramatically in recent years. In the modern world, an idea does not need years of dissemination before it is broadly accepted or rejected; thanks to the Internet, it can spread round the world instantaneously. It does not matter, as Giddens (1999, p 3) suggests, "whether you live in Beijing or Seoul or Africa many people can get the same sources almost immediately, usually using electronic technologies". Globalisation captured the sense of an increasingly convergent world due to the speed with which ideas, goods, money and people move across the face of the planet.

Globalisation has invaded every aspect and tier of human life from the truly planetary scale of economic organisation down to the way individual people experience life in the early years of the 21st century. Giddens (1990) identified three factors that shape globalism:

- the growth of transnational companies;
- growing economic integration;
- and the globalisation of communications.

At the centre of this new dynamic has been the imperative of the world economic order to create stable trading and monetary conditions compelled by the massive economic and political power wielded by transnational corporations, creating a convergent and increasingly integrated economic order. This is the core globalisation issue and its impact, particularly on a state like Britain, a trading nation (formerly the 'workshop of the world'), heavily dependent on financial markets and with its historical legacy of empire, is inescapable. As Evans and Cerny (2003, p 25) argue, the institutions of the state have been compelled "to conform to the anti-inflationary norms of the international financial markets". It was no coincidence, they argue, that the first major policy initiative of the first New Labour government, elected in 1997, was to cede control of interest rate policy to the Monetary Committee of the Bank of England, with a specific brief to meet inflation targets. The post-globalisation state is therefore not just about regulating and managing the political and economic system in the face of globalisation, but of *promoting* an open economy and polity in order to enhance the benefits of specific interests. From a policy analysis perspective, this points to one of the key features of globalisation: that it involves the distribution (and redistribution) of political power across the world. A main issue for us, therefore, is the extent to which the British state and, indeed, nation states in general have to react to the new centres of power, which cut across existing geopolitical boundaries.

Box 2.2: Globalisation in facts and figures

In 1999, the United Nations Development Program (UNDP) made globalisation the theme of their annual Human Development Report (UNDP, 1999). Among the stark facts it revealed were:

- $1,500,000,000,000,000,000 ($1.5 trillion) traded on the world money markets *every day*;
- foreign direct investment *seven times* the level it was in the 1970s;
- in 1997, General Motors' turnover exceeded the GDP of Thailand – a country of some 62 million people; the turnover of Ford Motor exceeded the GDP of the oil-rich Saudi Arabian economy;
- imports to the US economy had risen by 50% and to the Mexican economy by 200% since 1985;
- 70,000,000,000,000 minutes were spent on international phone calls in 1996;
- 70% of television programmes broadcast in Latin America were produced outside of the region – most imported from the US;
- the wealth of the 200 richest people in the world exceeded the income of the poorest 41% of the world population;
- the wealth of the world's *three* richest billionaires exceeded the *combined* GNP of all of the least-developed countries – some 600 million people in total.

Source: UNDP (1999)

And the nation state

One of the key features of globalisation is thus the debate about the extent to which domestic policy agendas remain in the close control of governments compared to the past. This is the central paradox of globalisation: that it simultaneously creates a convergent economic order while nation states are compelled to redefine their role and purpose in the face of these new challenges. Globalisation does not mean the end of the nation state – far from it. Rather, it changes by 'loosening' its structures, adopting new organisational forms and new ways of working that maximise the ability of the nation to keep pace with change, for above all globalisation is about greater speed, not just in the movement of information, services and currencies round the world, but in how ideas and policies can be moved from nation to nation in search of ever-greater efficiencies (see Chapter Ten). National economies in these circumstances are compelled above all to ever-greater efficiency in order to be able to compete on the world stage.

As we will see later in this book, this means that Britain's old-fashioned unitary state, which steered political life from Whitehall through most of the 20th century, has been forced to give way to something very different. The Blair agenda of devolution, breaking up traditional local government, reforming the House of Lords, initiating public–private partnerships for funding what used to be thought of as public services, enhancing quasi-autonomous agencies (QGAs) and creating new ones to 'deliver', is all part and parcel of this process. One of the most significant implications for the policy process of how New Labour is being forced to adapt to the globalisation agenda is the paradox that at one and the same time the government seeks to control the direction of policy but is compelled to leave delivery to a plethora of quangos and public–private partnerships over which its influence is relatively loose. Britain, in the words of Rhodes (1997b), has become a much more 'differentiated polity', not only in the sense that the government is less top-down but that this more fragmented structure operates through networks rather than hierarchies. In other words, *inside* the new polity the type of engine that operates the system is very different from in the past. These networks operate throughout the political system but have become characteristic at the delivery level (see Chapter Twelve). Inside the government's own machinery, 'agencies' have been established to take over from monolithic civil service bureaucracies that were the core of the old unitary state. New Public Management is their lifeblood, fed by the oxygen of performance-related pay, competitive tendering, appraisal, accelerated promotion and other management techniques drawn from the private sector which would have been unthinkable a few decades ago.

In short, the British state has been compelled to restructure from a centralised unitary system based around the Westminster model of government to a form of 'governance' that is much looser, more devolved and characterised by overlapping and increasingly detached policy networks.

And welfare states

The direction of key policies is also shaped, or at the very least has to take into account, the impact of this agenda. For example, some exponents of globalisation theory argue welfare states are being dismantled under pressure from competitive world markets. Corporations that operate in the field of tradable goods can threaten to move to low wage countries and have done so. Capital is now so mobile that it too can threaten to withdraw and seek higher returns elsewhere. It has been argued, therefore, that governments are compelled to reduce welfare state spending because of increased competition and have engaged in what Woods (2000, p 1) refers to as "a race to the bottom". Many commentators have disputed the truth of this assertion, not least because the evidence does not support a significant reduction of welfare state expenditure, at least in the OECD countries (see Swank, 2002). Even Mrs Thatcher's anti-welfare state governments in the 1980s did little more than contain the expansion in the rate of growth of state spending programmes (Castles, 1998, p 322). However, it is also clear that the New Labour 'project' has brought a globalisation-related spin to welfare state reform, embracing the shift of social policy towards a more contract-orientated, post-industrial welfare state and with an emphasis on the economic dimension of social policies apparent in its introduction of 'workfare' programmes designed to reintegrate the unemployed into the labour market. Moreover, the government's reluctance to increase income tax or to explicitly engage in debates about income redistribution signal a significant break with the egalitarian outlook of 'old' Labour's social policies.

The point here is that globalisation has undoubtedly compelled significant reappraisal of the post-1945 Beveridgian welfare state and caused a move to a more US-style workfare state. However, this does not leave the British state as the unwilling victim of forces beyond its control – far from it. Instead, the 21st-century state has to adapt and reinvent itself in the face of new economic and social forces that are global in extent; and, in so doing, it draws on and is necessarily influenced by its own unique traditions and historical legacies. As we will show later in the book there is a range of 'new institutionalist' theories that help explain how different countries have adapted to the power of the global economy. The deterministic idea of a 'race to the bottom' in cutting social budgets does not do justice to the reality of what has happened.

A fundamental point here is the recognition that globalisation does *not* imply a simple convergence of everything to some common endgame. Nor does it mean the end of the nation state and the takeover of the world by multinational corporations. Rather, it means that nations have to respond to globalisation pressures from within their own historical, cultural and political domains. National political institutions have significantly, indeed decisively, mediated the international economic agenda. The domestic reform of welfare states has been surprisingly resilient due to what Pierson (2001) refers to as 'institutional lock-in' (in which long-run traditions and institutional practices have become so embedded that radical change is difficult to achieve). This theme is taken up again in later chapters of this book.

Globalisation, although thought of in the orthodox accounts as principally a product of economic forces and the market, also has, therefore, a strong political dimension (as we will see in Chapter Six) through the development of multilateral agreements, intended to increase cross-border flows of capital and goods, as seen for example in the EU. The economic focus of much of the globalisation literature does not do justice to these political/institutional developments. New layers of governance have been laid down across the globe; new elite networks use the global highways to strengthen their power bases and often these networks are supranational – they are above the level of national boundaries. In a prodigious review and analysis of this, spanning three lengthy volumes, Castells (1996, 1997a, 1997b) argues that a new form of capitalism has emerged that is much more flexible than before and has created a **network society** in which the power of a new 'informational economy' interacts with social movements (that resist the imperatives of global power-mongers) resulting in macro-transformations of worldwide society and politics. The key to the network society is electronically processed informational networks.

Ironically, under these conditions, the nation state becomes bigger as it responds to these agendas through new layers of regulation and new interdependencies. Paradoxically, one of the complexities of this process of internationalisation is that the global polity itself is somewhat fragile compared to the nation state, creating compliance problems (McGrew and Lewis, 1992). As the SARS case study shows (see **Box 2.1**), the Chinese government only belatedly admitted to the problem and would not accept that the World Health Organisation should manage a crisis that clearly had transnational implications, and the same pattern was repeated with the outbreak of 'avian flu' in the early weeks of 2004. It would seem, somewhat perversely, especially in the less economically developed parts of the world, that the significance of the nation state has been sharpened as the sovereign state has become the effective, working, geopolitical unit of the global polity. The nation state, even if it fails to deliver good policy, remains the most important focus of decision making. As Parsons (1995, p 243) points out:

> Issues and problems may well be increasingly constructed in
> international and global terms, but decision-making and

implementation still remain domains which must be analysed within the context of nation states.

In short, one of the paradoxes of globalisation is the strengthening of nation states in the context of relatively weak global governance. Above all, it is the recognition that all levels of governance and society from the neighbourhood to local, to regional, to national, to international are inexorably connected in a way that was inconceivable only a few years ago.

How does globalisation work?

So, what makes globalisation different from previous discourses about world politics or international capitalism or even orthodox comparative social studies? Essentially, the difference is that in the postmodern epoch, societies have been compelled to embrace new technologies, new social processes, new alignments of existing economic forces and new forms of political process. It is the processes that knit these new forces and technologies together that are of the highest significance. As we will see later in this chapter, some scholars dispute its significance, saying that globalisation's impact is mainly confined to the countries of the more economically developed world and that the claims of the globalisation thesis are exaggerated. We argue that this case is increasingly

---

Box 2.3: Castells and the network society

In his three-volume study of the global information age, Castells (1996, 1997a, 1997b; also reissued as 2000b, 2000c, 2000d) sets out a grand narrative about the nature of the present. His main argument is that a new form of capitalism has emerged, clearer than ever about its goals and more flexible in its pursuit of them.

What makes 'networked capitalism' different is that it is built on new organisational formations arising from new information and communication technologies (ICTs). New forms of social network have been constructed through electronically processed information that are qualitatively different from previous social systems. This leads to a situation that goes beyond ideas of 'post-industrial society' or 'an information society' to one in which key social structures are organised around ICT-enabled organisational networks. It is the insertion of information technology into historically very different settings that has changed everything. As he says, "anything can happen at any time, it can happen very rapidly" (Castells, 1996, p 467).

New forms of social movements have also emerged, using the Internet, because loss of identity and cultural context has provoked a reaction, so that new social formations have emerged around the basic social identities of sexuality, religion, ethnicity and nationhood. (We take up some of the key themes of Castells' work in Chapter Five of this book.)

being shown to be redundant (although, as we have already shown, we do indeed doubt the idea of a world hurtling towards only one type of economy and society). Part of the claim that globalisation is a new phenomenon requiring its own discourse arises from the *processes* involved in what has happened, in the 'how' question just as much as in the 'what' question. For example, we have already referred to Giddens' idea that globalisation has involved the *stretching* of time–space pathways – that people around the world are connected to each other in ways that break from all previous historical eras opening up ranges of choice but also intensifying the related risks. By definition, this process also involves the speeding up of the means of communication and interconnectedness. Travel is quicker, of course (except in central London!), and air travel and other rapid transit technologies enable people to straddle the globe in ways and with a frequency previously impossible. However, it is the invention of digital communication technologies that has revolutionised interpersonal communication and trade in what Quah (1998) refers to as the 'weightless economy'. He calculated that the total volume of trade of all types has increased by about five times compared to 30 years ago and that the vast majority of this increase is due to weightless trading of services, particularly currency dealing mainly through electronic, 'virtual' means. Evidence such as this shows another side of the globalisation process: that the amount, the sheer volume, of economic activity in the world, not so much in manufactured goods but more significantly financial services and currency exchanges, has increased enormously in recent years, and uses the new telecommunications networks as its tool.

In addition to 'stretching', increasing 'velocity', and the growing volume of the weightless economy and movement of people across the face of the Earth, there is a fourth dimension which Held and McGrew (2000) refer to as *deepening*. This means that the effect of quite small, localised events can potentially have major repercussions elsewhere in the world. 'Deepening' also expresses the idea that globalisation processes loosen and sometimes reawaken cultural and social bonds that have in some cases been dormant for decades. The collapse of the USSR at the end of the 1980s was followed by a welling up across east and central Europe of nationalism built around centuries old cultural and ethnic bonds and rivalries. Globalisation is not only, or even principally, about new layers of transnational and regional governance and economic interests overlaid across existing geopolitical boundaries; rather, it gives rise to the divergence of societies each building up from their own cultural and historical foundations, challenged by globalisation but not subsumed into a uniform Big Brother state. As we show in Chapters Six and Nine, national political institutions are crucial to policy outcomes and this implies a very strong sense of divergence (rather than convergence) in the policy process, with different countries finding their own way through the process of modernisation.

As we said in Chapter One, the art of policy analysis is to be able to hold together the various layers and tiers of governance which shape and pattern differences between countries. We have to think of countries not as unique entities but as places moulded by cultural connections to their neighbours, bound by ties of history, language, religion and culture. This is the meaning of our meso-level, middle-range approach. What is it that connects societies and by the same token differentiates them? This is why the policy analysis approach is inherently and implicitly comparative. We can no longer think, for example, of the British welfare state as a model or paradigm for other welfare states but simply as one type, powerfully linked in its modern incarnation by culture and language to the American minimalist state but also looking to the social market model of our European neighbours. The idea that Britain can be studied and understood in isolation is no longer tenable (if it ever was). Ethnocentrism, by which the welfare systems or any other aspect of society is judged according to the paradigm of one's own country, was typical of applied studies of welfare states, housing policy, even economic policy. The globalisation agenda, however, compels us to see our own case in a wider context, not as part of a general convergence of states under the impact of a unifying transnational economy, but to consider as an empirical question the cultural and historical factors that draw nations together into clusters or families of nations and, crucially, *why* they differ from each other.

It is this process of 'deepening', of trying to explain the differences and similarities between nations using a broad range of data (both quantitative and qualitative) and sensitivity to historical and cultural contexts, that is the defining feature of the globalisation process (and is central to the argument of this book). The impact of the whole sweep of globalisation in the early years of the 21st century has been to intensify and deepen awareness of how culture is embedded in society but also to show how localised cultures and social relations are now able to transcend previously confined space and time. As Giddens (1999) puts it, 'interaction across distance' is possible in a way unimaginable in previous historical eras. The growth of local nationalisms in Europe and elsewhere is precisely a reflex arising from the pressures of globalisation to stretch geopolitical boundaries, so that nationalisms bubble into the vacuum, but also of the deepening arising from the nation state being shaken by global forces, rather as the Earth's crust fractures during an earthquake.

To sum up this section, it is the combination of these *processes* that is distinctive about the globalisation discourse and which compels us to rethink old certainties and orthodoxies. The processes affecting the social, economic and political life of planet Earth have been neatly summed up by Held and McGrew (2000) in four themes:

• *stretching* of economic, political and social activities across geopolitical frontiers;

- *intensification* or growing scale of the interconnections between trade, finance, migration and cultures;
- *velocity* of all these processes has increased dramatically so that ideas, capital, information and people relate to each other much more quickly;
- *deepening*, meaning that the effect of quite small local events can potentially have big repercussions elsewhere in the world; "In this sense, the boundaries between domestic matters and global affairs can become increasingly blurred" (Held et al, 1999, p 15).

Globalisation and the problem of the 'self'

Globalisation has invaded every aspect and tier of human life from the truly global scale of economic organisation down to the way individual people experience life in the early years of the 21st century. As Giddens (1999) puts it, globalisation is not only an 'out there' experience but is also an 'in here' phenomenon, meaning that everyone is challenged to live life in a more reflexive and individualised way: 'individualisation is the personal pole'; that is, the other extreme of the spectrum from transnational organisations. Giddens argues that modern cultures have created a more abstract, socially 'disembedded' world compared to pre-Enlightenment society when social relations were bounded by localised patterns of life. What distinguishes the era of 'high' modernity, according to Giddens, is the breakdown of traditional explanations of people's place in society – religious, tradition, 'that's how it's always been' – and the development of reflexivity. Reflexivity expresses the idea of rational, informed people making choices for themselves uninfluenced by old traditions and drawing on the new knowledge available in the Information Age. Information is to a very large extent what distinguishes late modernity; more even than that, it is what defines the condition.

Ontological security has thus been eroded by modernity and globalisation, because natural patterns of time and place have been disturbed. The idea of ontology is that human beings need to feel that the basic parameters of the natural world are secure and that their day-to-day place in the world has reasonably predictable boundaries, that they can have confidence in their identities and personal well-being. Globalisation has invaded every aspect of how humans relate to each other because of its impact on local culture. In a world bombarded by new choices and new risks, how do we make sense of our own self-identity? It is not surprising that the television is cluttered with makeover programmes which transform people's rooms or gardens, or that the voyeuristic *Big Brother* recorded more votes than the Labour government in winning power in the 2001 General Election, because they are all essentially about the same questions: who are we and how should we live in a world full of choices?

It could be argued that this kind of sociological evaluation of globalisation draws us away from the policy analysis approach, with its roots firmly embedded in political science. This, however, would be to miss one major lesson of policy analysis: that although its disciplinary roots are firmly embedded in political science, it is also an inherently interdisciplinary way of thinking and draws eclectically on the social sciences to support analysis of policy making and the wider nature of the state (and the welfare state). Understanding the 'personal pole', as Giddens puts it, is a good example of this cross-disciplinary sensitivity. It is important because it stands at the extreme end of the macro–micro spectrum but also because it is in the process of 'individualisation' that the social world is created and recreated. For example, many social scientists have written about the concept of 'home' – a familiar and everyday experience of going out from and coming back to the place where we keep our most treasured possessions and quite often experience our most intense relationships. It is closely bound up with creating and sustaining self-identity and where people (normally) find security from the risks and challenges of the world beyond the front door, a place where they can 'be themselves'. As G.H. Mead (1934), the founding father of symbolic interactionism, said, through knowledge of our 'boundaries', we come to know ourselves. Goffman's sociology of place expands on this idea showing that the home is a 'locale' in which social life is sustained and above all *reproduced* (Goffman, 1959). When men cut the lawns and check the antifreeze in their cars and women attend to the household's clothes and organise the cleaning routine in the house with barely a thought, gender stereotypes, social roles and social relationships are, as Saunders and Williams (1988, p 83) put it, "composed and contextualized".

This area of discussion is important, therefore, because it opens up the idea that the cultural level is crucial to patterning society and wheels on into any number of aspects of the policy process, for example, in the case of the 'home' whole areas of housing policy: what type and size of housing is appropriate to the type of households in society, where and how much housing do we need, why is it that we can put men on the moon but still live in a society where thousands of people are home*less*? One of the strong arguments in this book is that cultural contexts are key to understanding the nature of societies and how and why they differ.

Schools of globalisation theory

As with any discourse about society, new ideas and concepts need to be tested and, as time goes by, it is often the case that differing perspectives coalesce into distinct approaches or schools of thought. The debate about globalisation is no exception, especially because it has entered the social science vocabulary so quickly and with such a powerful impact. It has compelled social scientists to take up a position – broadly speaking, for or against. Clearly, it is a concept that cannot be ignored. One problem, however, is that the debate has generated

> **Box 2.4:** Globalisation and welfare services: micro-level impacts
>
> Holden (2002) points out that most analyses of globalisation and the welfare state focus on either its impact on the broad political economies of nation states (see Chapter Three of this book) or on the increasing role transnational organisations such as the UN, World Bank and IMF play in the policy process (see Chapters Six and Ten). However, as Holden argues, globalisation is having a visible impact on service delivery at the micro-level too, not least through the involvement of international companies in the delivery of key welfare services. He points out that in the field of long-term nursing care, for example, three internationalised companies (BUPA Care Homes, Ashbourne and Westminster Health Care) own or lease almost 500 of the UK's long-term nursing homes. Ashbourne, probably the most internationalised of the three, is US-based and owns homes in Australia, Germany and Spain as well as the UK and US. In the UK alone, it is responsible for over 8,000 beds and is the second-largest supplier of long-term care services in the country. The significance of this should not be underestimated: the services these companies provide would once have been regarded as falling within the domain of the public sector and as central to the activities of the (national) welfare state. Moreover, all have been characterised as what Holden terms 'market seeking', as they look to expand their reach in the UK and elsewhere. What is more, similar companies are looking to expand their reach too – both in this area of welfare services and in others. While Holden (2002, p 63) suggests that "Further research needs to be carried out into the policy implications of this", he feels "that such market-seeking behaviour means that internationalized providers will not be passive actors in any future development of private markets in welfare services". In other words, while globalisation is a macro-level phenomenon we should not lose sight of its micro-level impacts.

a huge literature and for newcomers it is difficult to know where to begin. However, Held et al (1999) have identified, broadly speaking, three main schools of globalisation theory: sceptics, hyperglobalists and transformationalists. A good starting point is to know in general terms what the characteristics of these three schools are.

The sceptics

This cluster of literature in essence asserts that globalisation is a myth, an invention of over-fertile imaginations. The sceptics argue that the world has not become any more integrated or 'networked' than it was in the past. The increase in economic activity, so they argue, is mainly confined to the advanced capitalist nations of the OECD countries and thus is not really a global phenomenon. More even than this, it is apparent that the major beneficiaries of the alleged globalisation are transnational corporations with very powerful right-wing political allies in whose interest it is to argue against high-spending welfare states on the spurious grounds that national economies need to be sleeker and more efficient if they are to be able to compete in world markets. Thus, globalisation is little more, according to some sceptics, than an illusion invented by neo-liberal economists to justify tax cuts and anti-inflationary reductions in public spending. No one wins in this world except the already rich and powerful. It follows from this position that the nation state remains the key geopolitical unit, that these states are autonomous. Hirst and Thompson (1999), for example, argue that the evidence for this is clear for all to see. There has not been any really major change in the trajectory of world economic growth over recent decades, certainly nothing that warrants inventing a new concept to describe it. Moreover, individual nation states have developed social policies that are distinctive with little evidence that they are converging on some common model under the impact of globalisation. Rather the world is breaking up into distinct groupings of nations each finding different ways through modernisation. In the post-Cold War world, the older, more powerful states have consolidated their hold on the world economy and polity.

Hyperglobalists

At the other extreme is a school of literature that argues that the whole world has been completely changed into a single global economy, which transcends every geopolitical boundary. Ohmae (1990), for example, refers to 'turbo-capitalism' and 'supra-territorial capitalism' in which the basic sovereignty of the nation state has been eclipsed. Globalisation has changed the world beyond recognition in a very short space of time. The key feature of this is that every nation on the planet is now inexorably connected to a fast-moving, powerful world economy. New markets have exploded and the Internet has created a massive potential for an intensification of competition between and across nation states. The information economy has driven a huge expansion in new forms of economic activity as well as speeding up and intensifying existing trade. What is very distinctive about the new global marketplace is the massive scale of 'weightless' trading in currencies and services.

According to Ohmae, this new world is rapidly smashing up orthodox political boundaries and the nation state is already in an advanced state of termination. In its place, the focus of political and economic activity has shifted towards subcontinental regions (for example, a corridor of new economic activity that has emerged across the south–eastern corner of England and stretches down towards Paris via the Channel Tunnel), and especially to a cluster of powerful cities – London, New York, Barcelona, Hong Kong, increasingly Beijing and other Pacific Rim cities. These great metropolises have become powerful magnets for the global economy, which increasingly operate across the old geopolitical boundaries and produce and consume around these great economic black holes. The idea of 'trading nations' in these circumstances has become redundant because being part of a nation state is no longer of much significance to what they do or how their economies in reality operate. Residual local economies continue to function but in a completely different paradigm. Thus it is quite normal in the great cities to find a new architecture, great cathedrals of capitalism towering into the sky, alongside squalid neighbourhoods clinging onto economic viability and crowded with the economically and culturally disadvantaged. For the time being, according to Ohmae, there is a two-tier world economy: the intensely competitive, dynamic global machine and the residual part of the old economy – slower, cumbersome, inefficient. The point is that globalisation has changed everything.

Transformationalists

In between these two extremes is a third school which accepts the logic and the fact of globalisation as a new social force, and is thus closer to the hyperglobalist approach than the sceptics. In broad terms, this is the perspective from which this book is written. Writers in this school argue that globalisation is not only an economic transformation of the world but involves the reprogramming of many aspects of social and political life. The nation state is not coming to an end but rather is being forced to reinvent itself under the impact of the new global forces. As Held and McGrew (2001, p 326) put it, the role of the nation state is having to be "re-articulated, reconstituted and re-embedded at the intersection of globalizing and regionalizing networks and systems". Nations are compelled to respond *but* from within their own cultural and historical frameworks. Thus the world is not converging, helter-skelter, towards some common superstate or being taken over by transnational corporations. New layers of governance have evolved across the world and new networks of power have to an extent transcended the nation state. However, the idea of loss of power or weakening of nation states is to misrepresent what may be new opportunities and to fundamentally misread change as erosion. Globalisation has not made politics redundant but has changed the nature of the political process.

It should also be noted at this point that there is a key methodological schism that distinguishes the hyperglobalist case, built around the global marketplace, and the transformationalist perspective which is more historically and culturally contingent in approach. The hyperglobalist case is essentially based around a rational choice logic; that the major actors in this, whether governments or private corporations, have no option but to follow the economically rational route, to maximise economic advantage. Unless this route is followed there is bound to be disinvestment and a 'flight of capital'. It follows from this that hyperglobalists downplay the role of culture and history as they follow the logic of neoclassical economic behaviour. The transformationalist approach, however, pays much more attention to the role of institutions as stabilising influences, as a means to creating barriers to change and mediating external forces. Reality is complex and values and ideologies also make an impact. Rational choice theory cannot (and has no need to) explain the influence of actors and political cultures on shaping outcomes; everything is bound into the logic of the marketplace. It is clear, therefore, that the difference between the hyperglobalist and the transformationalist perspectives is shrouded in a key methodological and behavioural discrepancy. We will return to this debate later in the book because it is perhaps our key claim that policy analysts must tease out the historically and socially contingent nature of social and public policies.

Giddens has been for many years a key advocate of the transformationalist perspective. He argues that the impact of the global marketplace needs to be precisely understood and not simply taken for granted. He argues, for example, that the communications revolution is separable from the global marketplace. As we saw earlier in this chapter, global communication has changed the way people across the world relate to each other and the fundamental pattern of social relations and individual self-identity. Globalisation is "not just dominated by economic forces, it's much more closely connected with communication ... it affects nations, it affects our personal lives" (Giddens, 1999, p 4). As we suggested, globalisation is a deepening experience that has awoken new forms of social movements and new local nationalisms often with long historic roots tapping into deeper layers of cultural meaning and experience. However, as globalisation 'pushes down' it also creates new opportunities for new local identities to emerge and, as the hyperglobalists argue, economic units that cut across existing territorial boundaries also bring the possibility of new cultural and social connections.

Thus the transformationalist school recognises both the power and extensity of the global economy and shows that social and political institutions have to respond and are indeed transformed by it – although not made irrelevant, far from it. In addition, new regional and global networks and forms of governance have emerged from these newly configured geopolitical units and these too have to be taken on board in policy analysis. We have already shown that the British state has undergone profound change in the last 20 to 30 years, changing from a centralised unitary form of government into a much more loosely bound and 'differentiated polity'. Later in the book, we will return to this theme when we examine it in more detail (see Chapter Six) and the historical/cultural foundation of nation states becomes much clearer through a reading of the new institutionalist literature (see Chapter Nine).

Conclusions

It is most important to realise that globalisation is not a single force pulling in one direction. It is not only about a world wrapped in a new economic order. It affects and forces the reinvention of all the major institutions of social life and the political state. As we have seen, globalisation is an 'in here' experience that challenges every human being to find for themselves, more reflexively, their own self-identity as the old certainties of status, class and tradition crumble. It affects every person and challenges him or her to define who he or she is in a world replete with choices. This is a fundamental fact of the age of 'high modernity'. We can, each and every one of us, reach out across the globe in ways unimaginable only a few years ago and this is just as important as the powerful economic forces unleashed in the process of globalisation. Of course, this is not to underrate the power of transnational, networked capitalism. Indeed, one of the key aspects of globalisation is its ability to redistribute political and economic power and there can be no doubting that in its current stage western capital – particularly the American economy – is the greatest beneficiary. However, globalisation per se does not increase economic and political inequalities. Through its processes of stretching, of increasing velocity, intensifying volume and deepening globalisation has challenged the whole of planet Earth and very few corners of it are untouched. Globalisation is fundamentally about the changing nature of relationships opened up by new communication networks and new power bases. It has re-patterned the way the world works and how people in different parts of the world relate to each other, from those we have never met to, equally, our closest partners.

Summary

- The invention of the Internet unleashed a tool of awesome power with information and communication networks operating at the speed of light. The globe has been wrapped in a 'virtual reality' web.
- The massive economic and political power wielded by transnational corporations, has created a convergent and increasingly integrated economic order.
- Globalisation involves the distribution (and redistribution) of political power across the world.
- Globalisation simultaneously creates a convergent economic order while nation states are compelled to redefine their role and purpose.
- Globalisation does not mean the end of the nation state. Nation states are forced to change by 'loosening' their institutional structures.
- The British state has been compelled to restructure from a centralised unitary system based around the Westminster model of government to a form of 'governance' that is much looser, more devolved and characterised by overlapping and increasingly detached policy networks.

73948

- Some globalisation theorists argue that welfare states are dismantled under pressure from competitive world markets. Many commentators dispute this, not least because the evidence does not support a significant reduction of welfare state expenditure. However, there are pressures towards more workfare-style welfare systems.
- It is the combined impact of the *processes* of stretching, intensification, velocity and deepening that is distinctive about the globalisation discourse.
- Globalisation has invaded every aspect of how humans relate to each other because of its impact on local culture. In a world bombarded by new choices and new risks, how do we make sense of our own self-identity? Reflexivity is a key response to high modernity.
- There are, broadly speaking, three schools of globalisation theorists: sceptics, hyperglobalists and transformationalists.

Questions for discussion

- On what grounds can it be argued that the nation state has been strengthened as a result of globalisation?
- Is globalisation essentially an economic process?
- To what extent is the terrorist threat a product of globalisation processes?

Further reading

Held, D., McGrew, A., Goldblatt, D. and Perraton, J. (1999) *Global transformations: Politics, economics and culture*, Cambridge: Polity Press.
Held, D. and McGrew, A. (eds) (2000) *The global transformations reader*, Cambridge: Polity Press.
Hirst, P. and Thompson, G. (1999) *Globalization in question* (2nd edn), Cambridge: Polity Press.

Electronic resource

www.polity.co.uk/global/links/htm

Political economy

Overview

Building on the issues examined in Chapter Two, this chapter considers the broad ideological shifts in the 'political economy of welfare' that have occurred in the past 25 years, developments that have often been fuelled by, but can be regarded as distinct from, globalisation. These shifts, which will be subjected to critical scrutiny, include:

- the collapse of Keynesianism and the consequently diminished role of the nation state in the economic sphere;
- the rise of the post-Fordist welfare state (or, as Jessop puts it, the move from the Keynesian Welfare National State to the post-national Schumpeterian workfare regime);
- the increased role of the private sector in welfare provision; the emergence of the Third Way as social democracy 'modernised' for the globalised, knowledge economy.

Key concepts

Policy paradigms; paradigm shifts; consensus; punctuated equilibrium; competition state; Keynesian Welfare National State; Schumpeterian workfare post-national regime.

Introduction

On 30 November 1999, policy makers from across the globe began to assemble in Seattle for a meeting of the World Trade Organisation. In a moment described as a 'coming of age' for the anti-globalisation movement, the meetings took place against a backdrop of mass protest and rioting: an international gathering of 50,000 demonstrators had descended on the city for what the media dubbed the 'Battle of Seattle' (see BBCi, 1999a). At the same time, matching protests were staged in major cities across the world under the banner 'N30 Global Day of Action', including a 500-strong demonstration in London where police and protestors clashed violently (BBCi, 1999b). These protests followed closely on the heels of the J-18 'Carnival Against Global Capitalism' that coincided with a meeting in Cologne of the leaders of the G8 nations on 18 June 1999; in the UK, this day saw the most violent demonstration in London since the anti-poll tax riots of 1990, with some £2 million of property damage caused in the City of London (BBCi, 1999b, 1999c).

What these clashes demonstrate so vividly is that **globalisation** has become a – perhaps *the* – defining concept of modern political discourse. Yet, as we noted in Chapter Two, little more than a decade ago globalisation was an obscure academic term. Indeed, from a British perspective, it is tempting to contrast the causes underpinning the capital's two most violent protests of recent times: the anti-poll tax riots of the Thatcher era that were concerned with a *national* policy issue about the funding of *local* government; and, the J-18 riots during the Blair era that relate to a *global* policy issue concerning *world* trade. To do so, however, would exaggerate the differences in the underlying themes of the protests for both, particularly with respect to the headline-grabbing violence, could more properly be seen as anti-capitalism demonstrations. Yet, this itself is of interest, for it highlights the fact that capitalist economies and their relations with the state change, as do the ideas and arguments that feature in debates about state–market relationships. For want of a better term, we have placed such debates under the heading **political economy**, and our aim in this chapter is to explore the broad shifts in political economy that have occurred over the past quarter of a century and to relate these shifts to changes in welfare policy – or, to put it another way, to explore shifting *political economies of welfare*. In this chapter, we examine recent changes to the political economy of welfare in the UK, then move on to consider some key theories about how the nature of the present economy constrains state action in the present day and then, finally, consider why and how political economies (of welfare) change.

Political economies of welfare

First, it is worth briefly stating why we think students of the policy process should be interested in political economies of welfare. Broadly speaking, our position is that decision makers' actions are in large part framed by the dominant beliefs of the era in which they live and, more specifically, that at any given moment in time an overarching **ideational** (or even ideological) **paradigm** exists which spells out accepted wisdom concerning the broad parameters within which state action can take place (see Heffernan, 2002). This is not to say that there is universal agreement about the validity of the dominant paradigm or that policy makers are absolutely bound to follow it; rather, it is to point to the fact that the major political parties often share many of the same core assumptions about what is possible and compete for votes by offering programmes which differ at the margins around these core assumptions. While these policy differences are certainly important and, empirically, have been shown to have a measurable impact on the nature of welfare state activity, it is rarely the case that major parties compete by offering manifestoes grounded in radically different world views; nor is it the case that parties remain rooted to the same policy positions year after year. Indeed, as we will show in a moment, the past century has seen some radical changes in the dominant beliefs about what the state can and should do – what we might call **paradigm shifts** of consensus opinion. We will discuss the causes of these shifts in more detail later, but it is worth briefly noting here that these shifts often come as a consequence of a perceived crisis facing the existing paradigm, its inability to solve new problems for instance. By calling into question existing assumptions, crises can open windows of opportunity, triggering a search for alternative frameworks of action. However, these windows are firmly sealed for the most part, and when they do open it is usually for little more than a brief period. It is the stability of these paradigms, then, that makes them important to policy analysts: by laying down the broad parameters of action, they play a key role in **setting the agenda** (see Chapter Seven). They are what Lukes (1974) refers to as the second and third faces of power – the often undebated assumptions that underpin political systems.

The post-war welfare consensus

To illustrate our argument, we might usefully consider the shifting philosophical basis of welfare policy in post-war Britain. The principles on which the welfare state was established in the immediate aftermath of the Second World War have been discussed at length by key social policy analysts such as Fraser (2003), Jones (2000), Hill (1993), Glennerster (1995) and Gladstone (1995). Following the Beveridge Report in 1942, the wartime coalition government and then the Attlee Labour government elected in 1945 introduced a number of key reforms which radically extended the scope of state action in the key spheres of social policy. For instance, in education, the 1944 (Butler) Education Act improved access to schooling by guaranteeing free education up to leaving age; in social security, the 1945 Family Allowances, 1946 National Insurance and 1948 National Assistance Acts rationalised, improved and extended state run income support schemes for those in need; and, in the health care sphere, the 1946 National Health Service Act created the NHS, making health care available free for all at the point of use (see Fraser, 2003, for an overview).

While there is disagreement over how far post-war developments represented a discontinuity with the past and over the precise causes of policy change, there is general agreement over some of the core features of the post-war welfare state.

First, the increased scale of **state intervention** that underpinned these new social policies reflected a view that government could intervene to tackle social ills. In other words, it was accepted that there were limits to what markets could achieve and that strong social policies were needed to protect people from the negative effects of markets. The Second World War itself had gone a long way to demonstrating the validity of this position, the marshalling of national resources in support of the war effort having led to improvements in access to health care, for example. In this sense, many of the post-war welfare policies were a continuation or extension of wartime practices, the break in continuity being with the more market oriented approaches of pre-war governments (Addison, 1994; Fraser, 2003; Hill, 2003).

Second, the new welfare state was heavily influenced by the recommendations of the committee charged with examining *Social insurance and allied services* – the so-called Beveridge Report (Beveridge, 1942). Summarising the implications of this landmark in welfare history is by no means an easy task, but its key contribution, arguably, was to emphasise the **social rights** that are implied by citizenship (see Marshall, 1950). Beveridge's position was that the state had an obligation to tackle what he called the 'five giants': want (poverty), squalor (inadequate housing), disease (or ill health), ignorance (lack of educational opportunity) and idleness (unemployment). The Beveridge Report captured the mood of the time – the desire to look towards a better world after the war – because it invoked a step change in thinking. Rather than considering social insurance as one of many separate, technical items of government expenditure, it argued the case for a more comprehensive set of interconnected policies for dealing with poverty and exclusion: in other words, for a *welfare state* rather than welfare policies.

Closely connected to this – indeed assumed by the Beveridge Report – was an endorsement of a **Keynesian approach to economic management**. More specifically, the new welfare settlement was underpinned by the belief that state intervention in the economic sphere could guarantee **full employment**: that by manipulating aggregate demand in the economy, government action could help smooth out the peaks and troughs of the economic cycle. As with increased intervention in the social sphere, the validity of claims that state management of the economy could be beneficial was boosted by the wartime experience, particularly the increasing levels of employment that resulted from the state-led process of rearmament in the run up to the war. Moreover, the harsh experiences of unemployment in the interwar period undoubtedly conditioned a general desire to avoid a repeat situation at the end of the Second World War. Indeed, for both social and economic reasons, the promotion of full employment became an official government policy after the war and the tools for achieving it the subject of one of Beveridge's less well-known works (Beveridge, 1944).

Similarly, the post-war social policy settlement was founded on a belief that careful management of the economy could – by ironing out the peaks and troughs of the economic cycle – ensure persistent and stable levels of **economic growth**. Although perhaps initially implied rather than made explicit, the feeling that continued prosperity was guaranteed meant it was easier to make the case for increasing levels of social expenditure than it would otherwise have been. Indeed, it was commonplace for policy makers to claim that spending increases were being funded through the proceeds of economic growth.

It is also worth adding that full employment at this time was assumed to mean full employment for men: although women had played a huge and crucial role in the wartime labour market, it was assumed they would adopt a more traditional child-rearing role in peacetime. In fact, more than this, the post-war welfare state was very much rooted in a **male breadwinner model**, for the social rights of citizenship implied in the Beveridge Report were gained by men through their National Insurance contributions while women and children were typically treated as 'dependants', gaining entitlements by virtue of their relationship with a male wage-earner. Similarly, the social policies of the era were based upon a particular view of the family unit too, the traditional nuclear family (see Chapter Four for a more detailed examination of employment issues).

In short, the post-war settlement was very much based around a political economy of welfare that presumed that state intervention could improve the management of the economy and, likewise, that taxation of economic activity and regulation of markets was necessary in order to guarantee the social rights of citizens. This marked a significant shift in thinking compared to the interwar period in which the state floundered in the face of economic problems as orthodox tools proved unable to combat the plunge into depression, where the response to mass unemployment could be characterised as little more than a weak attempt to ameliorate some of the worst side effects of the problem and in which emergent welfare provisions were curtailed and cut back at the very moment that rising unemployment created the need for an extensive set of social protections (see Fraser, 2003, for an overview).

Breakdown of the Beveridgian welfare state

Crucially, these core assumptions were largely shared by the two main political parties and formed the basis of a (the) **post-war consensus** during which welfare spending and state activity expanded under both Labour and Conservative governments. Indeed, commentators at the time coined the phrase 'Butskellism' to capture the closeness of the economic policies of the two parties (the terms being a combination of Butler and Gaitskell, the chancellor and shadow chancellor during the mid-1950s). While the precise extent and depth of this consensus can be questioned (Seldon, 1994) – and certainly it seems a little shallow when compared to the deeper and more enduring welfare consensus to be found in nations such as Sweden (for example, Baldwin, 1990) – there is little doubt that a paradigm shift in the political economy of welfare had occurred in the aftermath of the Second World War. However, the assumptions and beliefs upon which this new, pro-welfare state paradigm was based came under severe challenge from the late 1960s onwards as wider social and economic shifts began to undermine key elements of it.

First, it became increasingly apparent that the UK economy was facing some significant problems. While, at the end of the 1950s, the prime minister, Harold MacMillan, felt able to brag that the people of the nation had 'never had it so good', by the 1970s it was clear that Britain's economic power was on the wane as relatively weak growth rates meant the nation began to lose ground to its competitors. Indeed, rather than guaranteeing stable levels of growth, government policies had seemed to produce a **'stop–go' cycle**: sharp bursts of growth which pushed the economy close to its limits and so requiring active dampening of demand in order to prevent the economy overheating. Worse still, unemployment began to re-emerge. Indeed, by the late 1970s, it had broken through the psychologically important 'one million mark' and the perception that unemployment was out of control was a key factor in Labour losing power in the 1979 General Election[1]. Moreover, the political significance of this failure to deliver full employment was heightened by the fact that high levels of inflation accompanied it. One of the canons of Keynesian economics was that inflation and unemployment were inversely related: a rise in one would be connected to a fall in the other (the so-called 'Phillips Curve'). The emergence of **stagflation** – so named because it involves simultaneous economic **stag**nation and in**flation** – called into question the validity of Keynesian ideas.

On top of this, there were also suggestions that the UK economy was hampered by structural problems. Some felt that key industries relied on outmoded working practices and displayed poor productivity. Critics of the status quo argued that this in turn was a result of state intervention – particularly state support for (or even nationalisation of) struggling industries and a corporatist approach to economic management that gave unions a key role in shaping economic and social policies (see **Box 3.1**). Indeed, the view that the state had become so big that it had extended beyond its reach – the **state overload thesis** – began to gain ascendancy. Those asserting this position

[1] An iconic element of the Tories' 1979 election campaign was a Saatchi & Saatchi designed poster featuring a dole queue with the slogan 'Labour Isn't Working'. It was voted 'Poster of the (20th) century' by the advertising industry trade magazine *Campaign* and is often credited with having a key role in the election. See BBCi (2001).

Box 3.1: Corporatist economic management

From today's perspective, the corporatist approach to economic management that was a central part of the post-war consensus seems an alien one. For instance, while wage agreements are now largely seen as a private matter, all but two governments in the 1945-79 period felt the need to resort to a national incomes policy in order to help with the management of the economy; in principle, these were the outcome of negotiation between government and national leaders from business and trade unions, but at times policies were imposed by the state, or unions were unable to prevent agitation at local level against national agreements (Dorey, 2001). This was particularly the case in the 1970s, when the oil crisis placed the British economy in a precarious state and industrial relations were at a low point. So, for instance, the Heath government's strict incomes policy – which included a five-month period during which no wage increases were permitted – was in large part undermined by industrial action led by the miners. Similarly, the Callaghan government's imposed policy of (below-inflation) 5% maximum wage increases was thrown into disarray by the 1978-79 'Winter of Discontent'.

For many, both the attempts to impose such policies and, worse still, the failure to make them stick, seemed to suggest the country had become ungovernable. The level of industrial action reinforced such views: some 29.5 million working days were lost in 1979 (compared to just 235,000 in 1997; www.statistics.gov.uk). Certainly, Mrs Thatcher felt the country had become ungovernable and suffered from state overload and she exploited such concerns in the election campaign. For instance, her foreword to the 1979 Conservative Party election manifesto stated: "No one who has lived in this country during the last five years can fail to be aware of how the balance of our society has been increasingly tilted in favour of the State at the expense of individual freedom" (Conservative Party, 1979). The recently released draft manifesto began even more pithily: "The people of Britain have been suffering from too much government" (Conservative Party, 1978).

were undoubtedly assisted by two further significant events that undermined the credibility of the Callaghan Labour government. First, a persistent and significant weakness of the pound (£) and a related balance of payments problem resulted in the government seeking an emergency loan from the International Monetary Fund (IMF). Such action, more commonly associated with Third World economies in severe difficulties, was widely interpreted as a sign that the UK economy had well and truly slid down the ranks from world's richest nation to economic has-been. To make matters worse still for the government, however, the event created further problems in that the IMF attached conditions to the loan: in particular, public spending was to be reduced and the control of the money supply (and so, in effect, inflation) was to be made the top priority of economic policy. In short, this marked the end of the Keynesian-driven approach to economic management and the abandonment of the commitment to delivering full employment. Callaghan was quite explicit about this in his

Box 3.2: The party's over

Following the deal brokered with the IMF to assist with the UK's balance of payments crisis, Prime Minister Jim Callaghan delivered a landmark speech to the 1976 Labour Party Conference that explicitly spelt out the government's view that the Keynesian approach to economic management – and the assumption that economic growth could pay for continued expansion of public spending – was dead. In his speech he told assembled ranks of union leaders, party activists and MPs:

> We used to think that you could spend your way out of a recession and increase employment by cutting taxes and boosting government spending. I tell you in all candour that that option no longer exists, and even insofar as it did ever exist, it only worked on each occasion by injecting a larger dose of inflation into the economy, followed by a higher level of unemployment as the next step.

While many assume that the Thatcher government marked the end of the post-war political economy of welfare, this is not so: the reorientation of social and economic policy in fact began under the Callaghan government.

speech to the Labour Party conference in 1976 (see **Box 3.2**) but his attempts to cut back public spending were severely hampered by the second of the key events: the rising level of industrial action and, in particular, the 1978-79 'Winter of Discontent' (**Box 3.1**). Pay-related strikes by key public service workers (including the firefighters, ambulance drivers, refuse collectors and grave diggers) undermined plans for reducing public sector budgets and the credibility of the government's corporatist approach to economic management. Politically, they also handed the advantage to the key exponent of the state overload thesis: Mrs Thatcher.

From Thatcher to Blair

Famously, the aim of **'rolling back the state'** was central to Thatcher's programme of reform. Whereas the post-war welfare settlement was founded upon a belief that increased state intervention could improve economic performance and tackle social problems, Thatcherism was founded on precisely the opposite belief: that state intervention created more problems than it solved. Consequently, she launched a radical programme of free-market driven reforms that looked to reverse the gradual move towards collectivism that had characterised the previous century. This programme included the high-profile privatisation of many state-owned industries and utilities, drives to boost the efficiency and reduce the size of public-sector programmes, the marketisation of key public services, the tightening up of entitlement rules for key social security benefits – and a reduction in their rates – and a series of radical cuts in taxation (see Kavanagh, 1990).

Concomitant with this belief that state action was harmful was a revised view of citizenship in which social rights were de-emphasised, replaced by a stress on the importance of **individual responsibility**. For Thatcher, guaranteeing welfare was a matter for individuals and their families not the state. Indeed, as with the economic sphere, she felt that state intervention in the social sphere often caused more problems than it solved by, for example, discouraging people from saving for the future, seeking work when unemployed, caring for family members or volunteering in the community. Indeed, because high taxes were deemed to crowd out private sector activity and reduce incentives to work and, at the same time, because high social security benefits were seen as a disincentive to save or to seek employment, reduction of social expenditure was presented as an act that would both stimulate economic development and promote morally superior behaviour.

In terms of economic theory, Thatcher rejected the Keynesian approach and, instead, followed a **monetarist** approach that suggested that controlling the money supply – rather than attempting to manipulate aggregate demand – should be the priority for the state. In turn this entailed an emphasis on controlling the **level of inflation** rather than guaranteeing high levels of employment[2]. From this perspective, the government's true role in the economic sphere was to lay the conditions for economic success – to promote stability and certainty by keeping inflation in check. It was about operating on the **supply side** rather than the demand side of the economy, responsibility for growth and enterprise belonging to private industry and entrepreneurs.

In short, Thatcher's programme was based upon values that offered a mirror image of those that underpinned the post-war consensus. Rather than being a variation on a theme, her policies were supported by a paradigm shift in thinking about the political economy of welfare. Of course, this did not happen overnight or without struggle, nor did the consensus of opinion move as quickly as she did. However, powerful interests such as the Treasury, financial institutions, core parts of the media and public opinion and, abroad, organisations such as the IMF and the US government, played a key role in promoting and upholding this new world view (Hall, 1992). Although the Labour Party initially kicked against this shift – their 1983 General Election campaign saw them run on a manifesto that proposed an even greater increase in state intervention – under the leadership of Kinnock they began to move towards a position that accepted some of the key elements of this new paradigm. With the election of Tony Blair as their leader in 1994, this process accelerated and,

---

[2] Indeed, the former Conservative chancellor Norman Lamont famously proclaimed in parliament that a significant level of unemployment was "a price worth paying" if it helped keep inflation in check.

most famously, one of his first acts as leader was to reword the iconic Clause IV of the Labour Party's constitution on the grounds that its commitment to increased state intervention was outmoded (see Box 3.3).

None of this is to say that the course of action Thatcher took was the right one or to proclaim her approach as a success. Indeed, many of the problems she highlighted persisted despite her radical reforms. So, for instance, the boom–bust cycle repeated itself; unemployment increased dramatically; public expenditure proved difficult to roll back; tax cuts had to be financed by an increase in public borrowing – or, in effect, tax on future citizens. The point is that the consensus of opinion shifted towards the paradigm upon which her platform was based. While the problems and contradictions within the Conservatives' approach ultimately led to their losing power to Blair's New Labour government in 1997 – Blair made much of the fact that they did not "have the answer to the problems of social polarisation, rising crime, failing education and low productivity and growth" (Blair, 1998, p 2) – Labour returned to power only after undergoing a radical process of modernisation. Crucially, Blair's 'Third Way' was founded on the belief that Labour needed to draw from past failures and, where necessary, learn from what the Conservatives had achieved; indeed, the party even accepted some of the Thatcherite agenda it had so bitterly opposed at the time as "in retrospect, necessary acts of modernisation" (Blair, 1998, p 5). While critics have suggested that the New

---

Box 3.3: Clause IV

Amending Clause IV of the Labour Party constitution was a defining moment of Tony Blair's leadership. Printed on all party membership cards, the clause outlined the socialist aims of the party and included radical aims with respect to state ownership and the redistribution of resources. While its role was in practice largely symbolic – Labour governments never had a route map leading towards such radical ends – Blair's move to amend it was equally symbolic.

Old Clause IV

To secure for the workers by hand or by brain the full fruits of their industry and the most equitable distribution thereof that may be possible upon the basis of the common ownership of the means of production, distribution, and exchange, and the best obtainable system of popular administration and control of each industry or service.

New Clause IV

The Labour Party is a democratic socialist party. It believes that by the strength of our common endeavour, we achieve more than we achieve alone so as to create for each of us the means to realise our true potential and for all of us a community in which power, wealth and opportunity are in the hands of the many not the few, where the rights we enjoy reflect the duties we owe, and where we live together, freely, in a spirit of solidarity, tolerance and respect.

Labour agenda is nothing more than a shift to the right – an abandonment of traditional Labour values (Hay, 1999) – Blair (1998, p 1) is clear that "the Third Way is not an attempt to split the difference between Right and Left. It is about traditional values in a changed world", in which the emergence of a technologically driven, globalised knowledge economy has rendered traditional social democratic approaches obsolete.

For policy analysts, Blair's election has raised the difficult question of whether or not New Labour's Third Way is sufficiently distinctive from the programme followed by the Thatcher and Major governments to be viewed as another post-war paradigm shift, for, in many ways, there are strong similarities between the approach adopted by Thatcher and Blair's Third Way. Firstly, the Third Way is based on the assumption that there are **clear limits to state action**; Blair, for example, has suggested that "public expenditure as a proportion of national income has more or less reached the limits of acceptability" (Blair and Schroeder, 1999, p 2). Similarly, Anthony Giddens (2000, p 57) – the key theorist of the Third Way – has argued that the Third Way acknowledges a distinction between a big state and a strong state.

Second, in terms of citizenship, the Third Way takes on board the critique of the post-war model of social rights by emphasising individual responsibility. However, it goes beyond individualism in emphasising **rights and responsibilities** alongside each other. Here, Blair (1998, p 4) has argued that:

> For too long, the demand for rights from the state was separated from the duties of citizenship and the imperative for mutual responsibility on the part of individuals and institutions. Unemployment benefits were often paid without strong reciprocal obligations; children went unsupported by absent parents. [...] The rights we enjoy reflect the duties we owe: rights and opportunity without responsibility are engines of selfishness and greed.

Finally, in the economic sphere, again like Thatcherism, the Third Way rejects Keynesian economics in favour of a **supply-side approach**. Given this, it also rejects the idea that the state can guarantee full employment. Indeed, Blair (1999) has been quite explicit about this, arguing that the assumptions underpinning the Keynesian demand management model have "completely broken down". Given this, and the emergence of a more global, knowledge-based economy, Blair argues that "the top priority must be investment in human and social capital" (Blair and Schroeder, 1999, p 5). As Giddens (2000, p 73) puts it:

> The aim of macroeconomic policy is to keep inflation low, limit government borrowing, and use active supply-side measures to foster growth and high levels of employment.

Crucially, many of these supply-side policies – particularly those concerning unemployment benefits, education and training – were traditionally viewed as falling within the sphere of social policy, meaning "wherever possible invest in human capital ... is a guiding theme of welfare reform, as well as of the actions government must take to react to the knowledge economy" (Giddens, 2000, p 165).

For Giddens (2000, p 163), as for Blair, the Third Way "is not an attempt to occupy a middle ground between top-down socialism and free-market philosophy. It is concerned with restructuring social democratic doctrines to respond to the twin revolutions of globalisation and the knowledge economy". But, while the justifications for Thatcherism and Blairism may differ and, similarly, there are differing emphases on policies in particular spheres – particularly with respect to social policies – questions remain about how far the Third Way represents a change in direction or simply a variation on the theme of Thatcherism. Can, then, policy analysts help us in answering this question?

From welfare state to competition state?

In theorising the nature of this shift in the broad political economy of welfare over the post-war era, Evans and Cerny (2003) have developed the notion of a **competition state**. They argue that, in the post-war boom period, social policy was a relatively autonomous field of policy, a domestic issue that was unimpeded by wider economic concerns and so favourable to continual increases in state spending on welfare state activity. However, they argue that recent changes have undermined these conditions and that we have witnessed the emergence of the 'competition state' where government focuses its efforts on laying the conditions for economic success and looks to use all tools of policy – including its social policies – to promote this objective.

More specifically, they suggest that there has been a 'paradigm shift' that has resulted in "a new, loosely knit neoliberal consensus on the state's role in a global capitalist economy" (Evans and Cerny, 2003, p 21). In the economic sphere, this entails a rejection of Keynesian economics, an emphasis on free markets and supply-side economics, stricter controls on public spending and stringent attempts to combat inflation. In terms of social policy, it means a reduced emphasis on the social rights of citizenship (and an increased emphasis on individual responsibilities), the increased marketisation – or, sometimes, privatisation – of public services and the introduction of workfare style active labour market policies in place of insurance-style unemployment benefits.

While they suggest that the factors leading to the emergence of the competition state are both complex and multiple, they highlight one in particular: globalisation. Indeed, they argue that the "main challenge" facing "government all over the world" is the need to respond to globalisation (2003, p 25) and that "from the beginning, the impetus behind the emergence of the competition state was to adjust the economic policies, practices and institutions of the state to conform to the anti-inflationary norms of the international financial markets in order to prevent capital flight and make domestic investment conditions attractive to internationally mobile capital" (2003, p 25).

So, for them, Thatcher(ism) and Blair(ism) are both part of the same long-term trend in the shift from a Keynesian welfare state to a competition state for both see a more limited role for the state and emphasise the importance of adopting social policies that can help create the conditions for success within the global economy. Indeed, Evans and Cerny (2003) describe Thatcherism as the competition state Mark I and 'Blairism' – or the Third Way – as the competition state Mark II. In their view, both are, fundamentally, variations on the same broad world view: they share the same political economy of welfare. This is not to say that they are one and the same thing; indeed, Evans and Cerny (2003) suggest the two differ significantly with respect to the details of the social policies that underpin them. In effect, they underline that they share many core assumptions about what it is possible for the state to achieve and the kind of role it can perform in the contemporary era. Indeed, given this paradigm shift in the political economy of welfare this represents, Evans and Cerny (2003, p 24) go so far as to suggest that "the competition state is the successor to the welfare state, incorporating many of its features but reshaping them, sometimes quite drastically, to fit a globalizing world".

The post-Fordist welfare state

Evans and Cerny's work developed from the political science literature (and from the international relations literature in particular), but Jessop (1994, 1999, 2000), who draws more heavily on the sociological literature, has developed a very similar line of argument. In particular, Jessop has built on work from regulation theory and ideas embedded in the notion of 'post-Fordism' (see Burrows and Loader, 1994), which point to significant shifts in the ways in which the state guarantees the economic and social conditions required for capital accumulation. He argues that there have been fundamental shifts in the way in which the world economy operates that have forced governments to reform the bases of their economic and social policies in order to maintain national economic competitiveness and profitability. In particular, there has been a search for new ways of reconciling the demands for social policies that meet the needs of citizens with economic policies that meet the demands of the capitalist class. The result, Jessop (2000, pp 171-2) argues, is that:

> relative to the earlier post-war period, social policy is becoming more closely subordinated to economic policy ... and its delivery

has been subject to a partial rollback of the state in favour of market forces and civil society.

This is not least because the "opening of national economies makes it harder to pursue social policy in isolation from economic policy" (Jessop, 2000, p 182). More specifically, he claims that we have seen the death of the old style Keynesian Welfare National State (KWNS) and the birth of what he calls the **'Schumpeterian Workfare Post-National Regime'** (SWPR) (see *Table 3.1*). The SWPR differs from the KWNS along four key dimensions: the economic sphere; the social sphere; scalability; and its delivery mechanisms (Jessop, 1999).

In the economic sphere, Jessop (1999, 2000) argues that the Keynesian approach to economics – based upon demand management to produce full employment in a closed (that is, national) economy – has been replaced by a **Schumpeterian** approach in which the demands of an open (that is, international/globalised) economy mean that the emphasis is on supply-side policies which promote flexibility, innovation and economic competitiveness. In the social sphere, he suggests that the move towards an open economy

Table 3.1: *From KWNS to SWPR*

Keynesian welfare national state		Schumpeterian workfare post-national regime	
Keynesian	• Full employment • Closed economy • Demand management	*Schumpeterian*	• Innovation and competitiveness • Open economy • Supply-side policies
Welfare	• Welfare rights	*Workfare*	• Social policy subordinated to economic policy • Downward pressure on social wage • Attacks on welfare rights
National	• Primacy of national scale	*Post-national*	• Hollowing out of the state
State	• Mixed economy • State intervenes to correct market failures	*Regime*	• Increased role of governance mechanisms to correct market and state failures

Source: Adapted from Jessop (1999, 2000)

makes it difficult to sustain high-tax, high-spend welfare states. Indeed, Jessop argues that economic change has placed a downward pressure on the social rights that were at the heart of the post-war welfare settlement and that, consequently, social policies have been subordinated to economic policies, their role being to support economic competitiveness rather than guarantee social protection. He suggests, therefore, that we should talk about **workfare** rather than welfare when examining social policies. At the same time, he argues we can no longer talk about the nation state delivering these policies either – meaning both parts of the term 'welfare state' are redundant – because, in terms of his third and fourth dimensions (scalability and delivery mechanisms), these economic and social policies are increasingly operated above or below the national level and are delivered by a range of providers. The 'hollowing out of the state' (see Chapter Six of this book) means that we talk of 'governance' rather than 'government', and see supranational and regional government playing a bigger role within the state and, outside of it, Quasi-governmental agencies (QGAs), private corporations and voluntary sector bodies taking on more of the functions of the state too. So, rather than talking of policies that are national and state delivered, we have **post-national** policies that are governed by multi-sector **regimes**.

Jessop's characterisation of the shifting ideational basis of welfare chimes with the arguments made by Giddens and Blair about the nature (and underlying causes) of the Third Way. At the same time, it captures much of the nature of the Thatcherite project too. Indeed, Jessop (1999) conceives of both Thatcherism and New Labour as being variants of the same neo-liberal driven response to the emergence of the post-Fordist economy.

Paradigms and paradigm shifts

The consensus of opinion seems to suggest, therefore, that Blair and Thatcher operate from within the same paradigm. It is worth reiterating, however, that "to argue that contemporary politics embraces a neo-liberal consensus is not to claim Tony Blair is Margaret Thatcher reborn, only to suggest that ongoing policy continuities between the Labour government and its Conservative predecessors reflect a neo-liberal policy paradigm that constrains rather than determines government policy" (Heffernan, 2002, p 754).

Having looked at a case study of change, at this juncture it is worth expanding upon what we mean by a 'paradigm' when talking about shifting political economies of welfare. Here we are heavily influenced by the work of Hall (1992, 1993), Heffernan (2002) and Hwang (2002). As Hall (1993, p 279) puts it:

> Policymakers customarily work within a framework of ideas and standards that specifies not only the goals of policy and the kind of instruments that can be used to attain them, but also the very

nature of the problems they are meant to be addressing ... much
of it is taken for granted and unamenable to scrutiny as a whole.

It is this 'interpretative framework' to which Hall – like ourselves – refers to
when talking of a 'policy paradigm'. For the most part, politics revolves around
an accepted set of core beliefs – a *consensus* – that sets much of the agenda by
"diagnosing political and economic problems and prescribing policy solutions.
By providing policy makers with a compass [although] not necessarily a road
map" (Heffernan, 2002, p 743). In short, they set the **parameters of possibility**
within which political actors operate (Heffernan, 2002; Hwang, 2002).

One reason why policy paradigms are so important is they display immense
stability and only change periodically. In this sense, they are similar to the
paradigms of scientific knowledge described by Kuhn (1970; see also Hall,
1993; Heffernan, 2002). He argues that, for the most part, we operate within
the confines of 'normal science', proceeding on the basis of shared assumptions
about how the world operates. From time to time, however, our frameworks
for understanding the world break down as new discoveries and unexplained
phenomena challenge existing ideas. In such situations, new ideas ('radical
science') step into the foreground as a new framework for understanding the
world emerges; or, as Kuhn (1970) puts it, a 'paradigm shift' occurs. Policy
analysts have argued that much the same is true in the political world: that
policy paradigm shifts occur when the existing paradigm is in crisis. As
Heffernan (2002, p 750) suggests:

> If the paradigm 'ain't broke', radical ideational suggestions to 'fix
> it', existing in the form of circulating ideas and other forms of
> political discourse, will not find practical expression within the
> purview of the state. Only when a status quo is considered 'broke',
> and economic needs and political demands require change, can
> ideas be advanced to dramatically 'fix' it.

Similarly, Hwang (2002) has argued that 'new' ideas can become influential in
times of **uncertainty** when the dominant paradigm faces a crisis. Crucially, as
he points out, the term 'new' should be parenthesised: generally speaking,
emergent ideas are not 'new' at all insofar as they are likely to have been in
existence for some time; what is new is the heightened attention they receive
within policy making circles as decision-makers search for new ideas that can
help solve the crisis[3]. Here, he echoes Heclo's (1974, p 305) observation that,
in the making of social policies, "politics finds its sources not only in power

---

[3] So, for instance, the neo-liberal paradigm shift of the 1980s drew heavily on ideas developed by
Hayek in the 1940s (see, for example, Hayek, 1944). Similarly, Keynes lobbied heavily for his
ideas to be taken up by the UK government during the depression of the 1920s and 1930s but
had to wait until the 1940s and 1950s for them to be accepted by the Treasury.

Box 3.4: Pre-war paradigm shifts

In our discussion of political economy and paradigm shifts, we have focused primarily on the move from a Keynesian welfare state to the post-industrial competition state. However, it is worth briefly flagging earlier paradigm shifts in the political economy of welfare.

At the start of the industrial revolution, a non-interventionist **'laissez-faire liberalism'** typified state action. However, most industrialised countries in Europe witnessed a paradigm shift in the latter part of the 19th century as the growing awareness of the damaging social consequences of industrialisation led to calls for coordinated state action and the granting of the vote for working class men (male suffrage) boosted the political power of those most likely to benefit from increased state intervention. It is not surprising, therefore, that the first state sponsored social insurance programmes often concerned provisions for support in case of industrial accidents and that many of the earliest social policies were concerned with tackling public health problems related to urbanisation, insanitary living conditions and overcrowded slum housing.

It would be wrong, however, to give the impression that laissez-faire liberalism was replaced by a commitment to a welfare state as the 20th century approached – far from it. In most nations, the shift was towards a paradigm that might be dubbed **'reluctant collectivism'**. State intervention began to increase as elements of the modern welfare state emerged such as pensions, unemployment benefits, health and sickness insurance, state education and public housing. However, programmes were often patchy in their coverage or limited in their ambitions. In many cases, policies were only introduced after intense political battles and were often as likely to be instruments of social control as tools for redistributing wealth or promoting social solidarity. For example, in Germany, Bismarck's earnings-related, contributory social insurance scheme was very conservative in intent and socially divisive. Its aim was not so much to promote welfare as to secure the loyalty of the middle class – who gained most from his system – against an increasingly disruptive working class whose agitation threatened the stability of the newly unified German state.

In many European countries, with Britain being the exemplar here, it was only after the experience of the Second World War – when society was managed by the state and collective action was an imperative for national survival – that the legitimacy of state intervention was firmly accepted by the establishment. Likewise, the experience of 'pulling together' to defend the country brought down class barriers in society, allowing a more solidaristic vision of social policies to emerge. Only then were fully public solutions to welfare problems feasible and the more usual reactionary purposes of welfare states gave way to those of fundamental social change across the social classes. The wartime experience was critical in breaking down old barriers and ordinary people expected benefits and gains to their lives after the traumas of the war. This is the reason why the Labour Party decisively defeated Churchill, the great wartime leader and hero, in the 1945 general election. He delivered the nation from the war but could not be trusted to deliver the peace: locked into pre-war thinking, he missed the mood shift that underpinned the new collectivist, **Keynesian welfare state** paradigm.

but also in uncertainty – men collectively wondering what to do". Given this, Hall (1992) and Hwang (2002) have suggested that paradigm shifts are part of a process of **social learning** – the collective search for new ideas to solve policy problems. As Hall (1993, p 289) puts it in describing the breakdown of the Keynesian paradigm:

> The 1970s were dominated by collective puzzlement and uncertainty about the economy, and the effort to regain control over it was an intensely intellectual quest marked by highly sophisticated debate in the media, the political parties, and the City, as well as among policymakers. The play of ideas was as important to the outcome as was the contest of power. For these reasons, it seems highly appropriate to describe this process as one of social learning.

Conclusions: beyond the macro-level

Following Hall, one of the reasons we highlight the role of policy paradigms/ ideational consensuses/the political economies of welfare in the policy process is to bring the **role of ideas** in the policy process to the fore. Ideas often take a back seat in many policy analysis perspectives, the stress being placed on the power of political actors or social forces. Yet, ideas are at the heart of policy and, *prima facie*, ought to feature in analyses of the policy process. At the same time, however, it would be wrong to give the impression that ideas lead an autonomous existence within the policy process. As Heffernan (2002, p 749) argues, "ideas *explain* the form of change that is enacted, but actors, institutions and environments provide the *opportunity* for change to be effected".

So, for example, Hall (1993) has demonstrated the important role political institutions play in mediating paradigm shifts; in particular, he has pointed to the key role the UK's centralised, tightly-knit civil service played in hastening the switch from a Keynesian to a monetarist approach. Likewise, Hwang (2002) has highlighted the key role the presidential system has played in shaping social policies in Korea. The significance of this – as we will explore in greater detail in later chapters (especially those concerning policy networks and political institutions) – is that it implies that settings with different political institutions and different political organisations will produce variations on a given policy paradigm. So, while Jessop's (2000) notion of a Schumpeterian workfare post-national regime suggests welfare states are undergoing fundamental change and, in particular, that the values associated with traditional social democracy are under threat, he points out that this *does not* mean that welfare states will automatically begin to converge on a single neo-liberal model; indeed, he argues that many variations of the paradigm exist in practice. Similarly, Evans and Cerny

(2003) have argued that the idea of a competition state can be broken down into different subcategories, encompassing strong and weak variants rather than a single model of government. What this indicates, perhaps, is that while recent economic changes have placed high spending welfare states under pressure, we should not be too quick in jumping to the conclusion that this spells the end for welfare regimes that do not follow the neo-liberal path. This certainly chimes with the view of Esping-Andersen (1996, p 24) who, in a recent study of the impact of global economic change on welfare, has argued that "in most countries what we see is not radical change, but rather a 'frozen' welfare state landscape", thus confirming the view developed in his earlier work that there are a number of distinct types of welfare regimes within the capitalist world (Esping-Andersen, 1990) (see **Box 3.5**).

However, the thrust of Heffernan's argument is that, when paradigms do break down, institutions, past policy decisions, networks of policy experts and individual political actors play a key role in determining how wide the search for new policy ideas is and how long the window of change remains open. Again, we will explore such issues in greater detail in later chapters (especially Chapters Seven to Eleven). For now, however, it is worth emphasising a point we have made repeatedly in this chapter: that political economies of welfare display remarkable stability. The picture is one of **punctuated equilibrium** – long periods of stability interrupted by temporary periods of flux as the system readjusts following a crisis (see Chapter Ten). Moreover, even when paradigm shifts do occur, this does not mean that *everything* changes. Indeed, governments are severely constrained by past decisions and **historical policy**

Box 3.5: Worlds of welfare

In his seminal book *The three worlds of welfare capitalism*, Esping-Andersen (1990) argued that economically advanced capitalist nations could be split into three different **welfare regimes**:

- *liberal regimes*: weak social rights and high inequality (ideal type: US);
- *conservative/corporatist regimes*: strong social rights but limited role for state in addressing inequality (ideal type: Germany);
- *social democratic regimes*: strong social rights with egalitarian goals (ideal type: Sweden).

He argued that early debates about political economy – particularly the principles of state intervention and the nature of state–citizen relationships – fundamentally impacted upon future welfare development. At the same time, however, much also depended on political factors: the strength of working class political mobilisation and the depth of cross-class coalitions in a society (both, in turn, very much influenced by the nature of political institutions). In short, while different ideas underpinned the different regimes it was not ideas alone that led to these differences: institutions and networks were key also.

legacies heavily influence their action. Consequently, "one consensus will rework, not totally replace another" (Heffernan, 2002, p 755). In other words, there is often a not insignificant degree of overlap between the old and the new political economies of welfare, for "however they may change them, new paradigms build on past paradigms, reforming them and seeking to modernise them. The wheel is never reinvented" (Heffernan, 2002, p 755), in large part because interests, institutions and networks constrain the degree of change.

As this suggests, the analysis offered here is only partial and we will return to many of these issues about how institutions and interests filter ideas later in the book. What this also suggests is that it is difficult to pinpoint the precise nature of the role ideas play in the policy process: their role varies from time-to-time and place-to-place and they necessarily interact with other forces within the policy making process. However, while policy analysts have often struggled to develop theories and models that effectively articulate the role of ideas, few are in doubt that the role is a crucial one. For as Keynes (1936, p 383) famously proclaimed in his *General theory of employment, interest and money*:

> the ideas of economists and political philosophers, both when they are right and when they are wrong, are more powerful than is commonly understood. Indeed the world is ruled by little else. Practical men, who believe themselves to be quite exempt from any intellectual influences, are usually the slaves of some defunct economist. Madmen in authority, who hear voices in the air, are distilling their frenzy from some academic scribbler of a few years back. I am sure that the power of vested interests is vastly exaggerated compared with the gradual encroachment of ideas … soon or late, it is ideas, not vested interests, which are dangerous for good or evil.

Summary

- Policy makers' actions are often constrained by a dominant policy paradigm or political economy that lays down the broad parameters within which state action takes place.
- Policy paradigms display immense stability but can shift quite rapidly in times of crisis. This is sometimes referred to as 'punctuated equilibrium'.
- A pro-welfare state policy paradigm emerged after the Second World War; it was succeeded by a paradigm more hostile to the welfare state in the 1970s and 1980s. Evans and Cerny dub the new paradigm a 'competition state' – as opposed to a welfare state – and Jessop talks of a Schumpeterian workfare post-national regime having replaced a Keynesian welfare national state.

- Ideas are at the heart of the policy process but they play a complex role and are mediated by institutions, interests and networks.

Questions for discussion

- In terms of their broad political economy, how do the New Labour governments differ from the Thatcher governments?
- Why do paradigms change?
- What role do ideas play in shaping policy change?

Further reading

Evans, M. and Cerny, P. (2003) 'Globalisation and social policy', in N. Ellison and C. Pierson (eds) *Developments in British social policy 2*, Basingstoke: Palgrave, pp 19-41.

Hall, P. (1993) 'Policy paradigms, social learning and the state: the case of economic policymaking in Britain', *Comparative Politics*, vol 25, pp 275-96.

Heffernan, R. (2002) '"The possible as the art of politics": understanding consensus politics', *Political Studies*, vol 50, pp 742-60.

Jessop, B. (2000) 'From the KWNS to the SWPR', in G. Lewis, S. Gewirtz and J. Clarke (eds) *Rethinking social policy*, London: Sage Publications.

Changes in the world of work

Overview

One of the main consequences of globalisation has been the way in which centres of production of tradable goods has shifted to Asia and the southern hemisphere. Britain, once the 'workshop of the world', is now principally a service-based economy. This shift is critical to the shape of the welfare state, which, as we saw in Chapter Three, was devised to support a 'male breadwinner' model of society. This chapter considers the consequences of economic restructuring particularly on the way in which work is divided between men and women, the geographical shift of population and economic prosperity away from the old industrial centres and towards a suburban/small town locus, and the implications of this for the distribution of public services and the wider welfare state.

Key concepts

Labour markets; economic restructuring; Catholic cultural imperative; counter-urbanisation; suburbanisation; post-industrialism.

Introduction

One of the main consequences of globalisation over the last three decades has been acceleration in the restructuring of the world economy. A crucial feature of this in relation to the analysis of public policy is the changing structure of the global labour market. The big picture has been the shift of manufacturing away from the old industrial heartlands in northern Europe and the eastern seaboard of the US to an Asian–Pacific axis and a geographically diverse set of nations mainly in the southern hemisphere. This changing 'world' of work and the economic shifts that underpin it are major pieces in the puzzle of how welfare states have evolved in recent decades and so attention needs to be paid not only to the facts of how the global labour market has changed but what its impact has been on the shape of public policy.

The idea that there is a relationship between the nature of welfare states and the structure of the labour market is an observation that has been made time and again in the comparative public policy literature. One of the main stories of the 20th century was the evolution of large-scale welfare state spending to mirror and service 'Fordist', mass-production industries. An industrial worker adequately educated and housed and in reasonable health became the *sine qua non* of modern production methods. Sociologists and comparativists also pointed out that 'capital' was forced to an extent to concede improved conditions of life by organised labour. Here is not the place to debate the merits of this argument, but there is a *prima facie* case that, if the old-fashioned Fordist paradigm has changed as a result of globalisation processes, then the context for the development of modern public policy shifted too. Historical contingency is a central part of the way in which the story of modern public policy needs to be read. As we discussed in Chapter Three, policy directions reflect historical trajectories, the pathways of different nations as they progress through the process of modernisation. Key institutional concepts, such as path dependency and the 'punctuated' nature of social progress, are important conceptual hooks for understanding what has happened to the global labour market in recent decades and what the consequences have been for the shaping of modern welfare states.

This chapter begins by charting some of the basic facts about the development of labour markets in the post-Second World War period. We need to go back that far because the narrative is very much shaped by the outcome of the war and its aftermath. A war on that scale seems *prima facie* to be the likely cause of a major 'punctuation' point in social development and policy regimes. War is a time when the state takes charge of society and as a result also induces in the people a sense of 'pulling together' against a common enemy. It follows also that in its aftermath the people look to the state (rather than the private sector) to deliver the promised rewards and benefits for the suffering and traumas of the wartime experience.

This is a broad-brush approach aimed at showing key trends before we zoom in on the British case. The story involves looking at data on the changing structure of the economy (particularly at its growth), the balance between manufacturing production and the rise of the service economy, the distribution of new economic activity between men and women, and the geography of the modern labour market. In the final section, we consider the question of the extent to which public policy has been reshaped by the changing world of work.

The Second World War and its aftermath

The Second World War was the biggest and most extensive military/political conflict in the history of the world. Loss of life was numbered in millions and the economic impact was devastating for some countries, notably Germany, the USSR and Britain, but much less so for those countries involved as allies on either side but not directly affected by war damage. Indeed during the 1939-45 period, the economy of the US grew by over 3%. However, it is what happened after the war that concerns us most closely. One of the key features is that, in war-torn Europe, the state, having been at the centre of people's lives during the conflict in a way that was almost unimaginable beforehand, continued to exert a major influence over society and on the pattern of post-war recovery.

The economic and infrastructural reconstruction of European society was taken forward on a wave of collective action and state-led programmes fuelled by US dollars. In Britain, the Labour Party swept to power, ousting Churchill, on a political programme to bring to fruition Beveridge's wartime plan for a national health service, national assistance to those in need, a state education system and a programme of state housing. Although not uncontested, it was a remarkable expression of state over market-led solutions to the social crisis and above all the expectations created by the war. In the case of long-established industrial nations like Britain, it was all the more remarkable because the historical legacy was one of essentially private solutions to welfare, with a history traceable back to Victorian philanthropy and laissez-faire ideology. For more recently industrialising countries, such as Sweden or Austria, state intervention may have seemed a more natural way to tackle social problems.

One thing is very clear from all the data on the immediate post-war decades: the economies of the most affluent and most powerful trading nations grew exceptionally rapidly during the 1950s and 1960s. Summers and Heston (1991) estimated that the growth rate for the OECD nations between 1950 and 1960 averaged out at 3.3% per annum, and actually accelerated to over 4% up to about the mid-1970s. Castles (1998, p 32) estimated from a variety of sources that the world economy grew in volume more in the four post-war decades than in the whole of the previous 130 years. Castles also showed that this growth was not evenly spread among the industrial nations of the OECD. The economically strong countries built on their existing strength but during this period the weaker nations (Ireland, Italy, Spain, Portugal, Greece) were able to catch up so that entering the period following the post-war reconstruction – from the mid-1970s onwards – there was a more level economic playing field. This, of course, is highly significant for the development of public policy because of the link between economic affluence and spending on welfare programmes. At the very least it raises the question of how different countries constructed their welfare states from a platform of economic development that was historically much more uneven.

Economic restructuring and labour markets

One of the most important influences was the changing structure of economic activity and related changes to the labour market. Indeed, these changes were little short of revolutionary and require a brief explanation. Returning to the immediate post-war period, it is clear that, during the period of reconstruction and 'catch up' through unprecedented post-war growth (up to the mid-1970s), pre-war economic trading activity based on agriculture and particularly on manufacturing production reasserted itself. The post-war boom essentially was built around expanding manufacturing trade between the nations of the English-speaking northern hemisphere (and Australia) and 'old' Europe. However, in the period after the mid-1970s, major changes took place in the structure of the world economies, with the growth in significance of the Asian/Pacific Rim and other less economically developed nations as centres of manufacturing production and the switch of the more economically advanced nations from manufacturing to service-based economies.

Table 4.1 shows the pattern of change for a selection of OECD countries, taken from Castles' study (1998), in the balance of their industrial sectors (agriculture, manufacturing and services). It can be seen that, between 1960 and 1993, the share of employment in the UK accounted for by manufacturing declined by over 18 percentage points and the share of jobs located with services grew by 24 percentage points. Indeed, by 2000 services accounted for very nearly 75% of the UK labour market – ranging from jobs in retail outlets, banking and other financial services, education and higher education spin-off industries located on science parks, computing, leisure and tourism and, of course, public services and government itself. Recent government

Table 4.1: *Levels of change in the structure of employment*

| | % of civilian workforce by sector | | | | | | | | |
| | Agriculture | | | Manufacturing | | | Services | | |
	1960	1974	1993	1960	1974	1993	1960	1974	1993
UK	4.7	2.8	2.2	38.4	34.6	20.2	47.6	55.2	71.6
US	8.5	4.2	2.7	26.5	24.2	16.0	56.2	63.3	73.2
Sweden	15.7	6.7	3.4	31.5	28.3	17.2	44.0	56.3	71.1
Germany	14.0	7.0	3.5	34.3	35.8	27.1	39.0	46.3	57.9
Japan	30.2	12.9	5.9	21.3	27.2	23.7	41.3	50.1	59.8

Source: Adapted from Castles (1998, p 41)

statistics show that one in five of employed people work directly for the government and if outsourced work is included, such as Capita call centres, the figure is nearly seven million or one in four of the employed workforce (*The Telegraph*, 29 July 2003, p 32). The shift out of manufacturing (and also coal mining, which at its peak in the mid-1930s employed 750,000 men) has been dramatic and clearly shows up in this data.

Such dramatic change is not unique to the UK, of course, and is mirrored by the US whose shift out of manufacturing occurred earlier than in the UK, and also by Sweden which belatedly industrialised only in the post-war era but nevertheless still switched towards a service-based economy. A significant contrast between the US and Sweden in the narrative is that much of the growth in the Swedish service sector came about as the result of investment in public services through the establishment of its 'high tax/high spend' welfare state. Different stories can also be told for Germany and Japan, which is the only long-term Asian/Pacific member of the OECD. German agriculture clearly declined rapidly over the period, but the key feature of this case was that the switch out of manufacturing was much less dramatic than in Britain, Sweden or the US – down by only seven percentage points between 1960 and 1993 – although services still grew by nearly 20 percentage points. Germany has clearly tried to hold onto its manufacturing base and this is a significant fact we will return to later on in the discussion. By contrast to all the others, Japan expanded its manufacturing base by 2.5 percentage points, with the main change being the collapse of Japanese agriculture.

All of the advanced industrial nations show evidence of major economic restructuring, particularly in the decades after 1974. It is also clear that the detail of these changes conceals very different stories arising from earlier histories and cultural contexts. In the OECD countries as a whole:

- agricultural employment went down by two thirds and manufacturing by a quarter between the 1960s and the early 1990s;
- in 1993 there was no OECD country with less than half its workforce employed in services;
- growth in services employment was partly due to significant increases in state spending on health, education and welfare (Castles, 1998).

The new geography of manufacturing

The opposite side of the coin to the decline in manufacturing in the wealthy OECD nations is, of course, its **growth elsewhere**. This has been in the emerging industrial nations in the Pacific Rim – Singapore, Hong Kong, South Korea, Taiwan, Malaysia and including, as we saw earlier, Japan, and more recently in China, as well as a wide cross-section of so-called 'less economically developed' countries in the southern hemisphere. With the **liberalisation of**

world trade in the 1980s and the speeding up of economic globalisation, trade barriers were broken down and industries that had previously been protected by import taxes found themselves exposed to the full force of global competition. In Britain during the 1980s and 1990s, once-secure jobs in textiles, machine engineering, car manufacturing, horticulture and even primary products such as coal disappeared in a very short space of time.

By the same token, **manufacturing grew rapidly at this time in the less economically developed parts of the globe**. Examples of this are countries such as Bangladesh, Vietnam and Kenya. In Vietnam, 900,000 new jobs were created in manufacturing between 1990 and 2000 and a similar number were created in Bangladesh in the early 1990s (Jenkins and Sen, 2003). A very significant part of growth in these two countries was due to the opening up of the textiles and garment-making industries under the internationally agreed Multi-Fibre Arrangement, which regulates global production in these industries. The finished-garment industry accounts for 75% of Bangladesh exports and 50% in the case of Vietnam. Large companies, organised by the state in the case of Vietnam, have been able to reap the benefit of economies of scale, low wages and relatively poor working conditions to win large orders to supply goods globally in a rapidly moving, high-volume world market. A very large part of the growth in garment and textile employment in both Vietnam and Bangladesh has been of unskilled labour, almost entirely women who seem able to organise their daily lives to take on this role. Smaller companies and homeworkers, however, have found it very difficult to meet even the low international labour standards demanded by western companies and the International Labour Organisation, for example, risks being marginalised (Nadvi and Thoburn, 2003).

Other new markets have been created as a result of the **revolution in transport** and especially the growth in air transport. The production of fresh fruit and vegetables has become a very large-scale industry in Africa, supplying their produce to the European market, and especially the powerful UK supermarket chains. In Kenya and South Africa, for example, 20-30% of agricultural exports take the form of horticultural produce. This market grew rapidly in the 1990s. The stringent standards imposed by the supermarkets on quality and 'just-in-time' delivery has imposed significant pressures on this labour market, which is characterised by its informality, flexibility and insecurity. As Dolan and Barrientos (2003) observed, the pressures exerted by the supermarkets have tended to divert production away from the informal, smallholders and towards larger-scale units using casual labour. One consequence of this has been to pass on costs of insurance, sick pay and other benefits properly borne by the companies to local families and communities themselves. Once again, although this work is less gender-specific, the burden of casualisation of this production has been "disproportionately absorbed by women, who make up the majority of casual and seasonal labour forces" (Dolan and Barrientos, 2003, p 3).

The general point coming from these case studies is that there has been a dramatically changing world of work in recent years. The overall trend is for the shift of manufacturing to the Asian/Pacific Rim, to core Asian countries and to sub-Saharan Africa and South America while the industrially advanced nations have rapidly moved into 'post-industrialism' (see Chapter Five). In recent decades, globalisation processes operating through new technologies and the growth of international air transport have created new markets and new forms of trading of goods around the world. In most of the cases discussed earlier in this chapter, labour markets have changed dramatically with most of the new work engaging a largely unskilled, part-time and/or casual female workforce.

The second key lesson from these studies is that there are very contrasting experiences in terms of conditions of employment and wages across all these countries which reflects the increasingly integrated nature of the global economy and the ability of the deregulated market economy to adapt to rapidly changing trade environments. Each case needs to be looked at on its own merits. South Africa, for example, has *lost* a significant number of unskilled jobs in manufacturing in recent years with devastating consequences on an economy recovering from years of oppressive apartheid government and in which unemployment remains severely high (at about 30%).

The changing world of men and women's work

In Britain, the decline in manufacturing has been almost exclusively a decline in male participation in full-time jobs. This decline is partly explained by early retirements which is in effect a kind of unemployment ('go before you're pushed'), but is largely the product of wholesale closures of major industries, such as shipbuilding on the Tyne and Wear and on the Clyde, or the decimation of steel making in Sheffield and South Wales. Younger people staying in education longer can also account for some of the job losses. Thus, both older and younger cohorts are strongly influenced in behaviour by state spending in the first case on income transfer and in the second case on the expensive expansion of higher education with well over 40% of current 18 year olds staying on in education after their school years.

Thus, there is a strong case to be made for the influence of the (welfare) state in shaping and, at the very least, responding to economic transformation. As we discuss at various points in this book, the creation of the competition state in Britain was a response to shifts in the nature of the global economy. The emergence of the workfare state, the specific policies and programmes that were engineered by it, was a response to patterns of foreign direct investment into the UK, the draining of jobs from the traditional industrial heartlands and above all putting in place conditions in which the new services-based economy could flourish – requiring economic liberalisation, the establishment of a contract culture, and the break up of the old-fashioned centralised unitary state apparatus (see Chapter Six).

Female labour force participation

One of the most extraordinary features of the new global labour market is the extent to which work that used to provide full-time male manufacturing jobs has been taken over by part-time female employment in the countries of the Asian/Pacific Rim and sub-Saharan Africa. It is also the case that the vast majority of the new services employment in Britain is done by women, a high proportion of which is part-time work. It should be noted that, in the UK context, it is not true that women took men's jobs in the 1980s and 1990s. The economy restructured and the product of this in labour market terms was a precipitate decline in full-time male work almost entirely in 'old' manufacturing and an even greater increase in part-time female employment in the new services-based economy. As Castles (1998) observed, it should be noted that, in historical terms, women mainly did work outside the home until the 19th century. Before then, the family worked as a unit with a division of labour between men, women and children. Life was parochial and largely dictated by the seasonal round of seedtime and harvest and the other rites of passage which marked out the all too short route from cradle to grave. The factory system, however, was much more than just a revolution in production methods; rather, it resulted in a radical restructuring of daily life with the separation of work – done away from the house in factories – and domestic home life. Life began to be measured by 'shifts', and daily life became more fragmented and routinised (Harvey, 1973; Giddens, 1990). The feudal idea of treating the family as a single unit quickly died out as employers hired individual workers on the basis of weekly wage payments, and to whom they owed no other obligation.

Within this lengthy process of social advance the **function of the home** changed beyond recognition. In essence, the home became a female and child-centred domain providing nurture and comfort against an alien and often hostile economic sphere beyond the front door. Above all, for all social classes, the home became a bastion of respectability. The disruption, confusion and plurality of city life drove families into their inner home life and to try to live in communities with like-minded people. As Ravetz and Turkington (1995, p 4) observe:

> Social gradations became crucially important to identity and security, most particularly at borderlines between classes. The most

important of these in the eyes of Victorians, was that of separating 'respectability' from 'non respectability'.

So, women at home are a historical aberration; once again, in the 2000s, women are at the forefront of the labour market outside the domestic environment. The difference now is that they work for cash in their own right, implying greater independence and considerable changes in the balance of power within households.

In the post-Second World War era, the earliest and fastest growth in female labour force participation was in Scandinavian countries due to high levels of state spending on welfare. The decision to engineer a high-tax/high-spend welfare state arose from the strong and long-run social democratic control of society, dating back to the 1930s. Long-term party political incumbency is a key indicator of welfare state spending regimes. This in turn may reflect even deeper cultural foundations. In the case of female labour force participation, it was slowest to develop (as Castles and Esping-Andersen and others have pointed out) in societies in which the **Catholic Church** had a strong foothold – France and Italy, for example, and Germany to an extent (Esping-Andersen, 1990; Castles, 1998). The reason for this is that Catholicism is a confessional doctrine resulting in a hierarchical relationship between clergy and laity, and scepticism of civil society, especially in matters of moral teaching and family life. Protestant theology, on the other hand, emphasises the direct, personal bonds between God and individuals creating a greater sense of engagement with 'the world'. These major cultural configurations of European societies continue to exert an important influence even in an era when formal religious faiths have declined sharply (Flora, 1986). Attitudes to the state are deeply conditioned in different societies by such historic, religious and cultural allegiances. The point here is that countries influenced by the **Catholic cultural imperative** tended to create significant impediments to female labour force participation. Women should be at home bringing up the children while, insofar as the state should be active in personal life, it should support male breadwinners.

Castles' data showed clearly that, in the post-war era, female labour force participation grew fastest in countries with a Protestant tradition (such as Sweden) where civil society was unencumbered by the constraints of Catholicism and public spending on services was more extensive. Many of these services were directly related to enabling women to engage in the labour market and indeed were significant employers of women (such as crèches). By the same token, female participation in the workforce was slowest in Catholic-influenced countries such as Austria and Italy where public spending on services was low (Castles, 1998).

It was noted earlier that many of the new jobs, whether in the new manufacturing areas of Asia and the southern hemisphere or in the post-industrial services economies, are **part-time**. This raises further policy-related issues about the extent to which women have gained financial independence but at the cost of continuing domestic responsibilities in lives torn between work and the home.

The geography of work change in Britain

One of the key policy relevant features of economic restructuring has been the accompanying geographical shift of population. In Britain, this has taken the form of a process of **counter-urbanisation**, of a major movement of people out of the old industrial cities to smaller towns and suburban locations. Policy analysts should be very alert to such significant **demographic change** because the sociological literature traditionally drew attention to the association between urbanisation and the growth of the state. Britain holds a special place in this debate because it was the first example in history of a country industrialising on a large scale, which meant the depopulation of the countryside and the growth of towns and cities based around manufacturing. It also meant large-scale and sustained population growth. The population of England doubled between 1801 and 1850 – from 9,000,000 to over 18,000,000 – and the rate of growth never fell below 10% per annum until the 1930s. Britain was the first country in history to become urbanised on the basis of an advanced industrial economy. Astonishingly, by the time of the Great Exhibition in 1851, there were already ten urban areas in England with populations of over 100,000 each, accounting for 24.8% of the whole population and numbers continued to grow in frightening and unprecedented rates (Burnett, 1986, p 7). Urbanisation impacted dramatically on people's changing social horizons. It created new opportunities and new pressures on relations between the sexes, impacted on fertility, divorce and the whole shape of domestic and family life. It also significantly redivided society on the basis of social class. Important consequences of this were the extent to which different configurations of classes and trade-offs between classes impacted on policy choices and outcomes. At the simplest level, urbanisation led to the growth of state intervention, despite the culture of economic laissez-faire, in order to tackle public health and sanitation concerns, and, very soon, to other 'urban' issues such as street lighting, slum clearance and improving the quality of housing, eventually leading to a famous Royal Commission on the Housing of the Working Classes in 1884, the report of which sowed the seeds for the idea of housing subsidies and the need for the state to be involved in housing provision (Lowe, 2004).

The geography of the competition state

State intervention and the growth of 'public policy' (as opposed to private or local initiatives) are thus very much associated with 19th-century urbanisation.

It is this legacy that is the backdrop to contemporary social change, particularly the collapse of the 'old' industrial heartlands as centres of manufacturing production and the rise of the service economy. Disruption to a traditional pattern of population distribution on the scale we are talking about must imply significant issues for policy analysis, especially the role of the state in facilitating such large-scale change. The emergence of the competition state has been accompanied by geographical restructuring with major policy consequences. *Table 4.2* provides a summary of the population changes that have taken place between different types of location over a 15-year period.

The table clearly shows that employment has grown sharply in smaller towns and rural areas but has declined in the bigger cities. Old industries have been replaced by new ones but in different places. During the 1990s, about 40,000 people annually migrated out of the Northern and Midland conurbations, with much of this movement being to other parts of the same or adjacent regions, rather than the South of England. This data points to the fact that employment growth has been strongest in suburban areas.

Cross-tabulated to our other indicators of change – 'male versus female' and 'full-time versus part-time jobs' – Turok and Edge's (1999) data show clearly that this story of geographical change incorporates major social changes. Their analysis shows that male manufacturing jobs were lost everywhere, but especially in the conurbations. Between 1981 and 1996, 1.4 million manufacturing jobs were lost; that is, about one third of the 1981 total. The cities also had much lower rates of growth in other jobs, especially in services. Part-time jobs in services grew by 2.2 million between 1981 and 1996; that is, nearly 60% of the total of new jobs. As we might predict, this was a growth made up almost entirely of female workers, mainly in smaller towns and rural areas, including suburbs (Turok and Edge, 1999). Note also that around 7% of the workforce at any one time is employed in temporary jobs.

The overall picture told in this data, is that economic restructuring has been very geographically uneven in its impact. The short story is one of major job losses in the northern industrial cities with an attendant population decline. Jobs growth in the services industries by contrast has been in the smaller

Table 4.2: Change in the location of employment 1981-96 (000s)

Total employment	1981 (000s)	1996 (000s)	Change (%)
Towns and rural areas	11,278	12,953	+14.9
Free-standing cities	1,730	1,749	+1.1
Conurbations	4,497	4,208	−6.4
London	3,560	3,348	−6.0
Britain	21,064	22,258	+5.7

Source: Turok and Edge (1999, p 3)

towns and the suburbs especially, but by no means exclusively, in the south of the country. As Turok and Edge conclude, there has been "a net decentralisation of economic activity" (Turok and Edge, 1999, p 50).

Consequences for public services and the welfare state

In wider public policy terms, there are major issues linked to this pattern of change. For example, it follows that **suburbanisation** processes have been strongly associated with the expansion of home ownership during the 1980s and 1990s. This has been accompanied by the construction of tens of thousands of new owner-occupied properties on greenfield sites and close to the location of the new service industry jobs. Everywhere, out-of-town **shopping complexes** have been built, linked by ring roads and designed to be accessible by car, not public transport. **Science parks** related to local universities have sprung up incorporating partnership projects designed to exploit the commercial potential of new knowledge in the sciences and computing.

Box 4.1: Employment change in the Pennine towns

Over the period 1971-97, manufacturing in the Pennine towns declined by nearly 48% while services grew by 53%. In real terms, this means that this area of Northern England lost 40,000 manufacturing jobs in the space of 25 years (***Table 4.3***).

Sixty per cent of the service workers in 1997 were female and of these 85% were in part-time jobs. By contrast nearly three quarters of the employees in manufacturing were men, nearly all of them in full-time jobs.

This area was the cradle of the 18th- and 19th-century Industrial Revolution. The area was world famous for its production of fabrics, especially cotton and for finished garment manufacture, initially mostly done at home but increasingly in massive mills and factories. It has seen dramatic changes to its employment structure since the 1980s. It is typical of the story that could be told for any of the old, traditional industrial regions of the country.

Table 4.3: *Employment sectors in Huddersfield and Halifax (%)*

	1971	1977	1987	1997
Mining	1.8	1.9	1.7	1.4
Manufacturing	49.1	42.0	29.8	24.4
Construction	3.6	3.7	3.5	3.3
Services	45.6	52.3	65.0	69.8

Suburban home ownership has fed on these new jobs and households routinely have access to two substantial incomes by combinations of full-time and part-time working. By the same token, the inner-cities of the old northern industrial cities – such as Manchester, Leeds, Liverpool, Newcastle, Sunderland and Glasgow – have been through a period of dramatic decline with the loss of the economic heart of communities. As the case study in **Box 4.2** shows, this has led to the growing problem of low demand for housing in once-thriving neighbourhoods. Property prices slumped and public and private landlords have often found it impossible to find tenants for their accommodation. Those people left after the exodus to find work in the new economy tend to be elderly and unskilled or families disadvantaged in other ways by poverty and an inability to find work in the post-industrial labour market. Local authorities have been forced to downsize their council housing stocks by demolition. Housing built to accommodate the 20th-century industrial workforce has been quietly disappearing over the last decade. Webster reported that about 10% of Glasgow's council housing was demolished between 1981 and 1999 – some 20,000 units in all (Webster, 1999). Abandonment of housing in all tenures in the North of England was reported in a variety of studies (Lowe et al, 1999; Power and Mumford, 1999).

As with the case of the demise of British council housing, much of which is now owned and managed by a variety of quasi-public and fully private organisations creating what Mullins and Risborough (2000) refer to as a 'social

Box 4.2: Low demand for housing

One of the consequences of the decline of the old centres of manufacturing has been steady population decline resulting in the appearance of areas (mostly in inner-cities in the North and Midlands of Britain) where the demand for housing has declined. Council housing became 'difficult to let' because many households moved away to find work in the expanding suburbs, leaving many empty properties behind. Empty and abandoned housing became a target for vandals and these areas of low demand housing spiralled downwards – shops closed, bus services stopped running and the vitality of local communities ebbed away. Elderly people with few resources have stayed behind but saw their neighbourhoods become crime-ridden and where only the poorest people lived. These 'ghettos of the poor' contain the vast majority of the most socially excluded members of British society (Lowe, 2004).

For many local authorities, the only solution has been to demolish these areas. Between 1980 and 2000, Glasgow council demolished 10% of its housing stock, some 20,000 properties, and this pattern has been repeated all over the country. This problem also impacted on the private sector where house prices in some areas slumped and thousands of houses became virtually worthless. With average house prices in excess of £100,000, the contrast between escalating house prices in London and suburban communities all over the country could hardly be more dramatic.

business'; so with other publicly provided and run services associated with urban life. Transport, leisure facilities, road maintenance, the 'public' utilities and a whole range of services were closely connected to an urban way of life that spanned the whole of the 20th century. The services economy has to a considerable extent broken this historic connection between urban life and publicly provided services. As we show in Chapter Six, the long experience of government by a centralised unitary state has been fundamentally challenged and then largely replaced by a much more fragmented political system. A very large part of this necessity can be traced back to the need and ability to manage the delivery of an urban infrastructure and public services radically transformed under the impact of the changing world of work. Equally, as Graham and Marvin (2001) show, the deregulated, fragmented and often privatised 'public' utilities which serve urban areas have reinforced and exacerbated social divisions *within* urban areas: the division between the haves and have-nots becomes increasingly polarised within cities as a process of 'splintering urbanism' gathers pace.

To reiterate, the point here is that economic restructuring has had a very *geographically uneven* impact, with the major conurbations, the Pennine industrial towns and mining communities in the North of England very adversely affected. Depopulation, social decline and a spiralling down of the inner-city have been one legacy but set against the emergence of a new landscape and urban built environment that has been constructed around the new private service industries concentrated in small towns and the suburbs especially. Evidence of a North–South divide is also very much part of this debate, but it would seem that while the South of England has benefited to a large degree, so have the outer margins of many cities and large towns in the North. Late 20th-century suburbanisation and its impact on public policy has been a national phenomenon.

Conclusions

As we commented in Chapter Two, globalisation has brought the people of planet Earth into relationships hitherto unimaginable even a few years ago. Under its impact, the world of work has been transformed with its attendant consequences for the lives of millions of families. For the wealthier post-industrial nations such as Britain, there have been gains and some losses. Suburban families without a second thought buy fruit, flowers and vegetables in their out-of-town supermarkets, grown by casual, mainly female, workers in sub-Saharan Africa. The arenas of new manufacturing and horticultural production have spread across the less economically developed world. These people have been less well served because the evidence is of wages and conditions for many workers being driven down to minimally acceptable standards. Women in particular have borne the brunt of this changing world of work in long hours of toil both at home and in their places of employment.

The story is one of a dramatic shift in the social and geographical distribution of work across the planet. The specific case of Britain illustrates the transformation that has occurred in one of the advanced industrial nations. Here, the narrative is one of major disjuncture between an increasingly affluent suburban culture based on the new post-industrial services economy and decline in the population and prosperity of the old industrial cities in the North and Midlands of England. This new social and economic terrain has been instigated and managed by new organisational structures and new forms of governance (which will be discussed in more detail later in this book). For now, it is enough to recognise that, in Britain, the changing world of work has created a new social geography and new relationships between the sexes which both respond to steering by the state through public services and the wider welfare state and in turn reflects back the wider reality of the British economy transformed by the imperative of globalisation. A new suburban way of life based around a service economy has brought with it a new welfare state.

Summary

- One of the main consequences of globalisation over the last three decades has been an acceleration in the restructuring of the world economy.
- Manufacturing has moved away from the old industrial heartlands in northern Europe and the eastern seaboard of the US to an Asian–Pacific axis and a geographically diverse set of nations mainly in the southern hemisphere.
- The world economy grew in volume more in the four post-war decades than in the whole of the previous 130 years, mainly based on growth in manufacturing.
- In the UK between 1960 and 1993, the share of the labour market accounted for by manufacturing industry declined by over 18 percentage points and that occupied by services grew by 24 percentage points. By the year 2000, nearly 75% of the workforce was employed in service industries.
- Manufacturing grew rapidly in less economically developed nations in the 1980s and 1990s. For example, in Vietnam manufacturing employment grew by over 900,000 new jobs between 1990 and 2000 and a similar number were created in Bangladesh in the early 1990s, much of this work in textiles and garment making.
- Labour markets have changed dramatically with most of the new work engaging a largely unskilled, part-time and/or casual female workforce.
- In Britain, the decline in manufacturing has been almost exclusively a decline in male participation in full-time jobs while the new services industry jobs are mostly female and part-time.

- In the post-Second World War era, the earliest and fastest growth in female labour force participation was in Scandinavian countries due to high levels of state spending on welfare, reflecting a long-term social democratic partisanship and a Protestant cultural context.
- Economic restructuring in Britain has been very geographically uneven in its impact with major job losses in the Northern industrial cities, but jobs growth in the services industries in the smaller towns and suburbs especially, but by no means exclusively, in the South of the country.
- In Britain, the changing world of work has created a new social geography and new relationships between the sexes which both respond to steering by the state through public services and the wider welfare state (and in turn reflect back the reality of the British economy itself) transformed by globalisation.

Questions for discussion

- Why has manufacturing industry largely re-located to Asia and the Southern Hemisphere?
- What impact does the replacement of a manufacturing-based economy with a services economy have on welfare states?
- How far have women benefited from the new world of work?

Further reading

Castles, F.G. (1998) *Comparative public policy: Patterns of post-war transformation*, Cheltenham: Edward Elgar.

Dolan, C. and Barrientos, S. (2003) 'Labour flexibility in African horticulture', *Insights: Development Research*, No 47, Institute of Development Studies, University of Sussex.

Lowe, S. (2004) *Housing policy analysis: British housing in cultural and comparative contexts*, Houndmills, Basingstoke: Macmillan/Palgrave.

Turok, I. and Edge, N. (1999) *The jobs gap in Britain's cities: Employment loss and labour market consequences*, Bristol/York: The Policy Press/Joseph Rowntree Foundation.

Technological change

Overview

Technological changes – and particularly the emergence of powerful new information and communications technologies (ICTs) – have underpinned many of the developments outlined in Chapters Two to Four. Indeed, the idea of an Information Revolution is heavily connected with arguments about the increased pace of globalisation, the emergence of a knowledge economy and the rapid expansion of the service sector. This chapter considers claims that economically advanced societies have undergone (or are undergoing) profound change fuelled by new ICTs, from early ideas such as those put forward by Bell about the emergence of a 'post-industrial society', to more recent positions such as Castells' claim that we have seen the emergence of a 'network society'. This chapter relates these changes to globalisation and the broad shifts in the political economy of welfare identified in preceding chapters and examines the extent to which technologically related change is controlled by social forces.

Key concepts

Information Revolution; post-industrial society; network society; technological determinism; social construction of technology; actor-network theory; e-galitarianism.

Introduction

The Information Revolution

The claim that the last quarter of a century has witnessed a technologically driven, epochal shift in the structure of economically advanced societies is now commonplace, and a wide array of social theorists, popular commentators and politicians alike are ready to proclaim that we live in an Information Age (see Leer, 1999). Indeed, sociologists have for some time been engaged in a debate about the nature, extent and significance of changes facilitated (for some, *determined*) by the emergence of powerful new information and communication technologies (ICTs). A wide array of prefixes have been applied to 'society' in an attempt to encapsulate this change:

- Bell's (1974, 1979) notion of the knowledge-based, ICT driven **post-industrial society**;
- Masuda's (1980) road map for moving Japan towards a 'computopia'; that is, the first full articulation of the notion of an **information society**;
- Castells' (2000) argument that the term **network society** best encapsulates the nature of technologically driven change that we find in the 'informational' economy.

Much of this multifaceted and fragmented debate about the 'information age' (see Álvarez and Kilbourn, 2002) has taken place at an abstract, theoretical level, but many of the themes it engages with have been taken up by politicians keen to link their policy agenda with this popularly perceived opportunity for transformation and modernisation. So, for instance, Tony Blair (1998, p i) has argued:

> Information is the key to the modern age. The new age of information offers possibilities for the future limited only by the boundaries of our imaginations. The potential of the new electronic networks is breathtaking – the prospect of change as widespread and fundamental as the agricultural and industrial revolutions of earlier eras. (See also Leer, 1999)

Cross-party governmental institutions have also signed up to such views. For instance, in the mid-1990s, the EU (1994, p 3) commissioned an investigation into the implications of new ICTs for society that concluded:

> This [information] revolution adds huge new capacities to human intelligence and constitutes a resource which changes the way we work together and the way we live together.

At the same time, the UK's House of Lords (not an institution commonly associated with notions of modernisation) published a similar investigation that argued:

> The world is undergoing a technological revolution and entering the age of the Information Society. ... The potential technological, economic, and social upheavals resulting from the information

revolution could be of the same order of magnitude as those arising from the shift away from an agricultural to an industrial economy. (House of Lords Science and Technology Select Committee, 1996, para 1.6)

The long roots of the Information Revolution

Such claims, however, are by no means new. Indeed, the UK appointed its first Minister for Information Technology in 1982 and he made strikingly similar statements to those now made by Blair[1]. Moreover, the academic debate about the emergence of an information society dates back still further – to the late 1960s and early 1970s in fact, and the work of theorists such as Touraine (1969), Bell (1974) and Machlup (1962).

Daniel Bell (1974, 1979, 1980), for example, argued over a quarter of a century ago that we were witnessing "a revolution in the organisation and processing of information and knowledge, in which the computer plays a central role" (Bell, 1979, p 163) and, furthermore, that these changes were unleashing "an extraordinary transformation, perhaps even greater in its impact than the industrial revolution of the previous century" (Bell, 1980, p *ix*). He suggested that changes to the structure of the economy linked to technological developments – such as the increasing complexity of science, the rationalisation and codification of knowledge, the ability to store, process and transmit large quantities of information at high speed and low cost – were behind a shift in western societies from an industrial to a post-industrial structure that we commonly refer to now as the 'information society'[2]. Bell built on the work of Clark (1940) who argued that, while all economies consisted of a mixture of primary, secondary and tertiary sectors (relating mainly to extractive, manufacturing and service-based work respectively), the economic progress of industrialised nations could be measured by the various weights attached to each sector. He suggested that, as a nation's income increased, there would be a corresponding increase in demand for services and a consequent transfer of labour from the secondary to the tertiary sector. Bell (1979, p 177) argued that "in this fashion, Clark was able to chart the … change from a pre-industrial into an industrial and then into a service society".

However, Clark was arguing that as societies developed economically there would be an increase in the size of the service sector of the economy, not the emergence of a 'post-industrial society'. Where Bell diverted from Clark's thesis was in the importance he attached to *knowledge* and *technology*. He split the service sector into three further sectors: the tertiary (mainly services to

---

[1] For example, the minister, Kenneth Baker (1984, p 3), stated: "[The Information Revolution] promises to change society every bit as radically as the industrial revolution of the nineteenth century".

[2] Bell initially eschewed the term 'information society' (Bell, 1974), but soon began to use it and his preferred 'post-industrial society' interchangeably (1979).

assist industry, for example, transport and utilities), quartenary (mainly financial services such as banking) and quinary (areas such as science, research and education), and argued that the shift into the service sector would be concentrated in professional, technical and scientific occupations characterised by the knowledge intensive quinary sector. Moreover, he believed that the driving forces behind this change would be information technology and the increasing codification of theoretical knowledge. As Bell himself put it, "My basic premise [is] that knowledge and information are becoming the strategic resource and transforming agent of the post-industrial society" (1979, p 193), just as "the combination of energy, resources, and machine technology were the transforming agencies of industrial society" (1979, p 206) (*Table 5.1*).

At the time Bell was developing these ideas, modern computing was very much in its infancy, yet he was not alone in predicting a wide reaching impact. So, for instance, the popular writer Alvin Toffler published *The third wave* in 1980, in which he argued that "[We are entering the Third Wave], an event as profound as the First Wave of change unleashed ten thousand years ago by the invention of agriculture, or the earthshaking Second Wave of change touched off by the industrial revolution" (Toffler, 1980, p ix). Even more surprisingly, perhaps, in the late 1970s the French government had commissioned a broad

Table 5.1: *Bell's general schema of social change*

	Pre-industrial society	Industrial society	Post-industrial society
Key economic sectors:	*Primary* (extractive): agriculture; mining; fishing; timber	*Secondary* (goods producing): manufacturing; processing	*Tertiary:* transportation; utilities *Quartenary:* trade; finance; insurance; real estate *Quinary:* health; education; research; government; recreation
Key occupations:	Farmer; miner; fisherman; unskilled worker	Semi-skilled worker; engineer	Professional and technical; scientists
Key technology:	Raw materials	Energy	Information

Source: Adapted from Bell (1974, p 116)

ranging investigation into *L'informatisation d'société*. It considered the policy implications of the 'computer revolution' which, its authors concluded, would "alter the entire nervous system of social organisation" (Nora and Minc, 1980, p 3).

While the development of the personal computer around this time was undoubtedly a key cultural moment that brought with it some important social changes, it is since the emergence of the Internet in the mid-1990s[3] that we have witnessed a real explosion in theorisation about the implications of ICTs for society. This work encompasses a wide range of opinions, pitting prominent sceptics who feel the extent of technologically fuelled change is limited and, indeed, has been exaggerated (Golding, 2000) against evangelical exponents of hypotheses about 'revolution' who feel change has been earth-shattering and far-reaching (Angell, 2000). Similarly, the debate embraces a full spectrum of views about the direction of change too, from the utopian interpretations of those who see the new technology as empowering (Negroponte, 1995), to those who hold a distopian view of a future where humanity is increasingly undermined by technologically determined changes (Virilio, 1999).

In this mass of literature, there is, however, one theorist's work which has, more often than anyone else's, been held up as the defining work of the era: that of Manuel Castells. His notion of a 'network society' is one of the most widely cited theorisations of technologically related social change and it is to this that we now turn.

Castells' 'network society'

Castells' (2000b, p 28) starting point is his belief that:

> at the end of the twentieth century, we lived through one of these rare intervals [of major change] in history. An interval characterized by the transformation of our 'material culture' by the works of a new technological paradigm organized around information technologies.

Moreover, his belief (2000, p 9) is that "the vast majority of societies are affected in a fundamental way by these transformations" and that "All together they constitute a new type of social structure that I call the network society". This notion of a 'network society' which he offers is a far from straightforward position; indeed, it is laid out in great detail in a three-volume treatise stretching to over 1,500 pages (Castells, 1996; 1997a; 1997b; also reissued as 2000b, 2000c, 2000d). However, the essence of his position is that social relationships in the

---

[3] It is worth noting that the Internet was not invented in the 1990s; rather, it merely came to prominence then.

information age are characterised by 'networks' and that the economy, work, culture, politics and the state have undergone profound change as network relationships have taken hold.

Beginning firstly with his views on the economy, Castells argues that it has been transformed as a consequence of three profound changes. First, the economy is now **informational**, by which he means the ability to generate, process and act on knowledge and information are central in determining the productivity of businesses, regions or nations. Second, because new ICTs allow for instantaneous real-time communication of information and knowledge across the world, the economy is now **global**. Finally, the economy is now **networked**, not simply in the sense of being connected through ICTs, but in terms of the dominant mode of organising. Increasingly, he argues, businesses are now networks rather than single (hierarchical) organisations, typically involving a core unit that is surrounded by a periphery of competing units that supply parts or distribute goods (**Box 5.1**).

Linked to this transformation of the economy, he argues, is a transformation of the labour market. He claims (2000, p 9) that:

> induced by globalization, and the network enterprise, and facilitated by information/communication technologies, the most important transformation in employment patterns concerns the development of flexible work, as the predominant form of working arrangements.

Castells suggests that the rise of the new economy has brought about the decline of 'organisation man' and the rise of 'flexible woman' and that, moreover, it has created a divide between 'programmable labour' that is capable of reskilling itself and adapting to rapid change and 'generic labour' that is more disposable and can be replaced by machine technology. Further, he argues (2000, p 12) that "because of this structural divide [and] in the absence of a determined public policy aimed at correcting structural trends, we have witnessed in the last 20 years a dramatic surge of inequality, social polarization, and social exclusion".

Castells also believes we have seen a transformation of culture as interactive, multi-channel, multi-platform, round-the-clock forms of electronic media (including the Internet) have developed, producing a more fragmented, faster paced and often bite-sized approach. This in turn has impacted profoundly on the nature of politics as it becomes intertwined with the new media. Here he offers a somewhat disheartening vision (2000, p 12) arguing:

> Media politics needs to convey very simple messages. The simplest message is an image. The simplest, individualized image is a person. Political competition increasingly revolves around the personalization of politics. The most effective political weapons

are negative messages. The most effective negative message is character assassination of opponents' personalities, and/or of their supporting organizations.

Box 5.1: Dell: a networked enterprise in action

An excellent example of what Castells (2000b) calls the 'networked enterprise' is provided by Dell computing (www.dell.com). In less than 20 years, the company has gone from being a small one-man business to the world's biggest supplier of personal computers. Its success is in large part due to its flexible and networked organisational form that has allowed it to expand rapidly and respond quickly to technological change while keeping its investment and running costs to a minimum. The core features are as follows:

- *A direct relationship with customers.* Orders are placed over the Internet or via the phone; there are no intermediaries involved, reducing Dell's overheads and allowing them to pass savings on to the customer.
- *Products are built to order.* Rather than producing machines in bulk to meet anticipated demand, Dell only builds to order. Each machine only goes into production once a customer has placed an order for it. Eliminating the risks of overproduction means costs are cut and savings can be passed on to the consumer.
- *Flexible, tailored production.* Since products are only built to order, Dell can tailor each machine to the requirements of the individual customer, who can choose which facilities to include in the machine when they place their order.
- *Just-in-time production.* Information about orders directly feeds into assembly-line production which, in turn, feeds into Dell's own stock systems, allowing parts to be ordered as they are needed and on the basis of actual demand rather than being stockpiled just in case they are needed. This again cuts costs and also allows Dell to offer the latest technological components without running the risk of it writing off older stock.
- *Diverse supply chain.* The just-in-time production process is possible because Dell has a global network of partners who supply, assemble and distribute its products. These partners absorb many of the costs of production and are often in competition with each other for Dell's business. Dell does not own these companies but, instead, is the 'node' at the centre of a network and it can deactivate any of the other nodes if they cannot supply at the right price, right quality or right speed or if consumer demand for their components falls and vice versa. Operating in such a manner gives Dell maximum flexibility with minimal costs in terms of capital investment.

The model is in stark contrast to the old monolithic, hierarchical approach to production in which all elements of production were brought in-house within a single organisation. Here, much of Dell's role is a coordinating one and, crucially, its business model is only viable because of the instantaneous communication of information between different elements of the network made possible by ICTs.

So, politics increasingly becomes focused on personalities, on character assassination of those personalities and, ultimately, (the search for) scandal and corruption.

The state too, Castells (2000, p 14) claims, is transformed in the network society as:

> On the one hand, its sovereignty is called into question by global flows of wealth, communication, and information. On the other hand, its legitimacy is undermined by the politics of scandal and its dependence on media politics.

In response, it firstly "builds partnerships between nation-states and shares sovereignty to retain influence" (2000, p 14). Here he cites the EU as the most obvious example, but points to organisations such as the IMF, World Bank and UN too. Secondly, he argues, states also devolve power in order to bolster their legitimacy, be it through devolution, bolstering the power of sub-central government or the greater involvement of non-governmental organisations in the policy process. The upshot of all this is that:

> The state in the information age is a network state, a state made out of a complex web of power-sharing, and negotiated decision-making between international, multinational, national, regional, local, and non-governmental, political institutions. (Castells, 2000, p 14)

Significantly, Castells believes that two key factors have brought about these major transformations that he lumps under the 'network society' umbrella. The first is the emergence of new ICTs, which have fuelled the development of these networks. The second is the networks themselves, which have been energised by the new technology and have become, crucially, 'information networks'. As he puts it (2000, p 15):

> Networks are very old forms of social organization. But they have taken on a new life in the Information Age by becoming information networks, powered by new information technologies.

So, where once networks were an ineffective form of organisation – hampered by barriers of place (the difficulties that arose in having geographically dispersed groups of people working together) or time (the delays in communicating information between different parts of a network) – this is no longer the case. Indeed, he argues that fundamental to the emergence of the network society is the redefinition of time and space; or, more particularly, the emergence of **timeless time** and the **space of flows**, the former referring to "the use of new information/communication technologies in a relentless effort to annihilate time" (2000, p 13) and the latter to the "technological and organizational possibility of organizing the simultaneity of social practices without geographical contiguity" (2000, p 14).

The emergence of Information Age government

Assuming this transformation is real[4], how then is UK welfare policy responding to the emergence of this 'network' or 'information' society? What are the implications of this 'transformation' for the state? At the most basic level, we can point to the emergence of Information Age government. Shortly after coming to power, New Labour made clear their determination to modernise government services and the important role they felt ICTs had to play in this process (Cabinet Office, 1998, 1999, 2000). In particular, they announced a series of Information Age government targets, including a commitment to making 100% of government services available electronically by 2005 (Cabinet Office, 1999, 2000; Hudson, 2002).

Significantly, these plans for 'e-government' are underpinned by an ambitious programme for using new technology to reinvent government and elements of Castells' ideas can be seen at play throughout them:'timeless time' is illustrated in the desire to make services available '24-7'; the diminished importance of the 'space of place' can be seen in attempts to deliver services through call centres rather than high-street premises; and the notion of network organising can be witnessed at play in plans to use private and voluntary sector partners in the delivery of services. Indeed, Curthoys (2003, p 7) interprets the agenda as an attempt to boost the legitimacy of flagging government services by reinvigorating and reinventing them through the use of new technologies and network organising[5].

Beyond this, Castells' suggestion that, unless public policy seeks to counteract it, a divide will emerge between those able to adapt to new technology and those who are not is reflected in the Blair government's concerns over the emergence of the so-called *digital divide* – or 'information haves and have-nots'. Various initiatives have been established to address the divide including a Policy Action Team within the Social Exclusion Unit (DTI, 2000), the Computers Within Reach Initiative that aimed to place refurbished computers in 100,000 socially excluded households, trial schemes connecting entire estates

---

[4] We have noted already that sceptics exist. There is not room here to offer a full account of the sceptical perspective (but see May, 2002), but we offer some further qualifications later in this chapter and in subsequent chapters of this book.

[5] Interestingly, Curthoys (2003, p 5) suggests that, just as Keynes was the key theorist for Atlee and the post-war Fabians, Hayek for Thatcher and the New Right, Castells is the key theorist for Blair and New Labour.

under the Wired Up Communities Initiative, and the creation of some 6,000 UK-Online centres that offer community Internet facilities and basic IT skills training (Hudson, 2002). More importantly, Blair has made a commitment to delivering universal Internet access by the end of 2005, meaning not only that everyone who wants to should have access to the Internet by this date, but also that they will possess the skills to use it (Hudson, 2002, 2003).

E-galitarianism?

In truth, however, the New Labour government's plans for dealing with the digital divide are modest and, in the greater scheme of things, of fairly small importance. In terms of social policy and the Information Age, the bigger picture comes in terms of how the notion of an information society connects with New Labour's reconceptualisation of the role of the state and the notion of a Third Way. As Giddens (2000, p 23, 32) makes clear, "globalisation and the information revolution are … key concerns of third way politics", as it promotes the modernisation and reform of "social institutions" to "meet the demands of a globalising information order".

As we saw in Chapter Three of this book, New Labour's philosophy is based on the assumption that the old Keynesian-rooted approach to social democracy is dead. Blair (1999) has been explicit about this and also about his belief that it is globalisation and the technological revolution that have killed it off:

> Beveridge, like most of his contemporaries, was committed to full employment, delivered by Keynesian demand management. The assumption of enduring full employment held good during the 1940s and 1950s [but] began to come apart as early as the 1970s…. Today the assumption has completely broken down. Globalisation has placed a premium on workers with the skills and knowledge to adapt to advancing technology.

Here, his arguments chime with those of Castells: that the new economy of the network society requires a workforce that is able to adapt to the ever increasing, technologically fuelled pace of change; one in which flexible, programmable labour is predominant. So, for New Labour, 'education, education, education' becomes the priority as "the most important task of modernisation is to invest in human capital: to make the individual and business fit for the knowledge-based economy of the future" (Blair and Schroeder, 1999, p 2). As, Giddens (2000, p 52) says of the Third Way:

> [I]n the economic sphere, [it] looks to develop a wide-ranging supply-side policy, which seeks to reconcile economic growth mechanisms with structural reform of the welfare state [because]

in the information economy, human (and social) capital becomes
central to economic success.

So, the notion that the UK economy is undergoing (and has little choice but
to undergo) an ICT-driven transformation – and related claims that the
economy of the future will be increasingly knowledge based, skills based and
globalised – are central to the rhetoric of New Labour's Third Way. Moreover,
since policy is framed from a perspective that sees this technologically driven
revolution as inevitable, it aims to change societal institutions such as the welfare
state rather than to challenge the direction of technologically driven change.
For Blair, confronting the Information Revolution head on appears to be
about changing 'out-dated' beliefs and practices more than it is about defending
them; indeed, he argues (1998, p 4) that a key difference between Old Labour
and New Labour is that, for the latter, "new technology represents an
opportunity, not a threat".

Giddens (2001, p 178) acknowledges that this means, therefore, that there is
a break between the social democracy of the past and the present and that, in
particular, the Third Way assumes that "there is no future for the 'egalitarianism
at all costs' [approach of the past]". However, he argues (2001, p 8) that the
Third Way does "not give up on the objective of creating an egalitarian society"
and, instead, aims to update the methods for achieving it in light of the
emergence of the globalising information order. Hudson (2003) suggests that
a new label is therefore needed to highlight this shift in emphasis: he offers the
notion of **e-galitarianism**. 'E-' is a widely recognised signifier of a connection
between an 'old world' phenomenon and the ICT-driven electronic revolution,
and so 'e-galitarianism' encapsulates the centrality of the information revolution
to the Third Way philosophy and the close connection between technological
change and the perceived need for a restatement of the egalitarian vision.
Moreover, the segmentation of the word also hints at a discontinuity with the
past, signifying a fragmented (broken) variation of the egalitarian vision and
the dash can also be interpreted as a minus sign, meaning the term represents
a diminished, reduced, vision of egalitarianism.

Competing visions of the network society

It would be wrong, however, to presume that this process of change inevitably
diminishes the scope of welfare state effort. Indeed, Castells has suggested that
"the paths and outcomes of this transformation are extraordinarily diverse ...
there is no one model of the information society" (Castells and Himanen,
2002, p 3).

With respect to the information society and the welfare state, Castells and
Himanen (2002) draw a sharp contrast between the 'Silicon Valley model' and
the 'Finnish model'. The broad differences between the two societies are

relatively well known: the US places an emphasis on free markets and minimal state intervention, whereas Finland has a highly interventionist state and well-funded public services. The US is a relatively unequal society and has seen the gap between rich and poor grow over the last 30 years, while in Finland income is more evenly distributed and equality has increased in the last 30 years. In the US indicators of exclusion such as incarceration rates are relatively high, while in Finland they are relatively low (see Castells and Himanen, 2002, p 5-14). While it is also well known that the US is a rich country, Finland's wealth is not always so well known and it is certainly less well known that Finland rivals the US for the title of most technologically advanced economy (see *Table 5.2*).

In short, both nations have adapted their economy well to the demands of the network society. However, they have done so in different ways, with the role of the welfare state in facilitating this adaptation varying crucially. While many (such as Angell, 2000; Tanzi, 2001) feel the high-taxation welfare state is incompatible with effective economic exploitation of the information revolution, Castells and Himanen (2002, p 85) suggest that "in spite of the pressures of the global information economy, Finland continues to be a different form of an information society [to Silicon Valley], which combines with it a generous welfare state". However, they argue (2002, p 87) that "it is no longer the old species of welfare state, which was often just seen as the alleviator of the economy's worst effects and occupied a fundamentally defensive position against the economy". Instead, they believe Finland has flourished because it

Table 5.2: Competing visions of the network society: Finland and the US compared

	US	Finland
GDP per capita (PPP, 2000) (OECD avg: US$23,178)	US$35,619	US$25,240
UN Technology Achievement Index Rank (2001)	2nd (0.733)	1st (0.744)
Public and social spending (% GDP, 1998) (OECD avg: 20.8)	14.6	26.5
Gini Index (mid-1990s)	34.4	22.8
Scientists and engineers in R&D (per 1,000,000 – 1998) (OECD avg: 3,305)	4,099	5,059
Prisoners (per 100,000 – 2000) (OECD avg: 94.45)	468.49	49.55
Poverty (<50% median income – mid-1990s)	17%	4.9%
Mobile phone subscribers (per 1,000 – 2001) (OECD avg: 605)	451	804
Key high-tech company	Microsoft	Nokia

Sources: www.sourceoecd.org; www.undp.org; Castells and Himanen (2002)

has repositioned its welfare state in response to the technological challenge. Indeed, they also argue (2002, p 89) that "what we are seeing in the Finnish model is a new informational welfare state. The core is the virtuous circle of the informational economy and the welfare state". They argue that this virtuous circle encompasses the following elements:

- **Heavy investment in education, with a strong emphasis on science and technology.** Finland has a policy of free higher education but not necessarily free choice; it funds far more students in science and technology subjects than is the norm in OECD nations (and far fewer in the humanities and social sciences).
- **Generous state-run unemployment benefits.** These are essential in smoothing labour-market change, for they reduce the social and personal costs of any economic change needed to adapt to the network economy.
- **Strong role for the state in encouraging economic innovation.** This includes state subsidies/tax breaks for high-tech start-ups, strategic deregulation of key economic sectors (such as telecommunications) and heavy investment in science and technology research and development.
- **A role for the state in encouraging the take-up of new technologies and utilising new technologies themselves.** This includes an inclusive approach to the emergence of the Internet through attempts to boost Internet literacy among the community as a whole and the development of e-government services.

The relationship is virtuous in the sense that it is the high economic growth enabled by exploitation of technology that pays for the high welfare spending and, in turn, it is the high spending on welfare that facilitates a socially inclusive transition to a network society. It is in this sense that "Finland stands in sharp contrast to the Silicon Valley model that is entirely driven by market mechanisms, individual entrepreneurialism, and the culture of risk – with considerable social costs, acute social inequality, and a deteriorating basis for both locally generated human capital and economic infrastructure" (Castells and Himanen, 2002, p 167). There are, then, two crucial lessons to be drawn from their examination of Finland. The first (2002, p 151) is that "the Silicon Valley model is not the only way to build an advanced information society but that there is choice" – the network society does not have to be a free-market society. The second is that a high-spending welfare state is compatible with the network society; indeed, "Finland has seen the combination of the welfare state and information technology as a central expression of the information society" (2002, p 153). In short, while the Information Revolution has been at the heart of many social changes we have witnessed in recent years, choice still exists.

Technology: master or servant?

This issue about choice in the face of technological change carries echoes of a long running debate about the 'power' of technology and, more specifically, an argument about whether technology drives change to such an extent that it is outside the control of humans. Before we end our discussion of technology, it is worth briefly visiting this debate, for it can help further our understanding of how technology and social change are connected.

Arguments that privilege the 'power' of technology over the power of humans are generally labelled as being **technologically deterministic**. There are 'hard' and 'soft' versions of technological determinism, distinguished by the degree to which they concede a role for non-technological factors in the process of change. At the hard end are ideas such as **autonomous technology** which, according to Winner (1977, p 13), is "the belief that somehow technology has gotten out of control and follows its own course independent of human direction". It suggests that technology has an inherent, almost 'ideological', bias that "creates a relentless and constant pressure for change, but affords no opportunity to decide how" (Street, 1992, p 24). The perspective argues that the precise details of how new technologies emerge is irrelevant – the same process of change would have occurred anyway, be it faster cars, smaller computers and so on. It is a fairly distopian perspective, one in which technology places continual pressure on us to change, where human agency is diminished and people are powerless to resist technological change. The key exponents of the theory are technological pessimists, making wild predictions about a dismal, existential future[6].

Street (1992, p 29) argues "there are many problems with the theory of autonomous technology" and it is widely accepted that this is so (see MacKenzie and Wajcman, 1999). However, more moderate 'soft' technological determinism remains popular. Here, the argument is that technology is the driving force of social change, but "no particular claims [are made] about the ideological rationale provided by technology or about the extent of its impact" (Street, 1992, p 30). Rather, the technology *poses questions* for society and demands that people adapt. While it may be possible to resist change, to do so will often mean losing out to competitors who take advantage of the technology, making resistance somewhat futile. Adoption of the technology therefore becomes a necessity and hence no choice at all. While there seems to be little difference between the two, technological determinism is not so pessimistic – indeed,

---

[6] Marcuse (quoted in Street, 1992, p 29), for example, saw a world in which "all protest is senseless, and the individual who would insist on freedom would become a crank. There is no personal escape from the apparatus which has mechanised and standardised the world. It is a rational apparatus, combining utmost expediency with utmost convenience, saving time and energy, removing waste, adapting all means to ends, anticipating consequences, sustaining calculability and security".

many 'technological determinists' are quite positive about the impact of technology on society.

However, there are also problems with soft technological determinism. In particular, there is a problem with the vagueness of the theories. As Street (1992, p 35) puts it:

> It is noticeable that a wide range of verbs are used when describing the impact of technology on politics. Sometimes the word 'determine' is used, suggesting a fixed causal link, at other times words like 'shape' or 'guide' or 'influence' are employed, suggesting a less certain link.

The technological determinists are convinced that technology is driving social change, but are aware of the need to avoid a sweeping argument that ignores the importance of the 'genuine choices' facing decision makers in the course of technological and social change. However, rather than attempting to explore more fully the link between people and technology, the technological determinists are content with merely 'watering down' their claims, by moderating their language more than by adapting their theories.

MacKenzie and Wajcman (1999, p 4) argue "a simple cause-and-effect technological determinism is not a good candidate as a theory of social change" because "changing technology will always only be one factor among many others: political, economic, cultural and so on". There is a wide consensus that this is so and many theorists emphasise the **social construction of technology** (see MacKenzie and Wajcman, 1999; also Bijker, 1995). So, for instance, economic interests play a strong role in shaping technological change. We could ask why, for example, in the face of the environmental crisis it is contributing to, private motor vehicle travel continues to rise. This apparent conundrum could be answered by reference to a technologically deterministic perspective, highlighting the attractiveness and convenience of the technological solution to mobility that is the motorcar. Equally, however, we could point to the role powerful multinational motor vehicle manufacturers play in promoting the ideal of car ownership, the role oil companies play in promoting petrol-based vehicles and their power vis-à-vis advocates of alternative fuels or the role of governments reluctant to upset either voters or powerful business interests by restricting or heavily taxing automobile travel. This would give us a much richer and more complex picture of technological change – one in which different technologies are competing and powerful social interests are involved in promoting particular solutions.

However, social shaping often takes place at a far less explicit level than this (simplified) example, not least because the broad configuration of social relations in society will often impact upon the development of technology in less overt ways. Moreover, the process of social shaping is often unintentional. The

Internet, for example, emerged from a US government project to create a communication system that would allow the military to communicate following the mass destruction of a nuclear war, but ended up – via the tinkering of curious technicians, the activities of amateur computer buffs, the work of scientists wishing to communicate with each other about their work, and the vision of entrepreneurs seeing an opportunity to make money – into something completely different. MacKenzie and Wajcman (1999, p 16) argue that the outcome of technological experimentation cannot be easily predicted because "the social shaping of technology is, in almost all the cases we know of, a process in which there is no single dominant shaping force".

Significantly, more recent work has attempted to (re)promote the technology itself as one of those forces, particularly **actor–network theory** (Latour, 1999). This perspective, in essence, fuses technological determinism and social shaping into a whole. According to MacKenzie and Wajcman (1999, p 23), a central weakness of the social construction of technology perspective is "its neglect of the valid aspect of technological determinism: the influence of technology upon social relations". In other words, while it may well be true that technologies are socially shaped, this does not mean that when technologies emerge from this process they do not have an impact in themselves. Actor-network theory sees *both* humans *and* technologies as having an impact – both are 'actors' that constitute and are connected in 'networks' that shape, constrain, and enable action. From this perspective, "it is mistaken to think of technology and society as separate spheres influencing each other: technology and society are mutually constitutive" (MacKenzie and Wajcman, 1999, p 23). Consequently, the perspective grants humans and technologies equal importance in its analysis (what Latour [1999] refers to as the 'principle of symmetry'), and suggests we cannot simply view the world as being constructed by humans, for the artefacts we create have an impact too. Indeed, because the two are inextricably bound, they constantly interact with – and impact upon – each other.

Conclusions

A full discussion of theorisations of the technology–society interface is beyond the boundaries of this chapter (see MacKenzie and Wajcman, 1999). Instead, our objective has been to highlight the importance of adding a technological dimension to the analysis of the policy process and to point to the complex role technology plays in social change. Uttley (1991, p 148) has expressed disappointment with the fact that "technology and technological change have not featured prominently as a focus for direct attention in the range of explanatory models for the welfare state which have emerged", and his criticisms remain valid (Hudson, 2002, 2003). We need to make technology a key layer of our analysis, particularly given (as Castells highlights) the often profound nature of changes related to current technological developments.

However, as we have also suggested, we must be wary of ascribing too much weighting to technology in explaining social change. Technology is one of many factors involved in promoting social change and is itself shaped by social forces. In particular, we need to beware of arguments that technology is inevitably pushing policy or society down a particular path and leaving us without any choice about the direction of change. While suggesting that profound social change is occurring as the network society emerges across the globe, Castells (2000, p 9) also notes that "cultures, institutions, and historical trajectories introduce a great deal of diversity in the actual manifestations of each one of these transformations", and his work with Himanen highlights the potential diversity that can exist with respect to welfare policy in the Information Age.

Indeed, while there are those who believe that the emergence of the information society spells the end for the welfare state (see Angell, 2000), the truth is that a more complex process of change is at play. While some dimensions of welfare policy may be challenged by technological change, others might be strengthened. Although we have primarily considered ICTs here, the same arguments apply to other technologies too. So, while the advance of medical technologies presents challenges for the National Health Service (NHS) in terms of pressure on budgets as new, often costly, treatments emerge, these technologies can also relieve pressure on the NHS too as many will also cut the cost of procedures or increase the speed of treatment. Technological change rarely has a simple, linear impact.

Ultimately, the ways in which welfare policy responds to technological change will in large part depend upon the culture and traditions of a particular nation as much as the technology itself. Societies are different, so if technology is socially shaped then we should expect to see differing responses to technological change – as Castells and Himanen argue, there is no one model of the information society.

Summary

- Social scientists are becoming increasingly interested in the implications of technological change for society. Some (such as Castells) believe widespread social changes are emerging as a consequence of the development of new information and communication technologies.
- Interest in the topic is by no means new. For over 25 years, sociologists such as Bell were predicting widespread social changes would emerge as a consequence of new ICTs.

- Governments around the world are looking to exploit new ICTs in order to improve the quality of government services and boost economic competitiveness. Some believe that changes associated with the Information Revolution require governments to reorient the welfare state around a 'human capital' investment agenda.
- Claims of technologically driven revolution and transformation need to be treated with caution. There is more than one model of the information society and different societies will respond to the new challenges in different ways.
- Although technological change can be a powerful force for change, it is not beyond human control. Indeed, many commentators emphasise claims that technology is socially constructed.

Questions for discussion

- How does the notion of an 'information society' inform New Labour's social and economic policies?
- Can the tide of technological change be resisted?
  How far do Castells' arguments about the emergence of a 'network society' capture the reality of recent social change?

Further reading

Cabinet Office (1999) *Modernising government*, London: Cabinet Office.

Castells, M. (2000a) 'Materials for an exploratory theory of the network society', *British Journal of Sociology*, vol 51, pp 5-24.

Castells, M. (2000b) *The rise of the network society: The information age: Economy, society and culture, Vol 1* (2nd edn), Oxford: Blackwell.

Castells, M. and Himanen, P. (2002) *The information society and the welfare state: The Finnish model*, Oxford: Oxford University Press.

Curthoys, N. (2003) *SmartGov: Renewing electronic government for improved service delivery*, London: iSociety/Work Foundation.

Hudson, J. (2003) 'e-galitarianism? The information society and New Labour's repositioning of welfare', *Critical Social Policy*, vol 23, pp 268-90.

MacKenzie, D. and Wajcman, J. (1999) *Social shaping of technology*, Buckingham: Open University Press.

six

The changing nature of governance

Overview

In Chapter Three, we saw how the welfare state evolved into a workfare state under the impact of globalisation forces. In this chapter, we take the story one step further by showing how the whole of the British state apparatus has been challenged to develop in the face of the new political and economic realities. In place of the old-fashioned unitary state organised and managed from London, we now have a much looser, more fragmented system of governance in which the major direction of policy is set by the centre but delivery increasingly has been handed over to private and quasi-private agencies. British politics has been 'hollowed out' – the civil service has adopted New Public Management strategies derived from the private sector, traditional local government replaced by powerful mayors and cabinets, and an upwards hollowing out caused by the Europeanisation of British politics. By contrast, global governance has been unable to match the power of global economic advance.

Key concepts

Governance; democratic deficit; 'hollowing out of the state'; quasi-governmental agencies; New Public Management; Europeanisation.

Introduction

As we pointed out in Chapter Two, a central paradox of the globalisation process is that it creates both a convergent world economic order and has caused the nation state to become the core geopolitical institution of our time. This, we observed, was a consequence of the *processes* that underpin globalisation – stretching of time–space boundaries and deepening of the cultural/historical response to the challenges of a world connected by new technologies in a manner unthinkable even a few decades ago – except in the imagination of science fiction writers. Another feature of the paradox arising from this is that, despite the power of global economic corporations, global *governance* remains as yet relatively weak. It was not easy to mobilise a worldwide response to the threat of AIDS or of global warming, let alone the relatively minor problems caused by the spread of the new SARS virus and avian flu. The response to these issues has been and remains very much in the ambit of individual nation states that come together in large conferences to agree protocols, the enforcement of which is the responsibility of states. The reality is that individual countries argue about their 'national interest' and there is no matching authority to define let alone impose an equivalent global interest.

The wrapping of the world in a new 'networked capitalism', to use Castells' phrase, does not mean therefore that nation states, which were the principal form of governance in the 20th century, have been superseded or made redundant, as the hyperglobalists argue. Actually, their significance has been heightened. Neither does globalisation mean that the whole world is hurtling towards the same political and social endgame. Cultural and political difference remains central to how the world is evolving in the early years of the new millennium. Politics matters and a very large part of the direction being taken by the different nations is a consequence of their own policy-making process.

However, globalisation is a powerful force and the point that we are stressing here is that it compels nations to respond *from within* their own historical, cultural and political domains. At the same time, new layers of governance and new forms of politics have been laid down across the globe, new elite networks use the global highways to strengthen their power bases and often these networks are supranational; that is, they are above the level of national boundaries. Globalisation is thus not only about powerful *economic* forces, but also involves consideration of new political structures and the development of existing ones, national and supranational. In the British context, this involves evaluating the nature and reasons behind the dramatic changes to the British state in recent years, including Britain's relationship with the EU. Britain is a member state of the EU and so is politically and constitutionally integrated to a body that has considerable influence over the British policy agenda. Britain, for example, is a member of the Single European Market, which is intended to guarantee the free circulation of goods, services and capital around the 'internal market'. The issue here is to make sense of the influence of global markets against the political regulation of the economy created through Britain's membership of the EU. Globalisation meets Europeanisation.

The main focus of this chapter is on the newly reconstituted British state, its new structures and methods of operation, of how and (crucially) why it has been redefined and 'rearticulated' as Held et al put it (Held et al, 1999). The transformation of British governance over the last two decades, of course, has major repercussions for the welfare state itself, through the development of the competition state. The main question here, however, is the more general one of considering to what extent the British state has been rearticulated – or, in the words of Rhodes (1994), 'hollowed out' – in its response to the new economic realities of life as a service economy, inescapably bound into the logic of the global capital markets.

The idea of governance

This chapter is not only about the British government but spans a whole range of non-state as well as state-centred actors and agencies which together make up the functional reality of modern British politics. This is why political science increasingly has adopted the notion of *governance* to capture the different layers and tiers of organisations involved in the overall process (see Rhodes, 1996a, 1997). Inside the nation state, this means being alert to the boundaries between the public, private and voluntary sectors and how this configuration has shifted in recent years. There has been major structural change but crucially this has been accompanied by changing *processes*, especially the emergence of networking as the principal way in which policy is managed and delivered. Although this view is not uncontested (see Holliday, 2000), it is our belief that networks have become the engine-room of the modern British polity. The policy network literature will be discussed in more depth in Chapter Eight, but it is important at this point to recognise that the basic pattern *and method* of the old-fashioned unitary state, which served Britain well throughout the 20th century, has been radically dismembered. Networks are part and parcel of how the British polity has been forced to respond to the imperative of globalisation with its pressure for increased velocity of action, reflexivity and demand for flexibility.

One of the crucial implications of the notion of governance understood in this way is that these new inter-organisational structures have a significant degree of autonomy from the core state. The delivery and management of the public sector has to a considerable extent been ceded to networks. As Rhodes (1996a, 1997) suggests, they are often self-organising, and one of the key features of policy analysis in the real world is the empirical investigation of policy fields and the characteristics of the networks that operate within them. As Holliday (2000) rightly points out, systematic evidence documenting this shift is still somewhat slender. However, the resonance of the argument remains strong. Networks operate in a policy space that is to a large extent negotiated. The idea of a 'democratic deficit' is never far from the surface of this discussion. Thus, new governance embraces a variety of themes:

- **The relationship between the government, its core executive and the variety of quasi-state and non-state actors and agencies in the public, private and voluntary sectors.** To what extent has the centre lost its sovereignty? Has there been a separation of policy-making from delivery of services (of steering from rowing)?
- **The use of policy networks to connect the system involving a high degree of self-regulation.** The metaphor of the British state as a top-down hierarchy with chains of command up and down the system has largely been superseded by an image that stresses the linkages and interactions across the policy terrain and where top-down authority has been replaced by negotiation and contracts.
- **Policy networks are often self-regulating with considerable autonomy from the centre.** This raises issues about the (low) level of accountability in the system.
- **The role of networks as institutional filters, screening out policy change, directing the policy agendas and shaping incrementally policy directions.**

Within this switch, from an outmoded unitary state to a networked polity, traditional ideas of public service and citizenship have to a large extent been superseded by an ethic that stresses the logic of market exchanges, contracts and consumer choice.

The fragmented state

As we pointed out at various points in Chapters Three and Four, globalisation has radically changed the terms of how Britain engages in the world economy and has compelled the British state to spearhead the radical rebuilding of the British economy. In a nutshell, it has been transformed from a principally manufacturing-based economy to one almost wholly dependent on services including the vital role of the City of London as a conduit for global currency trading. Having been 'the workshop of the world' in the 19th century, the 20th century witnessed the gradual erosion of Britain's economic predominance based on its massive global empire. The point here is that this historical legacy made Britain particularly vulnerable to late 20th-century globalisation because the economy was and continues to be fundamentally built round overseas trading and foreign markets. In this process of change, the British state itself has also been radically overhauled in order to be capable of responding to the demands of the new economy and its more central role as an enabler of economic progress.

As we outlined in Chapter Three, the most useful and succinct explanation of the new governance is the idea of Britain as a 'competition state' (Cerny and Evans, 1999; see also Hutton, 1995). The essence of this idea is that the structure of modern government has been re-engineered in order that business elites, especially financial services, can enter the global economy proactively rather than defensively. This is a very different way of thinking about the role of the state, which for most of the post-Second World War era was thought of as a restraint on the power of the free market and with a strong redistributive purpose, the core of which was Keynesian demand management of the economy and the Beveridge welfare state. *Table 6.1* summarises the key changes that have occurred. The challenge – indeed, the threat – posed by globalisation compelled a radical redesign of the role and then, as a result, the structures of the antediluvian unitary state (that is to say, a system that was run and directed from Whitehall with no federal structures and, crucially, with all powers emanating from the 'centre') based on the increasingly ineffective 'Westminster model' of government. Dating from the second half of the 19th century, the Westminster model was the core, orthodox explanation of how the British polity operated. At its heart was the sovereignty of parliament incorporating cabinet/prime ministerial government, an institutionalised opposition, majority-party control over the executive and accountability via the electorate.

In the Thatcher/Regan era, the breakdown of the old model of government took the form, under the guise of the neo-liberal agenda, of restraining the powers of government in favour of the market. The Blair 'project' – to create a stakeholder society – responded to the same pressures and took forward the

Table 6.1: *Fragmentation of the state*

	1940s-1970s	1980s-2000s
Structure	Unitary state; the 'Westminster model'; strong central–local orientation	Fragmented state; devolved assemblies; weak local government; EU
Character	Bureaucratic; centralised; classic Weberian hierarchies	Quasi-governmental agencies; policy networks; centralisation of major policy instruments
Methods	Control of policy making and delivery; multilayered tiers of authority; macro-planning	Contracting out; New Public Management; public/private/voluntary networking; meso- and micro-focus
Culture	Interventionist state; Beveridge welfare state; Keynesian demand management	Stakeholder society; business orientation; neo-liberal ethos

Source: Adapted from Cerny and Evans (1999)

same agenda, albeit in rather different language and policy initiatives. Evans and Cerny (2003) called this stage the 'competition state Mark II', in which the Left embraced globalisation as potentially bringing benefits to all strata of society including the working classes. A precondition of this would be to increase the degree of regulation through New Public Management and to reconstruct government to be more responsive to bottom–up demands for inclusion while 'loosening' delivery of public services. This project also entails the redesign of the post-war welfare state and its replacement with what has come to be known as the post-industrial workfare state.

One of the key themes of the globalisation discourse is the extent to which welfare states are forced to dismantle under pressure from competitive world markets (see Chapter Two). We do not accept that globalisation has compelled a 'race to the bottom', because such deterministic explanations do not account for the idea of institutional lock-in or path dependency (Pierson, 2000). It is a key proposition of the new institutionalist literature that historically embedded institutions provide both filters for change and structures that are difficult to break down. Indeed, welfare states are famously stable institutions. In fact, *new* demands for state intervention were generated by the need for greater flexibility in the labour market (schemes to retrain workers made redundant by the loss of manufacturing work, demands for nursery facilities as more and more women entered the labour force). The New Labour 'project', the so-called competition state Mark II, was more sensitive to these pressures and embraced the shift of social policy towards a more contract-orientated, pluralistic system of welfare. Policies such as ending free higher education, the selling off of local authority council housing stock to quasi-private 'social businesses', and the introduction of expensive 'workfare' programmes designed to reintegrate the unemployed into the private sector labour market are typical of this approach.

The hollowing out of the state

As *Table 6.1* shows, the rearticulation of the modern state concerns both its basic structures and the way in which it operates, its processes and methods. One useful way of trying to express the changing shape of the British state is through the idea of 'hollowing out', advocated most forcefully in the work of Rhodes (1994, 1996a, 1997). His position on the nature and extent of policy networks as the central explanation of how the British political system operates is discussed in detail in Chapter Eight of this book. Fundamental to this is that the structure of the old unitary state has been and continues to be broken down. This is happening under the impact of the globalisation imperative, to create a more entrepreneurial style of government more suited to the needs of the 21st century. According to the hollowing-out thesis, power has shifted decisively *away* from the central apparatus. This is a key feature of Blair's period in office, despite an apparent tightening and expansion of the core Whitehall executive. The shape of British governance has been dramatically redesigned during the phase of the competition state Mark II. Key features are:

- The establishment of the Scottish Parliament, the creation of Welsh, Northern Irish (currently suspended) and London Assemblies have shifted the centre of gravity of the unitary state. English regional government was strengthened through the establishment of Regional Development Agencies (RDAs) in 1999 in nine locations and by the announcement, in the summer of 2003, of plans for referenda in Yorkshire, the north-east and north-west regions with a view to establishing regional assemblies.
- The reform of local government via the abolition of the traditional committee system and its replacement with powerful elected mayors and cabinets was also a key feature of the Labour government's commitment to create a slim, entrepreneurial-style polity. This major constitutional change was a prerequisite for the conditions in which there could be greater harmonisation between the public and private sectors in service delivery. This was also the motivation behind the call for English regional assemblies which will have only 30 elected members but entails the abolition of county councils and the incorporation of their functions – land-use planning, housing, transport and other core infrastructure – into the new assemblies.

Devolution, however, is not without risk to the centre. The election of Ken Livingstone as the first Mayor of London and the failure to get Blair's preferred candidate elected as Chair of the Welsh Assembly clearly backfired on the New Labour government and revealed the vulnerability of the centre to 'mistakes', or at least stretching the centre's capacity to control the newly devolved regional institutions. Political and constitutional reform as instruments of political modernisation loosen the ties between the central executive and the rest of the country and have apparently unpredictable results. This is especially the case when a proportional representation system of voting is used, creating, as it has done in Scotland, an assembly based on coalition politics. This inevitably leads to a politics of compromise and 'deals', such as the decision to ban top-up fees for Scottish students entering Scottish universities.

The instinct of the centre, especially the Treasury under Gordon Brown, is for top-down control. Holliday (2000) argues that Rhodes' 'hollowing-out' thesis is significantly flawed because there is strong empirical evidence that, not only is the central apparatus of government still strong, but that it has *increased* in size and influence during the Blair government. There are three times as many civil servants working in the Cabinet Office (the closest part of the Whitehall 'village' to the prime minister apart from his own office at No

10) in 2000 compared to 1975. "The core is now more substantial and more integrated than ever before", according to Holliday (2000, p 175).

Since the re-election of the Labour government in June 2001, modernisation of central government has moved up yet another gear. The prime minister put improvement of public services at the top of the political agenda, and saw the election result as 'an instruction to deliver'. In support of this mission, several new central units have been created that link the Cabinet Office to the prime minister. Following the appointment of Sir Andrew Turnbull as the new Cabinet Secretary in September 2002, all the main 'delivery' units were integrated into a single Delivery and Reform Team, incorporating the:

- **Strategy Unit** (strategic thinking and policy analysis at the heart of government);
- prime minister's **Delivery Unit** (monitors progress on the government's capacity to deliver its key priorities across education, health, crime and transport, ensuring that each department has a Delivery Plan);
- **Office of Public Services Reform** (a group concerned with more effective delivery of public services and reducing regulations);
- **Office of the e-Envoy** (responsible for online government services);
- **Corporate Development Group** (responsible for civil service management);
- office of **Government Commerce** (responsible for central government procurement and promoting private sector involvement in the public sector).

A more integrated centre is *not*, however, incompatible with the idea in the competition state thesis, that it is necessary to separate out delivery from policy making. If anything, the establishment of the Delivery and Reform Team underscores the idea of targeting implementation and working out how most effectively to engage the delivery agencies. The reality is that structural 'loosening' and the political imperative to deliver improvements in public service performance necessitates the separation of policy making from implementation, with its inherent risk of 'spillover' and loss of control.

This radical change to the pattern of governance, we contend, is neatly captured in the 'hollowing out of the state' thesis, or at least in the idea that this is the process that is shaping the modern agenda. This involved, through the 1980s and 1990s, the loss of functions by the central state to myriad agencies and implementation bodies, the introduction of New Public Management methods, privatisation of large parts of the publicly owned infrastructure, contracting out of services, blurring in the distinction between the public, private and voluntary sectors, all leading to a situation in which, as Osborne and Gaebler (1992) put it, the government 'steers rather than rows'. In other words, the centre guides the general direction of policy, especially through spending agreements and service targets, but delivery is largely contracted out and significant areas of governance devolved. Globalisation underpinned and accelerated the break up of Britain as a unitary state into a much more fragmented system – a 'differentiated polity', as Rhodes describes it. Government, he argues (1997, p 15), has substantially given way to governance, "to self-organizing, interorganisational networks characterised by interdependencies, resource exchanges, rules of the game and significant autonomy from the state".

Quasi-governmental agencies: the hybridisation of public services

The trend towards loosening of delivery had developed during the 1970s. It took the form of the establishment of what came to be called 'quasi-governmental agencies' (QGAs). These were non-elected agencies usually controlled by a central board appointed by the government. Funding was drawn from both the public purse and commercial activity. As early as 1990, a Charter 88 study counted 6,700 quasi-governmental bodies and delivery agencies with spending programmes in excess of £46 billion. The study was critical of the fact that many agencies were run by politically appointed managers, the low level of accountability to voters or to service users, and the massive increase in management costs due to new layers of administration (Charter 88, 1993). Normally a quango would be a single-issue body responsible for one area of delivery. An organisation such as the Arts Council, for example, became responsible for distributing finance to the major orchestras, regional opera companies and a host of smaller local art projects, theatre companies and music clubs. The Housing Corporation (HC) became responsible, following the 1974 Housing Act, for the rapidly expanding role of housing associations in the provision of social housing – the only real alternative in Britain to council housing. It had regional offices and a system for administering the funding to the associations and regulating their work. In recent years, the HC has overseen what in effect was the establishment of housing 'social businesses' incorporating the injection of large amounts of private capital into the social housing sector. This was the beginning of the process of separating steering from rowing. Although government established the broad parameters of policy the delivery end of the policy process was devolved to specialist bodies. This separation allowed a significant degree of commercial freedom and enabled governments to deflect attention from unpopular decisions onto the agencies, while enabling them to take credit for successes. This model also fitted well with large services such as the NHS where the function was on such a large scale that devolved management and significant loosening from the centre was generally welcomed. It also fitted with other more specialist functions such as nuclear power (the Atomic Energy Commission), forestry (the Forestry Commission), milk marketing (the Milk

Marketing Board) and so on, and the conversion of existing services such as map-making (the Ordinance Survey) and weather forecasting into more or less fully commercial enterprises and in all cases certainly brought formerly public services into close proximity with the private sector.

There is no standardised model for these quasi-governmental agencies, but it is very clear that the separation of steering from rowing created a revolution in the management and delivery of public services with a diffusion of power away from Whitehall and towards agencies consisting very largely of public–private sector organisational hybrids. Policy delivery increasingly slipped into the hands of unaccountable, professionally dominated elite groups outside government and provided the conditions in which the incorporation of the commercial private sector into public service delivery was eased. Thus, policy increasingly became the domain of inter-agency negotiation through policy networks.

The creation of the executive agencies: 'next steps'

One of the key features of 'hollowing out' has been the replacement of the centrally managed civil service by new agency structures that were deliberately engineered during the middle phase of the Thatcher governments. The establishment of so-called executive agencies arose from the abolition of the Civil Service Department in 1981 and the transfer of their functions into the Treasury and the Cabinet Office. This arrangement was further reformed in the late 1980s through the creation of the Office of Public Service to oversee an Efficiency Unit, the Next Steps reform of the civil service and the Citizen's Charter. The Efficiency Unit was established under one of Mrs Thatcher's guiding lights, Sir Derek Raynor, the chairman of what was then the highly successful Marks & Spencer retail chain. He soon gave way to Sir Robin Ibbs and it was Ibbs who in 1988 produced his radical report, *Improving management in government: The next steps*.

The three key recommendations of the Ibbs Report were:

- to separate 'steering from rowing' (that is, policy making from implementation). Policy, so it was argued, was best managed by decentralised management units working to predefined cost and performance targets;
- decentralisation to operate through: (i) the creation of semi-independent executive agencies devoted to specific functions; and (ii) the creation of contracts between government departments and agencies and between agencies and the private sector;
- market testing (the idea of using outside contractors through which the existing provider might or might not tender for the work they were already doing).

The reforms of the 1980s caused a radical shift from the old practices. Out went the idea of a unitary, hierarchical civil service of permanent staff and in came a system based on fragmented semi-independent agencies. Within five years, no fewer than 97 executive agencies had been created, employing two thirds of all civil servants. The uniform departmental hierarchies – with 15 general grades, from permanent secretary (the highest) to clerical assistant (the lowest) – were abandoned. In its place, a new Senior Civil Service was formed from the top five grades and career-managed from the 'centre'. All other pay and grading was decentralised to departments and agencies, and the central Civil Service Department was abolished.

Examples of the new agencies were the Benefits Agency responsible for the delivery of social security benefits, the Land Registry which logs and monitors the sales of land and houses, and HM Prison Service became an agency overseeing the running of prisons and other custodial establishments. There was no civil service function that was untouched (see O'Toole and Jordan, 1995). However, once the first flush of enthusiasm passed, a number of problems with a model of management derived from private sector practice surfaced, not least that many of these services were effectively monopolies and it was difficult to see how competitive tendering, market testing and other methodologies transferred from the private sector could be operationalised. Other criticisms were:

- **Increased flexibility but reduced accountability.** A major problem quickly became apparent that it was difficult to know *who* to blame when things went wrong. The Jennings Inquiry into the BSE virus (how 'mad cow' disease spread to humans) was scathing about this: if ministers have no direct control over implementation, how can he/she be held responsible?
- **The long tradition of civil service impartiality/anonymity was undermined.** It was soon apparent that loyalty to the public interest was not served in a situation that emphasised people's contractual relations to their employer rather than respect for professional competencies. Performance-related pay, short contracts and privatisation were uneasy bedfellows with the ethic of public service. Moreover, there was (and remains) little evidence that the introduction of private-sector management practice has actually improved public service delivery.
- **The rationale of government departments as centres of control was undermined.** A symptom of this was the emergence of uneasy relationships between government ministers responsible for areas of public policy and agency chief executives.

Crucially, this process of 'agencification' is by no means a peculiarly British phenomenon. As Pollitt et al (2001) have highlighted, many other nations – including Canada, the Netherlands, Japan, Jamaica, New Zealand and the US

– have implemented specific programmes designed to increase the number of agencies involved in policy delivery and others, such as Australia and Denmark, have implemented less formal programmes with similar end goals. The precise nature of the reforms, however, has varied from place to place, reflecting differing institutional settings and cultural practices (see also Pollitt and Bouckaert, 2000).

Box 6.1: New Public Management

New approaches to managing the public sector, designed to move away from traditional bureaucratic methods, made a major impact in the 1980s. New Public Management (NPM) is shorthand for various innovations that have spread across the globe (Pollitt and Bouckaert, 2000; Kettl, 2000). Key features are:

- performance measurement and monitoring;
- private-sector style of management;
- emphasis on output controls;
- distrust of traditional professions.

There is, however, no fixed doctrine associated with NPM and its application varies from place to place (Pollitt and Bouckaert, 2000). Some approaches are motivated by a desire to produce the conditions in which individuals and organisations can become 'excellent', implying no undue level of surveillance. Other versions suggest the need for the close control of behaviour in order to maximise efficiency. Some of these conflicting views can be explained away because they all subscribe to the idea that market disciplines in the end will impose their own logic. In Britain, NPM has a strong top-down ethos with little attempt to decentralise. 'Disaggregated units', according to Hood, have been subject to tight central control (Hood, 1991). The imposition of NPM regimes in local government, for example, has usually been accompanied by stringent financial and budgetary controls.

Despite its rise in prominence in the British public sector during the 1980s and 1990s, there is surprisingly little evidence in the literature about the results of NPM, whether, for example, 'market' philosophies and management practices have improved performance or not. If anything, experience tends to suggest that privatised public services run on the lines of NPM have required ever more external regulation.

Further reading
Hoggett, P. (1996) 'New models of control in public service', *Public Administration*, vol 74, no 1, pp 9-32.
Hood, C. (1991) 'A public management for all seasons', *Public Administration*, vol 69, no 1, pp 3-19.
Pollitt, C. (1993) *Managerialism and the public services*, Oxford: Blackwell.
Pollitt, C. and Bouckaert, G. (2000) *Public management reform: A comparative analysis*, Oxford: Oxford University Press.

The European dimension

The two key empirical claims of the 'hollowing out of the state' thesis are, first, that there has been a flow of power downwards and outwards in the internal British state, as we have described earlier in this chapter; and second, that there has been a flow of power and loss of sovereignty resulting from the UK's membership, from 1973 onwards, of the EC. This part of the hollowing-out process involved powers flowing upwards into a supranational tier of government. Europeanisation, so it is argued, involves the development of European governance, which draws the focus of decision making away from the national centres of power. In practice, the idea of 'them and us' has dominated Britain's approach to European integration; Britain opted out of Monetary Union and more recently opposed the introduction of qualified majority voting on the key issues of taxation and social security at the Nice convention, which was preparing the way for enlargement of the community by the accession of the post-communist states. In fact, such a black-and-white view of Britain in Europe (and Europe in Britain) does not do justice to the complexity of the relationships that have emerged, particularly since the development of the Single European Market (SEM) in 1986.

In line with our argument in Chapter Two on the 'stretching' and 'deepening' consequences of globalisation, we need to be alert to the interaction of the local, regional, national and supranational levels. As Hooghe and Marks (2001) suggest, we are dealing here with a system of multilevel governance with decision making dispersed across a variety of territorial levels. In this process, policy networks play a very powerful role in filtering and shaping policy outcomes. The same logic that applies to the rearticulation of British governance applies to the pattern of European-wide governance. Knill and Lehmkuhl (1999) show that this involves a number of key features:

- that there are some non-negotiable aspects of European policy that forces compliance on member nations;
- that the internal politics of EU members will be rebalanced and reconfigured as a result of membership giving some governments the opportunity to push through policies under the guise of conformity to EU rules. Such 'opportunity structures' vary from country to country so that there is no predetermined, blanket response across all the member states;
- there is a crucial ideational dimension in which established concepts and political discourses are challenged – or, as Rosamond (2003) expresses it, 'infected' – by a European dimension.

In the British case, these issues impacted against a specific historical/cultural context – as we have described it earlier – in which there has been openness to global trade, economic restructuring and the development of the 'workfare state'. This tension is at the heart of Britain's relationship with Europe.

Until the mid-1980s (and since the Treaty of Rome, which established it) the European Economic Community (EEC) had been a 'common market' with the aim of generally promoting common economic progress. The intensification of the global economy during the 1980s created pressure for an enhanced level of economic integration and the necessary constitutional framework to enable it. The Single European Act (1986) created a single market in which goods, services, labour and capital were free to circulate. The process of integration involving foreign and defence policy, monetary union and steps towards common social policies for all people in member states was further developed by the Treaty of European Union (the Maastricht Treaty) which came into force in 1993, establishing, in the process, the European Union. This period marked the high-water mark of the integrationist ambitions of the pro-European forces. The logic of the next step, the creation of a more federal Europe, has had a more chequered history, the establishment of monetary union being a major step forward, but the collapse of communism and German unification have fundamentally changed the playing field. Recent policy has focused on the constitutional issues raised by the prospect of incorporating the post-communist states.

The EU has engineered, therefore, a significantly deregulated single market, almost certainly freer than the trading conditions that apply to the global economy (with the exception of the electronically interconnected financial markets which by definition are extremely footloose). By the same token, the EU single market exerts considerable influence over production standards and increasingly over price so there is a tension between explanations that veer towards globalisation (free market) and those which are built round the social market, European dimension (a more political/institutional explanation). Different states respond to these pressures from within their own historical legacies. The French state, for example, with its Napoleonic legacy has retained a strong centralist character with powerful representation of the 'centre' in regional and local governance via the system of 'prefects'. In Britain, there is not such a clear demarcation between political and market-led imperatives because Britain has historically pursued both the neo-liberal/market transatlantic agenda and yet remains a core European state. These outcomes and responses arise from the path dependencies of the member states.

British engagement has arisen, therefore, rather less as a result of the establishment of the SEM in 1986 than by Britain's historic openly market-oriented stance. As Rosamond (2003, p 54) suggests, "there is little evidence of governments citing the imperatives set by the EU as the immediate cause of policy choices". In France, on the other hand, the requirements of the SEM and the preparations for European monetary union (EMU) have been consistently used as an excuse for public expenditure cuts.

Box 6.2: Britain in Europe/Europe in Britain

1957 The Treaty of Rome establishes the European Economic Community.

1973 Britain joins 'The Six'.

1986 The Single European Act establishes the European Union and sets up an internal market in goods, services and labour.

1992 Treaty on European Union (the Maastricht Treaty) set out conditions for monetary union and for greater political convergence; Danish referendum rejected further integration within the EU.

1995 Austria, Finland and Sweden join the EU.

1997 Treaty of Amsterdam, consideration of Qualified Majority Voting, common foreign and defence policy, the Social Protocol incorporated into EU framework following election of Blair government.

1998 Negotiations begin on the enlargement of the EU to include post-communist European states.

2000 Treaty of Nice sets out institutional reforms necessary for enlargement.

2002 The Euro currency (€) replaces local currencies in 11 of 15 member states; Britain, Denmark and Sweden remain outside the 'eurozone'.

2003 Rome Declaration published a Draft Treaty establishing a Constitution for Europe, but threats from Germany of a two-speed Europe.

2004 1 May accession of ten new member states, creating a EU of 25 states.

Britain's concern has been much more to do with the possible constraints on British parliamentary sovereignty and the possibility that further integration into the 'European project' might create barriers to engagement with the global trade outside Europe. The case made for British entry to the EMU thus hinges on whether or not joining the system would assist in combating the uncertainties of globalisation and not on further integration with Europe (Rosamond, 2003).

Membership of the EU has further 'hollowed out' the British state in the sense that another dimension has been added into the complex area of multi-layered governance, although the flows of power and policy making outputs are likely to feed back from the national level. A very good case of this is the development of social policy in the EU. The emergence of the competition state and welfare state retrenchment in the UK in the 1980s contrasted sharply with policy change in other EU nations, most of whom retained their traditional high tax/high spend welfare programmes, strongly influenced by the German model of the 'social market' (with a history going back to the Weimar Republic period). Britain opted out of the Social Chapter of the Maastricht Treaty, with John Major's government resisting the Europeanisation of British social policy. Other states, however, also effectively opted out of the social programme, fearing that the British position would undermine their own competitiveness

(Liebfried and Pierson, 2000). New Labour's emphasis on flexible Labour markets and the development of the competition state, with its post-industrial workfare social policies, has fed back through the EU institutions, creating a convergence of social policies around the British agenda. As Rosamond observes, in the treatment of the problem of unemployment among the member states, "... the means used to address these problems are largely consistent with British preferences and may reflect 'uploading' of policy ides to the European level" (Rosamond, 2003, p 59). **Policy transfer** (see Chapter Ten) of this type shows that the pattern of Europeanisation is not simply one of a flow of power from Brussels. As we argue throughout the book, the key point of the institutionalist approach is its sensitivity to institutional filtering and **policy learning** across and through interorganisational networks. EU policy is always mediated by British institutional filters, especially arising from the British tradition of parliamentary sovereignty, and the converse is equally the case: Britain in Europe and Europe in Britain.

It is not clear, therefore, the extent to which Europeanisation with its strong sense of politically and institutionally directed economic and social policies will trump the worldwide marketplace. Globalisation is a powerful disciplinarian of social and economic policies and it remains to be seen whether the British response built up from a long tradition of liberal free-market engagement is in practice the joker in the pack, especially after 1 May 2004 with the accession of the post-communist states who, in the main (but not all), have embraced the neo-liberal economic agenda. It may be that we are witnessing the 'hollowing out' of Europe.

Transnational governance

Despite the power of the global economy in reshaping world trade markets and its impact on nation states, global governance remains weak and relatively undeveloped. In the field of what can broadly be called public or social policy, very few new governance bodies have come into existence in parallel with economic expansion. The main trend has been for existing agencies to adapt to the new realities in much the same way as nation states. For example, the World Bank and the IMF have funded and developed major social programmes across the globe, recognising that globalisation has significant and potentially dysfunctional social costs (George and Wilding, 2002; see also Deacon, 2001).

However, social programmes generally have floundered in the face of the realities of national self-interest and the profit margins and power of multinational capital. The World Health Organisation (WHO), for example, was prominent in the campaign to stop the spread of AIDS in the late 1980s and 1990s (via the Global Programme on AIDS) and initially was successful in building a global consensus, but this project foundered as individual nations refused to accept what was happening or resisted the cost implications of combating the disease. Multinational drugs companies refused to make drug treatments available at low prices for less economically developed countries (LEDCs) and the legitimacy of the WHO stalled on this issue.

The International Labour Organisation (ILO) and the World Bank both have major projects to help monitor and alleviate the growth of poverty arising from labour-market changes. For example, the World Bank, established large numbers of projects in the former USSR and its satellite nations of Europe following the collapse of communism at the end of the 1980s. These projects were aimed mainly at helping the transition of these largely bankrupt economies to western-style free markets. This entailed the use of foreign consultants to help reshape local government finance, to establish properly regulated banking systems, improve the economic efficiency of factories and projects to help the transformation of state rental housing into an open market using mortgage funding (Struyk, 1996). The motivation was thus very much to do with importing neo-liberal economic methods and ideologies into the vacuum left by the collapse of communism. The degree of success of this project work varied enormously from country to country. This variance was to a considerable extent a consequence of the **path dependency** of pre-communist social and political forces in these countries and to the fact that each nation's experience of communism was different. There was no ubiquitous 'communist system' that was the same all over the world and some authors have noted considerable variations in how the countries of Europe came through the communist period and what subsequently has happened to them (see, for example, Lowe and Tsenkova, 2003, in relation to housing policy).

The reality, however, is that global governance is weak and, where it has progressed in recent years, implementation remains a key problem in the face of a vastly unequal distribution of global political power and economic resources. In post-communist Europe, the ideational battleground, as we saw earlier in this chapter, polarised around the European social market and the American-inspired neo-liberal free-market agenda. Global social programmes thus found themselves squeezed between competing paradigms as well as lacking legitimacy. As George and Wilding (2002, p 172) argue from their review of the progress in global social policies, "What exists is a plethora of very different organisations nibbling at a social policy agenda but in an essentially ad hoc and reactive fashion".

Care should be taken, however, not to overplay the 'power of global market forces' against the political impact, albeit 'weak', of global governance agencies to determine outcomes. An institutionalist perspective would suggest that there could be exchanges both up and down the global hierarchy. For example, in some circumstances, 'weak' global governance may impact on nation states, providing the opportunity for national governments to push forward their own reform agenda. This is more obviously the case, as we saw earlier, in the

Box 6.3: New social movements

An important phenomenon associated with new governance is the range of organisations that stand outside the formal political system. So-called 'new social movements' emerged in the 1970s and 1980s in response to the bureaucratic nature of formal decision making in western societies, campaigning on issues that were not captured by orthodox politics or were marginalised. These were often single-issue movements particularly associated with the environment, cultural diversity and peace campaigns.

What united these organisations into 'movements' was the aim they all shared to a greater or lesser degree to reconstitute civil society in a way that moved away from regulation and hierarchical control of society by elite interests and towards a more open, collective approach. To this end, they adopted distinctive forms of political activity; un-hierarchical modes of organisation, distance from formal party politics, and an emphasis on direct action and protest activity. 'Urban' social movements were particularly active during the 1960s and 1970s and spawned a large-scale literature among social scientists (Castells, 1977; Offe, 1985; Lowe, 1986).

Some writers have attempted to explain the scale of social movement activity as a consequence of the development of 'knowledge-based' societies (Melucci, 1998) or as a response to post-industrialism (Touraine, 1995). It is clear from this range of authors that the fundamental processes that underlie the development of social movements across the globe are those of broadening and *deepening* we recognised as characteristic of globalisation (see Chapter Two). Taking up these themes, Offe (1985) showed that it is the more dispersed nature of power, with the potential to harness local action into wider global alliances, that creates the claim of 'new' social movements to find non-institutional solutions to social problems. Offe claimed that 'new' and 'old' politics compete against each other and that the concerns of the 'new middle class' over the environment, public service provision, women's and other civil rights, world peace and so on created alliances with marginalised sectors of society (single parents, students, the unemployed) to challenge the orthodox political terrain.

More recently, Melucci (1996) has argued, building on Offe, that it is from globalisation processes – especially the creation of the Internet and intensive information flows – that new identities are being created that challenge the modern state. This arises from the massive diversity and plurality of choices available but also the attendant risk associated with increased surveillance and the problem of people being confined and controlled even while new possibilities become available. In this context information becomes increasingly powerful. New social movements impact directly on institutions by setting new agendas, changing the nature of political discourse and providing a base for political activists to penetrate the formal system. Thus, in a world in which political power has become more diffuse there are, for Melucci, increased opportunities for social movements to make a positive impact in the 'spaces' left by a looser, more networked system.

EU setting where the European Commission's aim to harmonise policy around an issue, such as best practice in labour relations, can open windows of opportunity for unpopular national reform programmes under the guise of pre-empting EU rules. In theory, the same opportunity is available from the programmes of other international bodies. Armingeon and Beyler (2003), for example, showed how the OECD's surveillance systems – its monitoring of trends, collection of comparative statistics and evaluations of policy effectiveness – were a trigger to new national policy because of the diffusion of new knowledge and ideas. In other words, what we are characterising as 'weak' international governance bodies may influence the pattern of individual state's policy programmes. These types of 'soft' triggers to reform are important and easily overlooked if due care is not taken to evaluate institutional impacts (Beyler, 2003).

Conclusions

There can be very little doubt that the British state has undergone a significant transformation in the structures and processes of governance over the last two or three decades. The old-fashioned unitary state which was suited to the conditions of life through most of the 20th century has largely been superseded by a fragmented polity, a hollowed-out state, in which despite the instinct of the centre to control there has been a significant loosening of policy making from delivery. It should also be clear that the manner in which Britain has responded to the challenges of globalisation is not the same as other countries. A key message from this book is the need to be very sensitive to the cultural and historical contexts of different societies and the 'path dependency' created by particular experiences. This is *not* the same as saying that every country is unique, the consequence of which would be that there would be no purpose in comparing nations or even in trying to understand the wider context in which the British case is situated. The policy-making process in Britain needs to be read not only against the changes in national political structures and processes but also against the wider governance of the globe and against the new global economy. As we have seen, one of the central paradoxes of globalisation is that it has strengthened the nation state and yet global governance remains fragile even though it is evolving rapidly. Even so, there are feedback effects from global governance organisations to the nation state just as there are in the case of the EU and Britain.

Summary

- The British state has had to spearhead the radical rebuilding of the British economy and the deconstruction of the outdated top-down unitary 'Westminster' model of government.

- The British state has been 'hollowed out', involving the loss of functions by the central state to myriad agencies and implementation bodies, privatisation of public services, contracting out of services, blurring in the distinction between the public, private and voluntary sectors.
- The separation of policy making from delivery of services has meant that power has trickled down to more specialised, elite agencies whose knowledge of and influence over policy implementation has caused a significant shift in the national power base.
- An 'upwards' hollowing out has occurred as a result of Britain's membership of the EU but the whole of European governance has been similarly affected by the creation of new networks and institutional structures. Europeanisation is a complex agenda and interacts with globalisation. Politically directed markets meet the free market.
- Global governance is weak and where it has progressed in recent years implementation remains a key problem in the face of a vastly unequal distribution of global political power and economic resources. There is, nevertheless, the potential for significant feedback effects and soft triggers to policy reforms in nation states.

Questions for discussion

- To what extent is there a 'democratic deficit' arising from the creation of a more networked polity?
- Does the UK need to integrate further into the European Union?
- On what grounds can it be argued that global governance is weak?

Further reading

Castles, F.G. (1998) *Comparative public policy: Patterns of post-war transformation*, Cheltenham: Edward Elgar.

Evans, M. and Cerny, P. (2003) 'Globalisation and social policy', in N. Ellison and C. Pierson (eds) *Developments in British social policy 2*, Basingstoke: Palgrave, pp 19-41.

George, V. and Wilding, P. (2002) *Globalisation and human welfare*, Basingstoke: Palgrave Macmillan.

Melucci, A. (1996) *Challenging codes: Collective action in the information age*, Cambridge: Cambridge University Press.

Rhodes, R.A.W. (1997b) *Understanding governance: Policy networks, governance, reflexivity and accountability*, Buckingham: Open University Press.

Electronic resource

New Social Movement Network at www.interweb-tech.com/nsmet/home.htm

Part 2: Meso-level analysis

Structures of power

Overview

The concept of political power is the core identity of political science as a discipline and as such runs throughout the book. Every part of the policy process is inhabited by an exchange of power. This chapter uses the idea that there are three dimensions to the concept, each one building up from the previous level. Classical pluralism is the first 'face' of power, theories that show how and why policy elites control the policy agenda is the second face and finally there is a 'deep-theory' approach concerned with how power is exercised over people by control of social discourses.

Key concepts

Power; pluralism; non-decision making; political elites; structuralism; hegemony; postmodernism.

Introduction

The key concept that runs from beginning to end of this book and weaves itself through the fabric of all the concepts we discuss is **political power**. This is not surprising since power is the core concept and epistemological identity of political science. In other words, the special focus and identity – or 'dimension' – that distinguishes political science as a field within the social sciences is its focus on explaining the nature and consequences of political power and how power is exercised through political institutions. Power, as Bertrand Russell described it, is how to create an intended effect, how to get someone to do what they would not necessarily otherwise do. Power can be likened to oxygen in the bloodstream; we cannot see it but its effects are felt all the time and without it the body would soon die. In just the same way political power circulates through the 'body politic'. Every choice made and decision taken and imposed through the policy process, even whether or not an issue comes onto the political agenda, is an exercise of power. In the policy analysis literature, the ideas associated with this core concept are often discussed under the heading of 'agenda setting', an early stage in the policy cycle associated with 'deciding to decide' and moving issues onto and off the political agenda. Our view, however, is that this is an unnecessarily restrictive approach to the discussion of power and does not enable us to show how power and the exercise of power is present at *every* stage in the political process.

Who decides, why and in whose interest do they decide? In more conceptual language, this can all be summed up in one word: power. In this chapter, we discuss the *nature* of political power. It takes us into the very heart of the political process: hence, this chapter appears in a pivotal position in the middle of the book, at the beginning of what we call the meso-level of the policy-making process. Power is moving all the time through political institutions and networks, across history; in one very subtle explanation, power is what defines relationships between individuals. In a curious sense, each of us is a source of power as we express it in our relationships between each other.

In order to contain the discussion of such a huge subject within the constraints of one short chapter (although many of the issues are taken further in following chapters of this book), we have opted to follow an idea originally proposed by Lukes in his influential book *Power: A radical view* (1974) in which he explains power using a three-dimensional model. The first dimension, and the base for the other dimensions of the model, is essentially pluralism and its variants (see *Table 7.1*). The second dimension deals with the idea that many interests are in reality excluded from the decision-making process by the power of 'non-decision'; and the third dimension considers a range of 'deep theories' which go beyond the pluralist paradigm and deal with schools of social science which consider how people are conditioned by the very language they speak to obey political elites. The rest of this chapter traces these three dimensions of political power.

Classical pluralism

Despite being subject to severe criticism from both left- and right-wing analysts, pluralism endured throughout the 20th century. Indeed, it has roots as a social theory dating back to the 17th century when the English Civil War provoked a debate about the power and nature of the state. Later on, during the foundation of the American political tradition, the idea of federalism with multiple centres of power and constitutional checks and balances (between the executive and judicial wings of government and between the presidential and congressional wings, that is to say between the 52 states and the central government) became the bedrock of the political system. People in American society were identified not so much by their social class, as in the European tradition, but by their membership of different religious and ethnic groupings and whether they supported, for example, slavery or were opposed to it. The constitution was structured around the assumption of plural centres of interest and was intended to balance them out. Pluralist theory thus has a strong association with the political philosophies and practice of the US.

Pluralism is essentially about difference and diversity. Its core tenet is that society is made up of myriad social groupings, organisations and interest groups, the latter ranging in the UK context from the big guns of industry such as the Confederation of British Industry, representing employers, and on the other side the trade unions representing the workforce, through to thousands of small local groups run by amateurs – cricket clubs, music societies, the 'Rat and Mouse Club of Birmingham', among so many others. Political power as a result reflects not *class* interests but this kaleidoscopic world of organisations. Power, as a result, is diffuse and the policy process is essentially driven by public demands and opinion. The state, therefore, has a very special role in classical pluralist thinking, not as a *source* of power but as an arbiter of competing interests. The institutional arrangements of the state ensure that there is no concentration of power in any one part of the system, thus according to pluralist orthodoxy there should be constitutional separation between the legislative, executive and judicial wings of government. There is also a clear separation between the state and civil society. As one of the greatest and most influential of the pluralist thinkers, the American political scientist Dahl, points out, "there are multiple centres of power, none of which is wholly sovereign" (Dahl, 1967, p 24).

The classical pluralist version of agenda setting derived from this is that the state acts as a referee to ensure that the rules of the game are adhered to and that differences are resolved through negotiation. By organising into groups, individuals can make their presence felt. It follows that many organisations are not permanent bodies but come into existence to represent particular interests at a particular point in time. The issue is raised, debated, resolved and the groups concerned dissolve, to be replaced by new issue groups. Recent UK examples of this are the organisations involved in fox-hunting, or the lobby groups representing the interests of the victims of the spate of rail crashes in the 1990s. Hence, the political agenda results from the reality of society and is finely balanced between the limited role of the state (including its dispersed centres of power) and the opportunity for minority groups and those with special interests to make their presence felt and influence the shape of policy. In normal circumstances, it is the role of political parties to represent the general will of the wider electorate at periodic elections.

Of course, not all pressure groups and interests have equal access to the policy-making centres, nor resources to campaign. As Dahl (1967) pointed out, business groups tend to get a favourable hearing from government but, he argued, this does not necessarily mean favourable access for the most wealthy

Table 7.1: Types of pluralism

	Classical	Institutional bias	Elitism	Network
Structure of the polity	Kaleidoscope of competing groups with equal access. No resource constraints.	Many groups in competition but unequal access to resources.	Many groups but dominance of a few powerful interests especially economic.	Many groups organised into clusters of interests.
Character of the state	Neutral referee of competing groups. No power base.	Referee but filters conflict before it occurs.	Represents and promotes interests of powerful insiders. Not neutral.	No central concentration of power but separation between centre and implementation levels. Intergovernmental linkages.
Power	Transparent and open. Diffuse.	Relatively open but biased in favour of insider groups through insider control.	Concentrated on few powerful insiders. Public as passive onlookers.	No central concentration of power but implication of democratic deficit.
Methods and ideology	Behavioural analysis of facts. No structural constraints. Ideologies non-existent/ implicit.	Behavioural analysis of facts. Ideological influences.	Behaviourist but strong deterministic tendency.	Behaviourist with important historical/cultural influence.
Policy agenda	Reflects public opinion. Peaceful resolution of conflict.	Safe issues only allowed, all others screened out.	Focus on economic agenda in support of business interests.	Managed by policy communities and increasingly designed by them.
Key authors	Dahl (1961, 1967)	Schattschneider (1960); Bachrach and Baratz (1970)	Mills (1956)	Rhodes (1997)

business interests, partly because they are busy competing with each other and partly because some individuals and weaker interests may be able to circumvent the normal channels of approach. Contrary to his reputation, Dahl did not believe that all interests were equally represented or that the state was a neutral arbiter in the simple formula of classical pluralism; but he did believe in the existence of 'countervailing' forces to balance the political process that was basically shaped according to public opinion and was open above all. Despite sharp conflicts of interest (notably between business and labour), there is a basic consensus about the nature of society, so that political stability is never really threatened.

Dahl's position was in part based on his extensive analysis of decision making within the US city of New Haven over a period of almost 200 years and on particularly detailed analysis of contemporary data he gathered at the time of his study (Dahl, 1961). He argued that, in analysing the key policy debates within New Haven, no single group's wishes dominated in terms of the decisions made with the city: winners and losers were spread out across groups as pluralist theory would predict. Moreover, he suggested that, from a historical perspective, a shift from elitism to pluralism could be identified in the case of New Haven. In short, Dahl's claim was that observation of the decision-making process supported the pluralist thesis.

Power as non-decision

However, during the 1960s and 1970s, this somewhat complacent view of the political process began to be eroded by events and by a new school of pluralist thinkers that challenged the idea of the state as a neutral, benign player. The book that made the most powerful critical impact here was Schattschneider's famous book, *The semi-sovereign people* (1960). Here, it was shown that the system has a strong permanent bias in favour of some groups over others and the strength of 'insiders' to shape the political agenda. Schattschneider argued that an essential power of government is to constrain and filter out conflict before it starts. Winners try to contain the scope of politics, losers to extend it. He thus challenged the view of the state as a neutral player and instead saw it as the domain of powerful political elites who between them manage and manipulate the political process to their own ends. As he famously argued, "whosoever decides what the game is about will also decide who gets in the game" (Schattschneider, 1960, p 105).

The idea that the system is biased against 'outsiders' and by extension the wider public was the key argument of Bachrach and Baratz (1962, 1963, 1970). They showed the existence of institutional bias so that key groups were excluded. Their work was based on a study of race relations in the city of Baltimore. It showed how a powerful business–political axis at the centre of the city's political system operated systematically to screen out the interests of the black minority. Many different types of tactics were used, including co-opting black leaders, state violence against others, labelling prominent black leaders as communists and troublemakers and using the media to invent scares. The 'mobilisation of bias', they argued, involved the ability of the state to manipulate the political agenda against relatively weaker groups, even to the point of the systematic exclusion of whole sectors of society.

Bachrach and Baratz used the term 'non-decision' to encapsulate this process and also to signal a methodological departure from the work of classical pluralists such as Dahl. They argued that Dahl's simplistic analysis of the outcomes of *overt* debates within New Haven's political institutions could not capture what they dubbed the 'second face of power': that is, the *covert* use of power outside of public fora to keep specific issues off the public policy agenda. In other words, Dahl had failed to accurately measure the distribution of power because his analysis did not account for the crucial role non-decisions – "a means by which demands for change in the existing allocation of benefits and privileges in the community can be suffocated before they are even voiced" (Bachrach and Baratz, 1970, p 7) – play in setting the policy agenda. His conclusion that New Haven confirmed the pluralist thesis was, therefore, based on flawed evidence.

It should be remembered that this critique of classical pluralism emerged when real-world events were challenging American society – the Vietnam War, race riots, the collapse of inner-city neighbourhoods. As we argue throughout this book, historical contingency is key to understanding the policy process and this applies equally to the evolution of concepts. Classical pluralism came under pressure not only from 'events' but also from the speeding up of the global economy. This was the beginning of the era of the multinational corporation wielding enormous economic and political power above the level of the nation state. An advanced version of pluralism, which expressed the increasing integration between economic and political forces, was the idea of corporatism. Corporatist governance was the result of a tripartite axis of power consisting of business, trade unions and government itself (Middlemass, 1979; Cawson, 1982).

In the British context, other pressures on the pluralist model emerged at this time based on the observable struggle of the central state to meet the demands and financial liabilities put on it by the large numbers of groups engaged in the modern political process. The so-called 'overload' thesis (see Chapter Three) argued that in order to win elections political parties were promising more and more but in government found it difficult to deliver such a large quantity of commitments. This was the basis of the New Right critique of the civil service, 'bureaucracy' and Mrs Thatcher's well known belief that there was 'too much government' (all of which interfered with the smooth functioning of the 'free-market' economy). The plurality that had previously been the bedrock of a stable, consensual democratic process was in danger of spiralling out of control. At the same time, insider groups and powerful new networks were threatening in effect to hijack the political system for their own advantage creating a 'democratic deficit' in which the electorate and most outsider groups became detached spectators (see Chapters Six and Eight).

Beyond pluralism

One of the key features of the idea of non-decision is the implication that people can be manipulated by powerful interests and are not at all 'free' as classical pluralists assert. Crenson (1971) pushed this argument beyond the boundaries of the pluralist paradigm when, in his study of air pollution, he claimed that there was an **ideological level** involved in the agenda-setting process. In other words, the way people responded to the issues was predetermined by a set of political values and ideas that created what he called a 'political consciousness' which shapes how people think about and respond to issues. In a similar vein, Lindblom (1977) argued that business interests benefited from a position that was more than simply privileged but was structured into the system: power is exercised by the *unseen hand of anticipated reaction* operating at an ideological level. Both Crenson and Lindblom, despite moving towards a radical left-wing perspective, nevertheless retained the core idea of pluralism that competitive groups are the bedrock of the political system, so that, as Smith (1995, p 224) points out, this form of neo-pluralism "represents a convergence between pluralism and Marxism". The elite pluralist analysis provides a more realistic explanation of how the state operates in the modern period than the earlier models. It opens the door to a sophisticated analysis of agenda setting but baulks at going through the door into a landscape where the pluralist paradigm is left behind. The point here is that pluralism, the existence of many competing groups, however it is reconfigured, cannot in itself explain *how* ordinary people acquire a political consciousness that predisposes them to certain solutions or disables them from reacting to issues.

Beyond pluralism there is, however, a collection of writers and social scientists that have observed what Lukes (1974) called 'the hidden face of power' and Parsons (1995) refers to as 'deep theory'. In other words, it is not people's observable behaviour that is important but, crucially, how power is exercised over them through the capture of their thought processes. This rather pessimistic interpretation can be found, for example, in the earlier writings of the French post-structuralist sociologist Foucault (see, for example, 1977) who showed how patterns of behaviour are learnt and internalised by individuals. At the beginning of *Discipline and punishment* (1977), he describes in gory detail the public execution of a regicide, the main purpose of which was to instil discipline into the population. A major crime against the state such as an attempt to assassinate the king would be punished by the codified dismemberment of the assassin's body and woe betide anyone else who tried it! Foucault showed that political power was exercised by the ruling elites by more than their control of the social and political structures of society: that is, by their control over the socialisation of the population, of how people think and more important still by providing the very language, the words and concepts, in which knowledge of the social world was discussed and evaluated. In his later work, Foucault goes beyond these ideas to show how power is present inside individuals and that this is essentially what defines it.

The idea of hegemony, associated with the Italian Marxist Gramsci, promulgated a similar thesis that it was the ability of the ruling class to use every institution of society – the Church, the state, education, the media – to construct a position of total control of one social class over another. The subordinate class was never wholly the unwitting subject of their rulers, according to Gramsci, because, however potent was their hegemonic control, the objective conditions of life pulled in another direction, so that the subordinate classes existed in a state of what he called a 'dual consciousness'.

Nearer home, the extraordinary novels of George Orwell, *Animal Farm* and *1984* (and a number of his essays), similarly were concerned with how totalitarian political systems (communism and fascism) used language and the power of the media to enter the mindset of its people. Big Brother was watching and controlled every corner of life even down to the sexual reproduction of the people. In our day, the mindset of the Taliban and other ideological fanatics (in other words, totalitarianism), the overwhelming influence of political spin (what Orwell called 'newspeak'), the ongoing tension between scientific discovery and morality and the power of globally managed multinational corporations, are testimony to the fact that the social control of the population remains the endgame of global power-mongers and that Orwell's agenda is alive and kicking.

Box 7.1: Foucault's *History of sexuality* (1999, vols I-III)

The French philosopher Michel Foucault wrote extensively about the nature of political power, which in his later work he saw as not emanating from political structures or even dominant classes. In his great, unfinished trilogy of works on human sexuality, he argued that power is dispersed, subjectless and is constituted inside people's consciousness, inside their identities and their very bodies. Power is the ubiquitous condition of human existence and exists not in institutions as such as in *knowledge*. In the trilogy, Foucault set out to explore the history of sexuality, showing that in different periods of history sexuality was the subject of a variety of discourses but that it was always a focal point for the transfer of power between men and women, parents and children, young and older people, clergy and laity, the population and administrators. It is a complicated and 'deep' theory but draws to our attention that ultimately the source of political power resides in the consciousness of every human being (Foucault, 1988).

Table 7.2: *The three faces of power*

Theorist	Conception of Power
Dahl (1961)	A has power over B to the extent that he can get B to do something that B would not otherwise do.
Bachrach and Baratz (1963)	Of course power is exercised when A participates in the making of decisions that affect B. Power is also exercised when A devotes his energies to creating or reinforcing social and political values and institutional practices that limit the scope of the political process to public consideration only of those issues which are comparatively innocuous to A.
Lukes (1974)	A may exercise power over B by getting him to do what he does not want to do, but he also exercises power over him by influencing, shaping or determining his very wants.

Back to the pluralist future

Postmodernism, however, has drawn a line under this type of social criticism by showing that inside the attempts to unify and control, the seeds of heterogeneity and 'difference' – a new postmodern pluralism – eventually germinated with explosive consequences. Since the collapse of the Berlin Wall and the political system that it symbolised, the idea of the state as a universal monolith impervious to individual criticism has been radically challenged. Indeed, so rapidly has social thought changed – partly as a result of the speeding up of information exchange through the Internet (see Chapter Five) – that the postmodern critique (that is, the challenge to universalistic, generalist modes of thought, the assertion of diversity over uniformity, of divergence over convergence, the dissolution of political ideologies, the challenge of multiculturalism over stereotyping) is itself being challenged. As Delanty (1999, p 182) very succinctly puts it, "the problem no longer consists of the dangers of false universalism ... but of an uncontrolled relativism". As Touraine (1995) argued, the issue for the world now is to find a pathway between the unfettered global economic marketplace in which individuals are counted as nothing except in their willingness to consume, and pure subjectivity (that is to say, an extreme focus on reducing everything to the level of the individual to choose their own morality without reference to anything apart from what they perceive as their own self-interest).

Here is not the place to push this argument further because it leads to conceptual complexity beyond our remit; however, students of policy analysis *should be alert* to these 'deep theory' questions. The recognition of diversity is an inherently pluralistic theme as we saw earlier in the chapter and a very much refined and reconstituted pluralism is now part of the contemporary discourse. It does in part lead back to the point we have made at various stages in the book about the role of cultural/historical sensitivity, for one of the answers to the question of where policy analysis goes now is, as it were, 'back to the future'. Our leitmotif of the significance of historical institutionalism in contemporary policy analysis – with its focus on path dependency, on the way in which the past leaves footprints which guide our futures, and on the significance of long-term cultural settlements – shows how the state, and with it the agenda-setting process, is marked by the past. In the language of deep theory, **culture meets subjectivity**.

We have also hinted at another part of the agenda we see as most useful to 'post-postmodern' scholarship in the discussion of the work of the theorists of the new Information Age. We have mentioned particularly Castells (see Chapters Two and Five), whose idea of the 'network society' suggests that the future, in a way that is paradoxical to our last comment about the significance of history and culture, is no longer predicated on historical trajectory but is already ahistorical because it no longer depends on a territorially defined platform. That is to say, rather in the manner of the hyperglobalists, that the critical role of the nation state has in part been superseded by a knowledge-based global 'multiculture'. Our society is thus much more *culturally* defined (in the sense of being concerned with social relations between people and groups rather than the fixed structures of state and society) because information exchange allows it, and is simply not dependent any more on the spatial and territorial divisions of all previous history. Castells points to the key role of new social movements as the agents of the future because the Internet and all the new technological interfaces have undermined the powers of the old establishment such as the state, the Church and even business (Castells, 1996).

The position we argue for is that the nation state has not been superseded but has undergone major surgery and continues to be reconstituted under the impact of globalisation. Networks and the network society fuelled by information is a powerful metaphor of the modern condition but to argue that society is nothing more than networks that are held together only by their ability to communicate (and that this is what defines society) is not a sustainable real-world case. Indeed, as our material on new social movements showed, the evidence is that these movements have not become an alternative political paradigm but have sought to promote their agenda within the context of the nation state. As we suggested, nation states have not been made redundant by globalisation but have been 'rearticulated' in response to these new economic and cultural agendas. More even than that they have become the focal point of the political process.

The suggestion that social movements play a key role in articulating the concerns of 'civil society' and stand outside the state is at once recognisable as a classical pluralist position. Civil society is a complex kaleidoscope of groups and movements that compete with each other for access to the state but also challenge the hegemony of the state because they represent a variety of alternative voices. The environmental movement represented by organisations such as Greenpeace, both seek to influence and shape government policy on issues such as the genetic modification of crops, global warming, threats to habitats and animal species, but at the same time argue that the 'real' solution to these problems lies in the construction of new forms of radical politics which is more inclusive and participatory. This is very different to the classical pluralist model with its emphasis on consensus and the role of the state as an arbiter of differing interests. The new movements make no attempt to defend the state and certainly do not consider its power to be neutral. Thus, they have a much more realistic view of the political process. But rather in the manner of the classical pluralists, the neo–pluralist approach fails to articulate precisely how their 'alternatives' will operate and in this sense are equally unclear about the true nature of state power and its ability to control agendas and screen out protest.

Conclusions

Structures of political power are a focal concern of policy analysis because they raise key questions about how and why an issue is picked up and dealt with in the political arena. Power is *the* central concept of all political science and, as we have shown, thinking about the various approaches sweeps us into some of the deepest and most complex recesses of social science. There is in our view no one magic-wand solution that answers all the questions about how and why policy enters (or does not enter) the agenda. We have, however, pointed strongly towards the elite pluralist model as the one approach that understands and accounts for the power of the state and how state actors relate to a range of stakeholders. In accordance with our view on the 'competition state' (outlined in Chapters Three, Four and Six), we see the modern state heavily influenced by the imperative of the economy to perform on the global stage. But within that framework, agenda setting remains a relatively open if messy affair. We do not discount the lessons of the deep theorists – that language and symbols are powerful weapons in the armoury of the political establishment – but cannot accept their deterministic conclusion. Neither do we accept wholly the postmodernist interpretation, which replaces the hegemony of monolithic states with an absorption into the 'text', the discourse of subjects uniquely lodged in time and place. The 'subject' may have been rediscovered but it has largely been at the expense of any sense of social responsibility or what we would see as the essentially political nature of humankind in the modern world. The new emphasis on plurality and 'difference' is refreshing after the generalist, ideologically driven dogmas that dominated the 20th century. One key part of this new pluralism and which takes us to the next chapter is the role of networks: that is, the connection of organisations, agencies and groups into clusters and communities of interest and which, as we discussed in earlier chapters of this book, lie at the heart of the reconfigured British state and its political process.

Summary

- Political power is the epistemological focus of political science.
- Pluralism is essentially about difference and diversity. Its core tenet is that society is made up of myriad social groupings, organisations and interest groups.
- Political power in the classical pluralist paradigm is diffuse and the policy process is essentially driven by public demands and opinion. The state, therefore, has a very special role: not as a *source* of power but as an arbiter of competing interests.
- Schattschneider's famous book, *The semi-sovereign people* (1960), showed that political systems have a strong permanent bias in favour of some groups over others and the strength of 'insiders' to shape the political agenda.
- Beyond pluralism, there is a collection of writers and social scientists who have observed that there are 'hidden faces of power' in which it is not people's observable behaviour that is important but crucially how power is exercised over them through the capture of their thought processes.
- Foucault showed that political power was exercised by ruling elites not principally by their control of the social and political structures of society but by their control over the socialisation of the population, of how people think and by providing the very language, the words and concepts, in which knowledge of the social world was discussed and evaluated.
- Postmodernism drew a line under deterministic, general theory by revealing the heterogeneity of social processes, its roots in cultural contexts and 'difference'.
- Neo-pluralist and elite pluralist approaches provide a much more realistic view of the state and the agenda-setting process than either classical pluralism or postmodern subjectivity.

Questions for discussion

- Can power ever be equally distributed?
- Who sets the social policy agenda?
- Describe some real world examples of the 'hidden face' of power.

Further reading

Dahl, R. (1967) *Pluralist democracy in the United States*, Chicago, IL: Rand McNally.

Foucault, M. (1977) *Discipline and punishment: The birth of the prison*, Harmondsworth: Penguin.

Kingdon, J.W. (1984) *Agendas, alternatives and public policies*, Boston, MA: Little Brown.

Lukes, S. (1974) *Power: A radical view*, London: Macmillan.

Orwell, G. (1949) *Nineteen Eighty-Four*, London: Secker and Warburg.

Policy networks

Overview
The idea of policy networks has become a key paradigm in the policy analysis literature during the last decade. Building on the earlier discussion of Castells and the global network society outlined earlier in this book, **network theory** is shown to be a powerful meso-level analytical tool linking the macro- and micro-level environments to agenda-setting theory and delivery analysis. The new governance described in Chapter Seven essentially comprises a collection of inter-organisational networks. This arises from the more fragmented polity, which requires new linkages but throws doubt on the ability of the centre to manage the system. Here, the origins of the policy network analysis literature is described and the literature is critically evaluated. Network analysis is shown to be a major contribution to the language, imagery and practice of policy analysis.

Key concepts
Policy networks; policy communities; issue networks; core–periphery; dialectical approach.

Introduction: networks in social science

In recent years, it has become almost impossible for a student of any social science to avoid **network analysis** of one form or another. The term 'network' has permeated the social sciences and variations on the network theme can be found, for example, in:

- **organisational studies**, where networks are viewed as increasingly prevalent coordinational relationships that cannot be characterised as either hierarchy or market-based (Thompson et al, 1991);

- **economics**, where the lowering of transactional costs are said to have made loosely connected just-in-time networks a more efficient production process than large, vertically and horizontally integrated firms (Williamson, 1985);
- **sociology**, where, as we saw in Chapter Five of this book, Castells (2000a, 2000b) suggests we are witnessing the emergence of a 'network society', promulgated by new information and communications technologies, in which network-style relationships are permeating virtually all social institutions;
- **policy science**, where the expansion of network governance is seen as a response by the state to the increasing complexity and intractability of policy problems (Kickert et al, 1997);
- **political science**, where, over the last decade and a half, the idea that the policy process is centred round interrelated, inter-organisational, interdependent policy networks has gradually gained ascendancy.

This list is far from comprehensive – similar developments have occurred elsewhere in the social sciences and, indeed, the physical sciences. Moreover, it should be noted that *within* specific fields of study there is an often "Babylonian variety of different understandings and applications of the … network concept" (Börzel, 1998, p 254).

However, while this proliferation of 'network theories' is often unhelpful insofar as it works against a desire for clear and concise terminology, the importance of the work that falls under this umbrella term means that we cannot ignore it in our analysis of how the policy process operates. In particular, the notion that policies are now shaped, made and implemented by 'policy networks' is central to many of the themes we are exploring in this book (particularly the argument concerning a shift from government to governance outlined in Chapter Six) and the **policy network approach** (PNA) is now a central part of the analytic armoury of most policy analysts. Indeed, in 1995, Dowding (1995, p 136) proclaimed that policy networks had "become the dominant paradigm for the study of the policy-making process in British political science"; it is this work that we analyse here.

The emergence of the policy network approach

Even in focusing on 'policy networks' rather than network approaches more generally, however, we still have a problem with terminological proliferation, for even within British political science there are diverse models of policy network analysis. Marsh (1998), for instance, distinguishes between four broad approaches with very different theoretical underpinnings:

- the *rational choice approach*, which models the behaviour and relationships of self-interested actors;

- the *personal interaction approach*, which adopts an anthropological approach that explores interaction between specific individuals;
- *formal network analysis*, which examines the actual structure of network based relationships;
- the *structural approach*, which analyses broad relationships between groups in society.

Here we focus on work rooted in the latter approach, in particular that which has built upon the so-called 'Rhodes model'[1], because this stream of work is undoubtedly the most influential and, via the Rhodes model, it also offers the most commonly understood articulation of the policy network approach (see Marsh and Rhodes, 1992; Rhodes, 1996b, 1997).

The Rhodes model

According to its key exponents (see Marsh and Rhodes, 1992; Klijn, 1997; Börzel, 1998; Evans, 1999), the Rhodes model builds upon Benson's (1982, p 148) 'seminal' definition of a policy network as:

> a cluster or complex of organisations connected to each other by resource dependencies and distinguished from other clusters or complexes by breaks in the structure of resource dependencies.

In many respects, this is a curious definition, not least because Benson's seminal definition is actually his definition of a policy sector rather than a policy network; indeed, Benson does not use the term 'policy network' at all in the paper from which this seminal definition derives. However, knowing this helps us a little in terms of understanding where the Rhodes version of the network approach is coming from. At its most basic (and much like the ideas about governance and governing without government outlined in Chapter Six), it assumes policy is made and implemented by a **group of organisations** that includes (but is not limited to) branches of the government; that these organisations – again including the government – are **dependent** on others in order to meet their goals; and, most importantly perhaps, that groups of organisations quite naturally develop clear **connections** with each other because of their shared interests. In this respect, 'policy sectors' and 'policy networks' could almost be interchangeable terms, but the latter captures more effectively the complex web of connections between organisations.

---

[1] So named because it developed from ideas expounded by Rod Rhodes (see, for example, Rhodes, 1990). However, Marsh and Smith (2001, p 540) suggest it is actually the 'Marsh and Rhodes model', given the key role David Marsh played in helping produce the contemporary models of the policy network approach that fall under the Rhodes model banner (see Marsh and Rhodes, 1992).

Indeed, this picture chimes with Rhodes' own (1997) articulation of what he now sees as the core assumptions of his approach:

- *interdependence*: networks exist because organisations are reliant on other organisations in order to meet their goals;
- *continuous exchange of resources*: members of a network have regular contact with each other;
- *game-like interactions*: members of a network employ competitive strategies within boundaries that form 'the rules of the game' in order to achieve their goals;
- *autonomy*: networks are self-organising and have no internal or external sovereign authority, though some groups may be more powerful than others.

As this makes clear, the Rhodes model characterises relationships as:

> a 'game' in which participants manoeuvre for advantage. Each deploys its resources ... to maximize influence over outcomes while trying to avoid becoming dependent on other 'players'. (Marsh and Rhodes, 1992, p 11)

Rhodes (1988, 1990) terms this the **resource dependency model**.

Types of policy network

The analysis of interdependency and the battle for resources, therefore, are key elements of the policy network approach. However, they also form the more abstract and esoteric side of the debate about what policy networks are and how they operate. To help flesh out what this approach means at a more practical level, Rhodes (1988, 1990) developed a categorisation of five distinct types of 'policy network' that we might expect to find when analysing different policy sectors: policy community; professional network; intergovernmental network; producer network; and issue network. These networks (summarised in *Table 8.1*) were distinguished according to the degree of integration in the network, the number of members within it and the distribution of resources among members of the network. Rhodes viewed the five types of network as representing a **continuum**, with the highly integrated and closed **policy community** at one end, and the more open and less stable **issue network** at the other, with the other three types – professional, intergovernmental and producer networks – being somewhere in-between the two extremes.

This typology of networks makes the application of the approach to real-world situations much clearer and allows us to quite quickly speculate that some areas of welfare policy might fit into some types rather than others; medical professionals, for example, have always played a strong role in the

Table 8.1: Rhodes' five-way distinction of the policy network

Type of network	Characteristics of network
Policy community/ territorial community	Stability, highly restricted membership, vertical interdependence, limited horizontal articulation
Professional network	Stability, highly restricted membership, vertical interdependence, limited horizontal articulation, serves interest of profession
Intergovernmental network	Limited membership, limited vertical interdependence, extensive horizontal articulation
Producer network	Fluctuating membership, limited vertical interdependence, serves interest of producer
Issue network	Unstable, large number of members, limited vertical interdependence

Source: Adapted from Marsh and Rhodes (1992, p 14)

development of health care policy (see Ham, 1999). Indeed, it has been suggested that health policy tends to serve their interests rather than patients' interests (see, for example, Alford, 1975); therefore, the health policy network might be sensibly classified as a 'professional network'.

However, Rhodes soon abandoned this categorisation of networks as the presentation of the five network types as a continuum was problematic, for "while it is easy to see why the policy community and issue network are at the ends of the continuum, the locations of the other types of network on the continuum are less obvious" (Marsh and Rhodes, 1992, p 21). Also, a continuum suggests that the network types are mutually exclusive and consequently "that there could be no such thing as a professional- or producer-dominated policy community" (1992, p 21). As a result, Marsh and Rhodes (1992, p 249) offered a simplified typology that abandoned the three intermediate groupings, focusing on the "distinction between policy communities and issue networks ... as the end points on a continuum". Moreover, at the same time as offering this simplification, Marsh and Rhodes (1992, p 250) also specified the key characteristics of these two ideal types of network. In so doing, they produced the definitive outline of the Rhodes model, 'policy network' being a generic term encompassing *all* policy areas – for they assume they are omnipresent – but with the precise nature of networks varying along a continuum from the tightly integrated, well organised and access restricted 'policy community' at one end to the loosely organised, more open and less coherent 'issue network' at the other. *Table 8.2*, drawn from Marsh and Rhodes' articulation of the model, summarises the two ends of the policy network continuum and the key features of each and so provides what they call a 'diagnostic model' that allows us to categorise real-world policy areas as being more akin to a policy community or issue network.

However, while this simplification of the approach made its applicability to the analysis of actual policy situations clearer, Marsh and Rhodes (1992, p 256) also added another layer of complexity at the same time, suggesting that all policy networks can have two tiers: a **core and a periphery**. Moreover, the periphery of a policy network may feature some self-contained issue networks. So, for example, a tight-knit policy community such as that found in healthcare policy may be surrounded by weaker issue networks interested in certain illnesses (for example, cancer) or a particular cause of ill-health (for example, smoking); the issue network may, from time to time, gain strong attention (in these cases, for example, if the issue of smoking in public places is under debate), but the influence of the issue network will, on the whole, be limited. This is an idea echoed by Smith (1993) who sees policy communities being surrounded by, and connected to, a series of issue networks – a messy scenario that replicates the messy business of policy making.

The impact of networks on the policy process

So, we have seen that the Rhodes model has undergone various revisions, that it is underpinned by well-refined assumptions and accompanied by a diagnostic model that allows us to categorise policy networks along the policy community–issue network continuum. However, there is still one crucial element missing from the picture: the issue of what this approach adds to our understanding of the policy process. In short, does knowing whether a policy sector features a policy community help us to analyse the policy process in that sector?

To help answer this question, Marsh and Rhodes and their collaborators undertook a series of empirical investigations structured around the Rhodes model (Marsh and Rhodes, 1992a, 1992d). Having done so, they suggested that policy networks exist to restrict access to the policy-making process, to routinise relationships between key stakeholders in the policy sector and, in so doing, to promote stability and continuity. Most significantly, they concluded that "policy networks act as a major source of policy inertia" (Marsh and Rhodes, 1992, p 260). More fundamentally perhaps, they concluded that:

Table 8.2: *Types of policy networks: characteristics of policy communities and issue networks*

Dimension	Policy community	Issue network
Membership		
a) Participants:	Very limited number; some groups consciously excluded.	Large number.
b) Type of Interest:	Economic and/or professional interests dominate.	Encompasses a large range of affected interests.
Integration		
a) Frequency of interaction:	Frequent, high-quality, interaction of all groups on all matters related to policy issue.	Contacts fluctuate in intensity and quality. Access fluctuates over time.
b) Continuity:	Membership, values, and outcomes persistent over time.	A measure of agreement exists, but conflict is ever present.
c) Consensus:	All participants share basic values and accept the legitimacy of the outcome.	
Resources		
a) Distribution of resources – within network:	All participants have resources; basic relationship is an exchange relationship.	Some participants may have resources, but they are limited, and basic relationship is consultative.
b) Distribution of resources – within participating organisations:	Hierarchical; leaders can deliver members.	Varied and variable distribution and capacity to regulate members.
Power	There is a balance of power among members. Although one group may dominate, it must be a positive-sum game if community is to exist.	Unequal powers, reflecting unequal resources and unequal access. It is a zero-sum game.

Source: Marsh and Rhodes (1992, p 251)

> networks affect policy outcomes. The existence of a policy network, or more particularly a policy community, constrains the policy agenda and shapes the policy outcomes. Policy communities, in particular, are associated with policy continuity. ... In brief, policy networks foster incremental changes, thereby favouring the *status quo* or the existing balance of interests. (Marsh and Rhodes, 1992, p 262)

To put it differently, policy networks matter because they tell us a great deal about the ways in which power is distributed among different groups in a particular policy sector. The importance of this can be illustrated by considering varying responses between policy sectors to common pressures such as globalisation, economic change or the development of new technologies. So, for example, in Chapter Five we examined the increasingly important role played by information and communication technologies (ICTs) in the delivery of government services. Often, but not always, the increased use of ICTs in the delivery of services is unpopular with front-line staff because it can involve closer (electronic) scrutiny by managers of working practices, the increased collection of data about individual performance or reductions in staff levels as computers undertake tasks that were previously completed manually. Unsurprisingly, therefore, resistance to change is commonplace. Indeed, government computing projects in the UK have a poor track record, many having failed to get off the ground or to be fully implemented, not least because of this resistance (see Hudson, 1999).

However, if we take a longer view of events and look at how technologically related change has impacted on particular sectors of UK welfare policy over the course of the 1980s and 1990s, an interesting picture emerges because the extent to which resistance to change has succeeded varies across government (Hudson, 1999). More specifically, policy sectors where a policy community exists, such as in healthcare or social care, have witnessed a much slower pace of change than sectors where the government is surrounded by an issue network such as in social security policy. This is significant, for while there were examples of strong resistance to changes in each of these three policy networks – including some long-running strikes in the social security sector – and some high profile attempts by the government to introduce radical ICT-related policies, the policy networks with strong professional groups at their core (medics in health policy and social workers in social care) acted to slow the pace of change through bargaining within their well established policy communities, while the issue network to which front-line social security workers belonged lacked equivalent high level linkages with the government and, ultimately, they had technology imposed upon them (Hudson, 1999).

Marsh and Rhodes (1992d) made a similar argument with respect to the impact of Thatcherism on public policy. In examining the impact of Thatcherite policies on a range of policy sectors, they concluded that their impact varied from sector to sector. Some, such as housing, had witnessed widespread change, while others, such as health care policy or agricultural policy (that is, those with strong policy communities), had displayed quite a high degree of continuity. Marsh and Rhodes pointed to the crucial role of policy networks in explaining this variation and argued (1992d, p 186) that, in sectors where change had been muted, "continuity has been preserved, in part, because of the ability of the policy network to prevent radical policies being brought forward [and the ability] of policy networks [to prevent] the successful implementation of policies once they were introduced".

Policy networks as a meso-level concept

Crucially, the above examples illustrate that the PNA brings its greatest insights when combined with some account of macro-level change; or, to put it differently, the PNA sits at the **meso-level**, occupying the space between broad macro-level issues, such as globalisation or demographic change, and the micro-level issues of what occurs at the ground level, such as how particular individuals or groups bargain over specific issues or how particular individuals carry out the duties they have to perform in the delivery of specific policies. Marsh and Rhodes (1992b, p 268) are explicit here, arguing that "the meso-level concept of 'policy networks' needs to be clearly located [alongside] a number of macro-level theories". Moreover, they further illustrate this with respect to arguments about the emergence of post-Fordism (see Chapter Three), arguing (1992b, p 267) that because policy networks impact on policy change, the changes related to post-Fordism "occur at different rates and lead to different practices in different countries". Moreover, they suggest (1992b, pp 267-8), therefore, that "a meso-level concept like 'policy networks' is central to understanding resistance to such changes and the ways in which political institutions and practices adapt" because "policy networks are political structures which filter or mediate the change [to Post-Fordism]".

Metaphor or theory?

However, while exponents of the policy network approach extol its virtues, it has fierce critics too. Dowding (1995, 2001) in particular has forcefully put the case that the approach lacks explanatory power. He argues that Rhodes et al simply use the term 'network' in a **metaphorical sense** and that the Rhodes model simply labels policy sectors rather than explaining the dynamics of network relationships. He argues (1995, p 136) that "while we have learned much about the policy process by cataloguing the policy world into different types of network, the approach will not, alone, take us [far]". This is because, he claims (1995, p 137), the approach "fails to produce fundamental *theories of* the policy process ... because the driving force of the explanation, the independent variables, are not network characteristics *per se* but rather characteristics of components within the networks".

To put this another way, what Dowding is arguing is that, despite all the talk about 'networks' being of crucial importance, when exponents of the PNA analyse a policy sector, with a view to placing it somewhere along the issue network–policy community continuum, they pay no real attention to the actual *structure* of the network. He argues that if the network itself is the key explanatory variable then the approach should involve mapping out the precise structure of networks – the number, direction and intensity of connections between actors for instance (see **Box 8.1**) – in order to determine the impact of specific network configurations on the policy process. A more formalised approach that developed along these lines – which would be akin to the mathematical approach to network analysis conducted by some sociologists (such as Wellman, 1992; Knoke, 1998) – would, he argues, move beyond metaphor and become a genuine theory of the policy process, not least because it would properly map relationships of power.

As it stands, Dowding remains sceptical of the value of network analysis. Indeed, he argues:

> the nature of the policy process and the network of interests from which it emerges can be explained without recourse to the **language of networks**. The language ... is that of bargaining strategies, power resources and coalition possibilities.... Policies emerge through power struggles of different interests. (1995, p 145)

He concedes that, in its initial conception, the Rhodes model placed the issue of 'power dependency' at its heart, but argues (1995, p 146) that in its more recent conceptions, the model has "developed away from considering the resources of actors in a game" and moved instead towards a more classificatory approach that is heavy in metaphor that is useful for describing, rather than explaining, the policy process.

While Richardson (1999, pp 189-90) has suggested that "Dowding's critique of the network approach ... might yet turn out to be a watershed finally marking the intellectual fatigue of ... policy community and network analysis in Britain", most exponents of the approach have offered a stern defence of it and responded to Dowding's criticisms quite forcefully (see, for example, Rhodes, 1996b, 1997; Evans, 2001; Marsh and Smith, 2001). At the most basic level, Rhodes (1996b) has simply refuted Dowding's claim that the approach lacks explanatory power, arguing (1996b, p 13):

power-dependence is [and always has been] a central feature of policy networks ... the distribution, and type, of resources within a network *explains* the relative power of actors ... the different patterns of resource-dependence *explain* differences between policy networks[2].

A dialectical view of policy networks

Others, however, have responded by modifying the approach in order to strengthen its explanatory power. In particular, there has been an important debate over what theorists have termed the **dialectical** view of policy networks (see Marsh and Smith, 2000, 2001; Dowding, 2001; Evans, 2001). Marsh and Smith (2000, p 5), the key advocates of this approach, suggest "a dialectical relationship is an interactive relationship between two variables in which each affects the other in a continuing iterative process". They argue there are three key dialectic relationships that policy network analysts need to be alive to: between the structure of the network and the actors within it; between the network and the context it is operating in; and between networks and policies (2000, p 20).

In essence, their argument is that, while policy networks affect policy outcomes, filter broad macro-trends and provide a structure within which the actions of individuals take place, these relationships are two way. So, for instance, we considered earlier how policy networks had impacted upon the intensity of ICT-related change within different policy sectors in the UK and noted that powerful professional groups such as medics had used their privileged position within their policy network to resist change. However, we could also have considered other ICT-related trends in the sector too. For instance, we could have examined arguments that the easy access to health-related information on the Internet has made patients more willing to challenge the judgement of their doctors and removed some of the mystique that bolstered their power (see, for example, Hardey, 1999) or we could have considered arguments that the placement with private corporations of large contracts for public sector computing applications has brought a new player into policy debates. Both developments have weakened the power of medics a little *despite* the existence of their strong policy network. In other words, while the health care policy network has been effective in resisting ICT-related change, it is also true that ICT-related change has been effective in reshaping the health

---

[2] Smith's analysis would also suggest that power *is* at the heart of the PNA. He suggests (1993, p 64) that "in a policy community power is a positive-sum. In other words a policy community does not involve one group sacrificing power to another. It could involve each group in a mutual expansion of power as each increases its influence over policy. In an issue network power is unequal and there are likely to be losers and winners. As the losers have few resources they can do little if their interests are sacrificed in the development of policy".

Box 8.1: A formal approach to network analysis

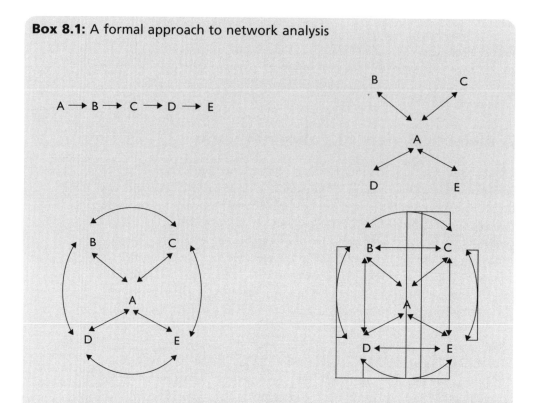

Dowding's arguments about the need for a more formal approach to network analysis can best be explained by reference to a simplified example (see also Dowding, 1995). Above, we find four examples of a relationship between five different actors (A, B, C, D and E). In the first example, we have a hierarchical relationship. Information or commands flow from A to B to C and so on; it flows one way only. Clearly A is in charge here and enjoys a position of power. In the second example, information or commands still flow from A, but A now speaks directly to each of the others. Moreover, the others can speak directly to A too as the flow is now two-way. Here the relationship is more complex but A is clearly at the centre and, therefore, the most powerful, being the only actor in contact with all the others. In the third example, other actors now have the ability to communicate with each other, B being in contact with C and D, and E with C and D. Here A's power is weakened as other actors on the periphery of the network can communicate with each other rather than via A. Finally, in the fourth example, all actors are connected to each other. In this example, A remains in the centre – as with the second and third examples – but A is no longer in a position of power because the structure of the network (that is, the connections) have changed. In this example we lack a dominant player. The point here, then, is that all the examples contain the same group of actors and, with the exception of the first example, the same broad layout, but that the nature of the connections between these actors matters a great deal in terms of their power and authority.

care policy network too. The effects and interactions are two way; that is, dialectic.

The same arguments can be applied to a consideration of the role of individuals in networks. So, to continue with our example, the action of individual doctors in disputes about ICT use have been structured by the nature of the health care network – by, for instance, the British Medical Association (BMA), as a key node in the network, instructing doctors to resist specific developments (see Hudson, 1999). Equally, however, the actions of specific individuals has an impact on the nature of the debate and the ways in which key elements of the network have acted; here we might point to the work of computer security expert Ross Anderson, whose report examining how new ICT systems threatened patient privacy (see Anderson, 1996) helped convince the BMA to resist key changes[3]. So, again, networks provide a meso-level structure that shapes the actions of individuals at the micro-level, but individuals constitute those structures and can and do, therefore, affect them through their actions. Similarly, policy outcomes affect networks as well as networks affecting policy outcomes. So, while the health care network was very effective in resisting ICT-related change in the 1980s and much of the 1990s, the Blair government's decision to make increased use of ICTs a central part of the modernisation of government has shifted the agenda somewhat and made resistance more difficult because the issue is higher up the policy agenda. Consequently, there are signs that more recently the network has been forced to concede in some areas it had previously won victories. Once more, we can see the dialectic at play here, with both policy and networks affecting each other.

The development of this dialectical perspective is important for two key reasons. The first is that it helps explain change more effectively than previous work. The Rhodes model was a little static, viewing networks as semi-permanent structures that filtered policy trends. Marsh and Rhodes (1992) conceded this was a weakness of their approach and their attempts to overcome it focused on pointing to external factors that might temporarily unbalance a network and require it to adjust to new circumstances brought about by technological change, economic change or the emergence of new ideas or new ideologies (Marsh and Rhodes, 1992). The dialectical view advances our thinking here by offering a more dynamic view of networks that are in a continual state of flux – albeit with changes generally taking place at the margins of networks perhaps.

The second key point is that the dialectic approach responds to one of Dowding's central concerns that what really matters is not the networks themselves but the actions of the individuals that constitute them. According to its exponents, the dialectic view allows us to consider *both* agency (the

---

[3] Or at least bolstered the BMA's arguments against them.

actions of individuals) *and* structure (the impact of networks) and, therefore, not only deals with Dowding's concerns, but in fact takes our understanding a stage further by fusing an approach that reflects his interests with those of Rhodes et al.

Perhaps inevitably, Dowding (2001) refutes Marsh and Smith's refutation of his refutations. He does not believe the dialectical approach adds to our understanding and, moreover, feels (2001, p 102) it is time we "put an end to pointless theorizing about policy networks, 'dialectical approaches' and (while we are at it) all the other hopelessly vague theories about the policy process such as the 'new insitutionalism'". (Here we must apologise to Dowding: the latter forms the subject of the next chapter of this text!) He believes (2001, p 89) that most of the findings produced by network analysis are trivial and merely confirm what we already know from more casual observation of the world. Marsh and Smith (2001), of course, provide further refutations of these refutations. Significantly, the central point of their counter-argument is that there are different ways of investigating the policy process that are rooted in very different **epistemologies**; that is, different views about how knowledge is generated. This, in essence, is what much of the debate between Dowding and the network theorists has been about – a clash of cultures over how research should be conducted and knowledge developed. Whereas Dowding advocates a formalistic, quasi-scientific approach centred around modelling the behaviour of individuals (in essence the **rational choice approach** – see Ward, 2003), Marsh and Smith (2001, p 535) are happy to see a more descriptive approach that invokes metaphor as part of its attempt to interpret and explain the world, their view being that "metaphor and analogy are widely, and usefully, used in social science" (see also Evans, 2001). They suggest, of course, that their approach is more than mere metaphor; but the central point is that there is a strong tradition of excellent work in political science that does not share Dowding's epistemological base, and that he is wrong to dismiss work out of hand which does not begin from the same point as his own[4].

Blind alleys?

While we sympathise with both viewpoints – and feel that Dowding is right to suggest that the approach relies very heavily on metaphor, but that Marsh and Smith are correct in arguing that metaphor can help us to understand the policy process – we feel that this debate has been something of a blind alley and has diverted British policy analysts from a more fruitful road of debate. To our mind, there is no doubting that something has changed over the last 20 years in terms of the delivery of social policies and that inter-organisational

---

[4] As they put it (2001, p 530), invoking a sporting metaphor, "In effect, Dowding wants to set the rules, referee the game and send off anyone he regards as ineligible".

networks have become increasingly important in the delivery of policy. As we argued in Chapter Six, echoing Rhodes, empirically the state has become increasingly dependent on others as society has become more complex and policy problems have proved intractable. Consequently, we have witnessed the emergence of 'a new governance' which "blurs the distinction between state and civil society [and in which] the state becomes a collection of interorganisational networks made up of governmental and societal actors with no sovereign actor able to steer or regulate" (Rhodes, 1997, p 57).

Much empirical social policy research has confirmed this, but potential links with the more abstract theories about policy networks have not been effectively exploited. Indeed, social policy research often talks about networks or partnerships and their implications for policy and policy research but uses the terms in a *very* loose and metaphorical sense that does not build on the work of Rhodes, Smith, Marsh, Evans et al (for example, Duke, 2002). Writing from a Dutch perspective, Kickert and Koppenjan (1997, p 35) highlight the irony of the extent to which this blind alley has dominated the debate on policy networks in the UK, observing:

> it is remarkable that ... consideration is given to networks, their characteristics, factors which affect their formation and – to a lesser extent – their effects on policy outcome, whereas the impact of the existence of networks on governance and public management hardly receives attention.

In stark contrast, the work of Kickert et al has very much focused on what the emergence of policy networks means for those working on the front line of public services – how it changes their working practices, its implications for management processes and so on. In other words, their work (examined in Chapter Twelve) considers how policy networks impact on the *implementation* of policy at the micro-level. Indeed, the real strength of their contribution – and its advantage over the work that has dominated the debate on policy networks in the UK – is its bold attempt to think through the implications of networks for governance and to offer strategies for maximising their potential for improving the quality of public policy. Indeed, Rhodes himself (1997b, p xiii) concedes that such issues remain "a minority interest in Britain" and that "too few are aware of the pioneering work being carried out by Kickert [et al]".

What is also very interesting about the Dutch work is that, via notions such as 'network management', it makes it clear that the state – as a key node at the centre of policy networks – has a huge role to play in managing networks, configuring networks and steering them towards particular policy goals. This chimes well with empirical research conducted in the UK about attempts to develop partnership networks in areas such as urban regeneration (for example,

Skelcher et al, 1997), yet the theoretical literature devised by Rhodes et al emphasises the idea of networks as 'self-organising', a notion used to support the idea that networks are self-governing and lack a dominant player meaning we have witnessed the emergence of 'governing without government' (for example, Marsh and Rhodes, 1992d; Rhodes, 1996, 1997; Evans, 1999). While such phrases nicely capture the general thrust of change, they also risk overemphasising the decline of the state, which remains hugely powerful. Rather than having diminished, its role has changed and it is clear that networks are often created by government rather than emerging from outside of it. Indeed, Rhodes (1997, p 51) hints at this when he argues that "as British government creates agencies, bypasses local government, uses special-purpose bodies to deliver services, and encourages public-private partnerships, so networks become increasingly prominent among British governing structures". Of course, in part this is a response to macro-level changes outside of the state's control such as globalisation and technological advancement, but it is also a change that is being invoked by different governments at different rates and in different ways. In short, it is the result of a complex, iterative process.

Conclusions

As Kickert et al (1997) argue, networks are, and will remain, a key part of the policy process. So, while there are clearly some problems with the PNA as it stands, it seems to us that the attempt to further refine and develop a theory of the policy process that has networks at its core is of crucial importance. Moreover, we also believe that further developing our understanding of how policy networks operate and how they might be managed is also of real importance. While it is beyond the scope of this introductory chapter to develop a synthesis of existing network theories in order to aid analysis of this increasingly prevalent policy trend, our brief review has nevertheless highlighted a number of important themes that any student of social or public policy can reflect upon in order to aid their understanding of how the policy process operates.

The first key lesson is that policy networks matter because they affect policy outcomes. They act as filters that shape the ways in which specific policy sectors respond to common pressures such as globalisation, technological change, economic changes or the emergence of new ideas. Categorising policy sectors along the Rhodes model continuum, therefore, can help us to understand why common trends have had varying impacts and can help us to predict how far current trends are likely to impact on particular sectors in the future. However, the effects of networks are complex so any predictions we make must carry a health warning. Networks interact (or have a dialectical relationship) with their surroundings – with the macro-level contexts within which they operate, with the individuals who constitute the networks and with the policies they produce.

Crucially, therefore, policy network analysis should not be operated in isolation from other forms of analysis. It is designed to occupy the meso-level that sits between macro- and micro-level analyses. It is at its most powerful when combined with other explanations of change and used, for instance, to explain why broad changes have had more impact in one policy sector rather than another. It is worth emphasising too that the policy network approach has a real strength in highlighting resistance to change and the ways in which change is resisted. While those interested in macro-level change sometimes have a tendency to emphasise the transformatory potential of phenomena such as globalisation or the 'information revolution' (see Chapters Two and Four), the policy network theorists remind us that the impact of such changes is constrained by political structures (policy networks) that exist to routinise political relationships, consolidate political power, protect (vested) interests and limit policy change. In short, they deter radical change and foster **incremental change**.

Finally, we should note that there is much work to be done in terms of thinking through how policy makers at the ground level are responding to the move towards network working. While Marsh and Smith's dialectical model is an advance insofar as it conceptualises networks as being in constant flux, we need to explore more thoroughly how those creating, implementing and managing policy seek to utilise inter-organisational networks and partnerships.

Summary

- Policy networks affect policies. They act as filters that mitigate the impact of broad macro-level trends and steer policy towards particular goals. They tend to foster incremental change and bolster the status quo.
- In the Rhodes model, policy networks are conceived as a continuum with policy communities at one end and issue networks at the other. Policy networks might also feature a strong core surrounded by a periphery of issue networks.
- Some commentators doubt the value of the policy networks approach (PNA), arguing it is nothing more than metaphor. More formal approaches exist that differ radically from the Rhodes model.
- The policy network approach is a meso-level approach that makes most sense when combined with theories of macro-level change. It is particularly strong in explaining why responses to macro-level changes vary between different policy networks.

- Marsh and Smith argue that policy networks have 'dialectical' relationships with macro- and micro-level events. They interact with the broad context in which they are located, with the individuals that constitute networks and with the policies that they produce.
- Policy networks need to be managed. Participants in networks might need to engage in strategies that can activate networks or reorient them towards specific goals.

Questions for discussion

- Why do policy networks matter?
- How do policy networks constrain policy change?
- Would a more formal version of the policy network approach deliver substantial analytic gains?

Further reading

Dowding, K. (2001) 'There must be an end to confusion: policy networks, intellectual fatigue, and the need for political science methods courses in British universities', *Political Studies*, vol 49, pp 89-105.

Evans, M. (2001) 'Understanding dialectics in policy networks', *Political Studies*, vol 49, pp 542-50.

Marsh, D. and Rhodes, R.A.W. (1992c) *Policy networks in British government*, Oxford: Clarendon Press.

Marsh, D. and Smith, M.J. (2000) 'Understanding policy networks: towards a dialectical approach', *Political Studies*, vol 48, pp 4-21.

Rhodes, R.A.W. (1997b) *Understanding governance: Policy networks, governance, reflexivity and accountability*, Buckingham: Open University Press.

Institutions

Overview

This chapter examines the central role of institutions within the policy process. It offers a guide through the new institutionalism literature that has become increasingly important in political science over the past decade-and-a-half. In particular, it emphasises the role institutions play in framing the 'rules of the game' that political actors face and their role in restricting policy options and fostering stability. Drawing on multi-country comparisons to illustrate the importance of institutions in shaping policy outcomes, ideas such as path dependency, policy feedback, the mobilisation of bias and punctuated equilibrium are explored.

Key concepts

Path dependency; policy feedback; increasing returns; veto points; mobilisation of bias; unintended consequences; punctuated equilibrium.

Introduction: does the organisation of political life matter?

It is increasingly common to hear people express the view that politics does not matter anymore, that democracy is a meaningless process, that all governments – all political parties – are all the same nowadays, that big business drives the agenda rather than the government, that the important decisions are made in Washington and imposed on the rest of the world, that globalisation has brought the end of the sovereign nation state. This widespread cynicism about politics and the role politicians play in society is reflected in opinion surveys. For instance, MORI have regularly surveyed British citizens' opinions of ten key professional groups: nurses, doctors, dentists, teachers, judges, lawyers, accountants, politicians generally, government ministers and the police. In each of the surveys conducted between 1999 and 2002, all groups have been deemed to be providing a satisfactory service (often overwhelmingly so), with the significant exception of politicians and government ministers who have been consistently perceived as producing a dissatisfactory service (www.mori.co.uk).

Such sentiments have manifested themselves in declining turnout rates at elections: in the UK, for example, only 59% of voters participated in the 2001 General Election, compared with an average turnout for the post-war period as a whole of just over 75% (*Social Trends*, 2003; see **Figure 9.1**). This headline figure says a lot, but the picture is even more pronounced within certain groups. For example, 73% of young women (those aged 18-24) voted in the 1983 General Election; however, in the 2001 General Election, only 46% of the same group did so. While the collapse is greater for young women than young men (60% in 2001), it would be wrong to assume that the latter have retained significant levels of engagement with the political system. Indeed, official statistics show that the proportion of young men who express an interest in politics has slumped from a figure of 28% in 1986 to just 13% in 1999 (data source: British Social Attitudes Survey, 2000; and British Election Study, 2003; both at www.statistics.gov.uk).

Although such figures are far from unique to the UK (a recent survey showed that 40% of Europeans are dissatisfied with their nation's democracy, with figures running at 70% for Ireland, 46% for Greece and 41% for France: Eurobarometer, 1999, p 12), it is curious that disengagement in Britain has risen at a time when the nation has had a government committed to a programme of constitutional modernisation that has included:

Figure 9.1: Voter turnout at post-war UK general elections

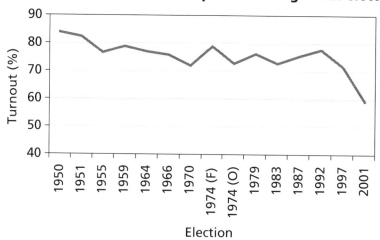

Note: 1974 (F) = 1974 February; 1974 (O) = 1974 October.

- devolution of decision-making power over key policy areas to democratically elected institutions in Scotland, Wales and London, with proposals for additional bodies in the English regions;
- a concerted attempt to revamp decision-making processes within local authorities through the introduction of elected mayors and/or cabinet style executives;
- experiments with e-democracy and e-voting and extensive use of governmental websites in order to make information about policies and policy proposals more widely available (see Chapter Five).

While it is undoubtedly the case that these reforms could have been more radical in their intent or, in the case of devolution, further reaching in terms of their geographical scope, the fact is that none have genuinely captured the public imagination. Even in the case of the most radical reform, the Scottish Parliament, satisfaction levels are depressingly low: fewer than one in three are satisfied according to a recent (2003) MORI poll (www.mori.co.uk). Meanwhile, proposals for high-profile elected mayors have been quashed in many cities by public disinterest in such experimentation and, worse still, in many places where they have been introduced they have at times merely highlighted dissatisfaction with the political process. In Hartlepool, for example, the first mayoral election was won by the local football team's mascot[1].

What all this suggests perhaps is that, whatever form it takes, politics is seen as an empty process; that whatever the institutional arrangements in place, politics is thought to make little difference to the issues that matter. Moreover, we know too that, in part at least, this is because there is a general perception that the hyperglobalists' thesis (see Chapter Two) is correct: in a recent poll of EU citizens, some 65% of those giving a firm answer[2] agreed that globalisation is outside the control of governments (Eurobarometer, 2001, p 3).

In defence of politics

Such feelings of disengagement are by no means new however; indeed, Crick (1962) felt sufficiently moved by similar apathy in the early 1960s to pen the classic book *In defence of politics*, and many political scientists since have followed in his footsteps by focusing their research efforts on investigating the extent to which politics matters – that is, whether or not it makes a difference to our lives (see Castles, 2001). Crick's work was primarily a philosophical account,

---

[1] The mascot, a monkey named H'Angus, made free bananas each day for all school children in the town one of his key election promises. In what could be a novel case study of the difficulty of delivering policy change he has had to renege on this promise due to the cost and complexity of delivering it – despite a last minute post hoc rationalisation of this promise as a serious public health measure!

[2] That is, when excluding the 28% of respondents who answered 'Don't know'.

highlighting the virtues of a society that values tolerance and open debate. More recent research, however, has aimed to cast light on the role of political institutions in filtering change, in ensuring (as we hinted in Chapter Two) that, when faced with common pressures – such as globalisation, deindustrialisation, rising unemployment, an ageing population, changing family forms – states respond in distinctive, divergent ways that reflect different historical traditions or political cultures. In other words, they have aimed to demonstrate that while macro-level forces heavily influence social and economic policies, politics still matters. Much of this research has been focused around a body of work dubbed the 'new institutionalism' (Hall and Taylor, 1996) that aims to highlight the role of institutions in the policy process (see **Box 9.1**). Some of the most exciting work in the field of public policy analysis is located here and it is this body of work that we examine in this chapter.

What is the 'new institutionalism'?

At its most basic, the new institutionalism is an approach that aims to "illuminate how political struggles are mediated by the institutional setting in which they take place" (Thelen and Steinmo, 1992, p 2). The approach is 'new' in the sense that much early social science work often emphasised the importance of institutions too, but did so in a rather rigid and formulaic way that underplayed human actions (agency) and overplayed the role of institutions (structure). The new institutionalism tries to emphasise *both* agency and structure, pointing

---

Box 9.1: What are institutions?

Institutions
- are **meso-level structures**: they are devised by individuals but constrain and structure the actions of individuals;
- have **formal and informal** dimensions: they are rules and laws but can be customs or norms;
- show **stability and legitimacy** over time: they are valued in themselves.

Examples
- election rules, voting systems
- party systems and structures
- relations between branches of government
- structure and organisation of key economic or interest groups
- welfare state agencies and delivery systems.

Sources: Thelen and Steinmo (1992); Lowndes (1996)

in particular to the role of institutions in structuring interaction between political actors (as the earlier quotation from Thelen and Steinmo suggests).

The new institutionalism began to emerge in the 1980s (when March and Olsen, 1989, for example, wrote of *Rediscovering institutions*) and has strands in most of the social sciences, including economics (such as Williamson, 1985), sociology (DiMaggio and Powell, 1991) and political science (see Hall and Taylor, 1996). To make things more complicated, there are often sub-strands within each of the social sciences too; Hall and Taylor (1996), for instance, suggest there are three strands of relevance to political science. All, however, are united by the belief that an examination of institutions provides the key to understanding social and political life.

However, as all this suggests, there is a considerable diversity of viewpoints within the new institutionalism, and it is important to note that the new institutionalists do not offer a coherent conceptual tool kit for analysing the world; instead it is better to see the approach as one that joins those with a common belief in the importance of institutions. Indeed, two of the key writers in the field describe it as simply an "empirically based prejudice" (March and Olsen, 1984, p 747), a belief that what they have seen suggests that institutions are a key variable in explaining the outcomes of political life.

As we have hinted in earlier chapters of this book, we share this belief that institutions matter and feel that they have a major impact on the policy process. We have also suggested that history matters too and that the past has a strong impact on the present. For this reason, we will focus our exploration of the new institutionalism on one of its key schools of thought – historical institutionalism. We believe that the historical institutionalists have produced the most powerful work to emerge from the new institutionalist school, not least because they have emphasised the role of history in shaping policy outcomes. In addition, it is the historical institutionalists who have focused their attention most heavily on the issue of the welfare state (such as Baldwin, 1990; Immergut, 1992a; Skocpol, 1992; Pierson, 1994, 2001; Castles, 1998). Their work, therefore, marks an obvious starting point for our discussion about the role of institutions in shaping social policies.

Institutions and stability

At the heart of the historical institutionalist perspective is the claim that institutions foster stability, not least because institutions themselves have a high degree of 'stickiness' and are difficult to remove or reform. Krasner (1988, pp 73-4) sums this up neatly, arguing that "an institutionalist perspective implies that something persists over time and that change is not instantaneous and costless". Consequently, institutionalists often emphasise the high degree of continuity of public policy and the generally incremental nature of policy change. As we will see, institutions often act as a barrier to policy change or, more subtly, they guide change towards a particular direction, making it difficult for governments to deliver policy reforms (particularly radical reforms). As Krasner puts it (1988, p 74): "changes, from an institutionalist perspective, can never be easy, fluid, or continuous".

Significantly, it is precisely this belief that *stable* institutions shape policy outcomes that results in the historical institutionalists giving their work a strong temporal dimension. They argue that because institutions persist over time, so too do their effects. Consequently, if we are to understand the impact of institutions on policy outcomes then we need to understand the role they have played in shaping policy over the long durée. This is important, for other schools of thought within the new institutionalism think it is enough merely to regard institutions as providing the context (or the arena) for political action that is occurring at this moment in time – that is, they adopt an *ahistorical* approach. By contrast, the historical institutionalists regard it as a methodological necessity to understand the ways in which policies have developed over time and tend to use detailed historical case studies in order to explore the complex ways in which institutions have shaped processes of policy development.

Path dependency and increasing returns

Why then do historical institutionalists believe that policy tends to evolve quite slowly and in an incremental manner? In part, they believe that this is so because policies themselves tend to create sticky institutions – such as pension funds or health insurance funds – that are difficult to reform and so often act as barriers to change. Building on such ideas, key thinkers such as Pierson (2001) have argued that the stickiness of institutions results in policies displaying **increasing returns**. This notion is meant to contrast with one of the basic laws of economic theory – that of 'diminishing returns' – which suggests that once a certain point of attainment is reached, additional effort is likely to bring smaller and smaller rewards. Here, the logic is reversed, and the argument is that once the decision to take policy down a particular route has been taken, the benefits (and the ease) of travelling further down the existing route tend to *increase* – as do the costs of switching to an alternative route, importantly. In part this is because, once a social right has been conferred, the process of removing it is always likely to be politically controversial. (Indeed, the historical institutionalists have argued that the politics of welfare retrenchment that have characterised social policy debates in recent decades are very different from the politics of welfare expansion that we witnessed in the earlier post-war period for this very reason. See Pierson, 1994.)

Myles and Pierson (2001) illustrate the notion of increasing returns well with the example of pension reform. They argue that all western state pension systems have been facing pressure to reform since the 1980s as the proportion of pensioners in society started to increase and the proportion of wage earners began to decrease, particularly given that most schemes have been funded on a Pay As You Go (PAYG) basis – meaning pensions for the ever growing number of elderly are having to be paid by taxes on the decreasing number of wage earners. This situation, combined with other factors such as the onset of globalisation, led many, including the World Bank (1994), to predict that radical reform would have to occur in order to reduce the state's responsibilities in this field; in particular, the privatisation of pension responsibilities was seen as the way forward.

However, having examined the reality of pensions policy in OECD nations, Myles and Pierson argue that, contrary to predictions that pensions systems would converge on a more privatised model, two paths of policy have been evident since the 1980s. On the one hand, some nations have indeed taken the radical route, with countries such as Australia, Denmark, Switzerland and the UK increasing the role of the private sector in pensions provision. However, on the other hand, many nations (including the US, Germany, Italy and Sweden) have undertaken more modest reforms which, while retrenching provision to a degree, has not involved a radical shift towards private provision. Significantly, the nations that fall into each of these categories do not neatly correspond with existing categorisations of those nations' political culture or historic welfare regime (see, for example, Esping-Andersen, 1990). So, for instance, social democratic Denmark is found in the basket of countries that have undertaken radical action while the liberal US is found in the group that has taken more modest reform.

Myles and Pierson suggest that examining pre-existing pension arrangements provides the best explanation for the paths of reform chosen. They argue that in nations with well-developed PAYG state pension systems that had existed for some time, reform invariably followed the route of modest tinkering with a view to cutting down on some commitments at the margins. On the other hand, in nations where such systems were in their infancy or had not been effectively developed, policy makers took more radical action that favoured increased privatisation. They argue (2001, p 313) that "how far one has gone down the path of PAYG provision is critical for delimiting reform options" and that "the options open to policy makers, whatever their politics, are constrained by institutional and programmatic designs inherited from the past" (p 306). In other words, despite facing common pressures to reform pensions systems, policy makers have had to adopt different solutions to this problem because those nations with well established institutions (that is, pension funds) regarded the dismantling of those institutions as beyond the scope of what they could reasonably achieve.

This idea of 'increasing returns' links with another fundamental notion within the historical institutionalists' cannon: **path dependency**. Indeed, Myles and Pierson (2001, p 306) argue that "pensions policy is a *locus classicus* for the study of 'path-dependent' change", by which they mean, "processes in which choices made in the past systematically constrain the choices open in the future". In the case of state pension systems, the crucial decisions came in the 1950s when many states responded to growing post-war affluence by extending state pension schemes. Countries that took such a route created a widely based core of beneficiaries who, when the schemes came under threat in the more austere economic climate of the 1980s and 1990s, expressed a strong political preference for the continuation of those schemes. This contrasted markedly with the political climate in nations without mature systems, where the numbers of people who felt a strong attachment to state schemes was smaller. In short, nations responded quite differently to the common pressures facing their pensions systems because they were 'locked', in effect, into one of two paths of policy development three or four decades earlier.

Policy feedback

What the notion of path dependency illustrates is that past decisions constrain and impact upon future decisions. Historical institutionalists often refer to this phenomenon as **policy feedback** (Skocpol, 1992; Pierson, 1994). This term is designed to encapsulate the view that policies, rather than merely being the *outcome* of the policy process, can and do become a central part of the policy process itself. This is particularly so for social policies, because so often they involve the large-scale (re)distribution of resources, creating large communities of interest that seek to defend the existing settlement.

One of the best illustrations of this argument has come from Swank (2002), who has argued that each nation's post-globalisation debate about welfare reform and/or retrenchment has been fundamentally shaped by the welfare provisions that already exist in a given nation. He suggests that factors such as the way in which welfare states are organised, the extent to which resources are redistributed and the degree to which people are given democratic control over social policies are crucial in determining how far pro-welfare supporters are able to resist challenges to welfare in the post-globalisation era. So, for example, while in the UK most of the key areas of the welfare state are controlled directly by central government, in Germany there is considerable decentralisation of both administration and decision making; this difference in institutional arrangements directly impacts upon the configuration of policy networks in specific fields and on the power of non-governmental actors within those networks[3]. So, as Swank (2002, p 52) puts it, "aspects of

---

[3] So, for example, while the NHS in the UK is a single organisation funded centrally through general taxes, the German healthcare system is based around social insurance to a whole series of decentralised parastatal funds that cater for different groups in society and offer varying benefits. Over 1,000 funds exist and beneficiaries have democratic input into the management of their funds (see Bolderson and Mabbett, 1997).

programmatic structure have substantial impacts on the representation and the relative political capacities of pro-welfare interests".

In other words, welfare policies create communities of interest that will then seek to defend the institutions of the welfare state against attacks from government (or, indeed, from supranational organisations) making it difficult for policy makers to alter decisions made by their predecessors. As Skocpol and Amenta (1986, p 149) put it:

> not only does politics create social policies; social policies also create politics. That is, once policies are enacted and implemented, they change the public agendas and patterns of group conflict through which subsequent policy changes occur.

A comparison could be drawn here with the ideas found in the policy networks literature (see Chapter Eight), which points to bargaining between government and key groups who either deliver or receive the benefits of particular policies. Both approaches emphasise the fact that policies create interests that will then seek to defend the status quo, making change difficult to achieve and so favouring incremental adjustments to policy. (Indeed, Rhodes, 1995, has argued that the new institutionalism and the policy network approach are one and the same thing.) However, the (historical) institutionalist perspective goes beyond the policy networks approach insofar as it sees politics as *more* than a resource bargaining issue. Swank (2002; see also Rothstein, 1998), for example, is keen to emphasise the role previous policies play in shaping *values* as well as *interests*. The two are crucially different, for the historical institutionalists are keen to embrace a model of human interaction that sees people as more than self-interested actors pursuing their own interests and instead to allow for a view of the policy process that assumes people act on a broader set of motivations, including ideals and beliefs based on moral views of what is right and wrong (see Steinmo and Thelen, 1992).

Unintended consequences

For the historical institutionalists then, policy feedback can have extremely powerful impacts on the nature and direction of policy development. It should be noted, however, that the precise nature of policy feedback is impossible to predict and so historical institutionalists also emphasise the **unintended consequences** of policy decisions. Indeed, many key writers in the field are keen to highlight the somewhat haphazard and unplanned nature of policy development. This point is perhaps best illustrated in Baldwin's seminal analysis of the origins of European welfare states (Baldwin, 1992). Central to Baldwin's work is the belief that we too often assume that our current justifications for social policies relate to the original intentions of those who introduced the policies – in other words, that policies have met their intended goals. To illustrate this point, we can consider one of the policies Baldwin examined at length in his study: that of Sweden's generous basic state pension. The system, which was one of the first proper state pension schemes to be introduced, dates back to 1913 and, from the outset, was universal and funded on the basis of ability to pay through general taxation. The system is often regarded as an example of a pioneering welfare policy that was underpinned by socially just altruistic ideals and an early indicator of the solidaristic principles that are at the heart of Sweden's political culture and which sustain its highly generous, social democratic welfare state.

However, Baldwin argues that the lofty ideals of social justice and social solidarity or the principles of (modern-day) social democracy had very little to do with the debate about the nature of the pension system when it was first introduced. Indeed, social democrats were divided over the issue of whether or not to support a universal pension scheme, many preferring a scheme that focused only on the urban working class. In fact, much of the pressure for a universal system came from better-off agrarian groups, aggrieved at the prospect of missing out on state subsidies that the urban workers were to receive. Significantly, much needed measures to address poverty among the elderly were held up for over two decades as wrangling about the distribution of resources occurred in parliament and the introduction of a universal, tax-financed pension scheme was not the starting point of the debate but, rather, the compromise introduced in order to break through this deadlock. Baldwin (1989, pp 23-4) argues that, while "both of these characteristics – universality and tax financing – did, in fact, later become progressive, solidaristic aspects of welfare policy ... these features were the result of demands put forth by the emerging agrarian middle classes on their own behalf". In short, Sweden's present-day pension system, which is extremely generous, universal, and funded through redistributive taxation, is a classic example of unintended consequences at work. It emerged as a result of the self-interested actions of the better off, was opposed by much of the (urban) working class who are now its key beneficiaries and was the product of a quite grubby and unprincipled debate about the distribution of resources; yet, is now held up as the ideal-type, socially just pension system. Baldwin (1989, p 24) sums up the deep irony of this beautifully, pointing out that, in this case: "The origins of virtue turn out to be mundane. The solidarity of one age has its roots in the selfishness of another"[4].

---

[4] In examining the factors that resulted in Sweden ending the 20th century with what he regarded as the most generous social security system in the developed world, Esping-Andersen (1990) also emphasised the absence of a coherent policy blueprint – even among the strongest advocates of generous social policies – for taking Sweden from a market economy to the ideal-type social democratic welfare regime, instead pointing to the long and intense process of political bargaining and struggle that underpinned the development of the Swedish welfare state.

Institutions as 'rules of the game'

These examples should make it clear that, in creating welfare state institutions such as pension or health insurance funds, past policy decisions can and do have a significant impact on current debates and future decisions. Not least, past decisions make reform (particularly retrenchment) difficult and so help foster stability, bias politics towards the status quo and encourage changes that are generally incremental in nature. In turn, this allows for radically different paths of policy development to exist in different nations. Early decisions about (say) pensions policy or health care provision have lasting consequences that bias the direction of future policies, unleashing a logic of development that favours one path over others, albeit a logic that is very difficult to predict or foresee.

However, institutions play a crucial role in shaping policy *before* decisions are made, too. Indeed, in establishing the **rules of the game**, they often limit the scope of possibilities open to policy makers at the outset, blocking off some paths of policy development *before debates have even begun* about (say) the nature of early pension schemes or health care systems. To illustrate this, consider one of the most fundamental sets of rules: electoral rules. Clearly these rules vary quite widely from place to place and from time to time. Whether a party needs to win 60% of the vote to form a strong, single-party government (as in, say, Sweden) or can do so on just 40% of the vote (as in, say, the UK) matters a great deal in terms of the strategies that parties might deploy in order to fight a successful election. In the UK, we might argue, it makes sense for a party to adopt an adversarial approach that looks to discredit the opposition in order to secure the 40% of the vote that will allow them to govern alone and enjoy the fruits of power. By contrast, a party in Sweden knows its chances of gaining 60% of the vote are slim and that even if they gain the largest share of the vote they will probably have to govern in coalition with other parties after the election. Here, robust debate would still be expected, but it makes sense to adopt a more consensual approach that allows agreements to be reached where possible and for good working relationships to be established. This single difference in the rules of the game (between a first-past-the-post or a proportional voting system) can have a massive impact on the nature of policy debates and the outcomes of those debates. In short, such rules have a major impact on the nature of the policy process and imply that because the rules of the game vary considerably from place to place, so too will the policy process. The institutionalists go still further, however, arguing that the rules of the game will inevitably favour some particular players over others too, for different sets of rules will empower different sets of actors at the expense of others (another reason why different institutional arrangements will produce different policy outcomes). This argument is neatly encapsulated within the phrase **'mobilisation of bias'** and, as we will see in the following sections, institutions mobilise bias in many complex ways.

Institutions as veto points

Immergut's work examining the emergence of European health care systems illustrates this point very well (Immergut, 1990, 1992a, 1992b). In Chapter Eight, we examined policy networks and the key role that non-governmental actors play in shaping welfare policy. Here, the powerful position of the medical profession in shaping health care policy was noted, medics often being cited as the classic example of a powerful group upon whom the government is dependent in order to meet their policy goals. Although our discussion there focused upon the UK, the same observation could be made about the medical profession in any economically advanced nation. However, while the power of the medical profession is a universal phenomenon, it would seem that the impact of medics on the development of health care systems varies dramatically, for there are widely differing health care systems in operation across Europe.

This observation forms the starting point of Immergut's work; she explores the issue of why we see such variation by examining the historical development of three health care systems:

- *Sweden* (highly socialised, state-run universal service funded through general taxation);
- *Switzerland* (highly marketised, minimal state role, primarily private);
- *France* (generous funding via social insurance, strong role for parastatal groups).

She suggests there are three obvious reasons why the nature of these systems might differ. First, it could be because different ideas dominated the debates in each nation. However, this is not the case. In each nation the initial debates were very similar – with the government looking to socialise medicine – and in all countries the medical profession responded by trying to block attempts to socialise medicine. This factor, she argues, can be discounted therefore. This conclusion then prompts a second factor: that the medical profession mobilised more effectively in some countries. She argues that this was indeed true, but that it cannot account for the variation in policy outcomes because medics had much larger and more established representative organisations in France and Sweden than they did in Switzerland, yet it was in the latter nation that the solution favoured by the medics (minimal state intervention) was adopted. This suggests, therefore, that factors other than the power of the medical profession were at play. Finally, Immergut suggests that differences in the power of groups supporting increased state intervention might be an obvious factor for explaining the different outcomes. Here she examines the power of the working class, who were indeed pushing for reform and whose power did vary between the three nations. Once again, however, she argues that this factor cannot explain the different outcomes. At the time of the early debates, it was the Swedish and the Swiss working class that were the most effectively mobilised, and while the Swedish working class achieved their goal, the Swiss working class were far less successful than the French working class despite being more effectively organised.

Given this, Immergut argues that we need to turn our attention to the organisation of the state, it being the remaining key actor in the analysis. Crucially, in each of the three nations the 'rules of the game' were very different: a strong executive typifies Sweden; a strong parliament typifies France; and Switzerland has had a strong tradition of direct democracy, with referenda being a key feature of the decision-making process. Immergut suggests that it is these differing institutional arrangements that best explain the differing development processes with respect to health care policy. She argues that all democratic political systems posses **veto points** – opportunities for groups to voice opposition to policy proposals and exert their influence over them – but the extent and nature of veto points varies radically from place to place. In Sweden, the centralised nature of the political system allowed the executive to push through plans for the socialisation of medicine with relative 'ease', there being comparatively few veto points within the political system. At the other extreme, the Swiss medical profession were able to take advantage of the system of direct democracy to mobilise opposition to the executive's proposals for the socialisation of medicine. They called frequent referenda in order to block and delay legislation with the end result being extremely watered down proposals that left the status quo largely intact. Although less well organised than their Swedish counterparts, the Swiss medics were able to take advantage of the numerous veto points in their political system in order to resist change. Meanwhile, the political system had fewer veto points in France than in Switzerland but more than in Sweden, which corresponds with the extent to which proposals for socialisation were achieved, the French health care system also being midway between the Swedish and Swiss arrangements with respect to state involvement.

What is important about Immergut's work is that it demonstrates the way in which institutions can favour (or, conversely, disadvantage) particular outcomes over others. While the effects of institutions are complex and often unpredictable, it is clear that institutions impact upon a government's room for manoeuvre and upon its power and autonomy. Indeed, presuming we accept Immergut's interpretation of the evidence, then it is possible to suggest that there is a real sense in which institutions in fact set the agenda of what is politically possible. Moreover, if we can make generalisations based on her findings, then this suggests that political systems with numerous veto points produce collective action problems that, in turn, limit the chances of a generous welfare settlement succeeding, while in systems with relatively few veto points the opposite is true.

Institutions and the creation of interests

Approaching a similar issue from an alternative angle, Pierson (1995) has explored the implications of federalism for the development of social policies. He too suggests that the fragmentation of political systems may create collective action problems that can make generous welfare provisions difficult to deliver. However, he argues that constitutions not only set the rules of the game, but can also **influence the interests** of political actors too, adding a further dimension to the mobilisation of bias. In the case of federalism they do this by institutionalising regional interests and, in turn, placing issues surrounding the regional distribution of resources permanently on the agenda. Examining the development of social policy in the US, Pierson argues that the need to accommodate the regional agenda has negatively impacted on welfare state development in three key ways. First, it has often resulted in the politics of the lowest common denominator – policies having to account for the objections of the least enthusiastic players in order to be successful. Second, it has produced institutional protections; that is, guarantees that prevent policies associated with specific states from being overturned. Finally, it has led to a search for escape mechanisms: opt-out clauses that allow certain states to be exempt from specific dimensions of welfare policy. In short, the 'dilemmas of shared policy making' have fundamentally conditioned the nature of policy debates in the US by opening up avenues for conflict that do not exist in unitary states. More specifically, federalism has created a significant political cleavage (between regions) and, in doing so, both created another hurdle for policies to clear and strong regional interests that are a fundamental dimension of key policy debates.

However, Pierson cautions against assuming findings from studies of one or two nations are generalisable, arguing that the impact of specific institutions is very much dependent upon the context within which they are located. With respect to federalism, he argues (1995, p 473) that it "operates in conjunction with other important variables: the structure of party systems, the nature of a particular political economy, the geographical distribution of minority groups", which, he suggests, "is bad news ... for those hoping to get powerful statistical results by slapping a 'federalism' variable into a quantitative study". So, while "the institutional rules of federal systems have major implications for social policymaking" (1995, p 450) these implications are far from straightforward and require careful, qualitative analysis on a case-by-case basis.

Institutions as policy filters

In essence, what all of this adds up to is an argument that institutions **filter** change. Institutions sit at the **meso-level**, operating between the macro-level trends such as globalisation or technological change and, at the micro-level, the individuals who make or implement policy decisions or who, as citizens, experience the impact of these trends. Furthermore, because institutions differ from place to place, so too do the 'filtered' experiences of globalisation or economic change.

In one of the most ambitious pieces of work to emerge from the new institutionalism, Swank (2001, 2002) has attempted to demonstrate the systematic ways in which institutions have filtered the impacts of globalisation on welfare states. In something of a departure for work in this field, he supplements historical case studies with a sophisticated quantitative analysis of time-series data. Swank's (2002, p 275) analysis of this data produces the hugely important conclusion that globalisation (by which he means the increasing international mobility of capital) "is not systematically and directly related to social welfare policy change in the contemporary era". This is not to say that globalisation has *no* impact on welfare, but instead to argue that there is nothing preordained about its effects and that arguments that welfare will *inevitably* converge on a neo-liberal model as a consequence of globalisation are misplaced. Instead, the evidence gathered for Swank's (2002, p 279) study suggests that "the direction and magnitude of social welfare effects of international capital mobility are significantly shaped by domestic political institutions". More specifically, he points to the crucial role played by "the structure of systems of collective group and electoral representation, the structure of decision-making authority in the polity, and the structure of welfare state institutions" in this process (**Box 9.2**).

Conclusions

Of course, as in any field, the work of the historical institutionalists is not without its problems. One of the most fundamental criticisms is that the approach lacks consistently clear lessons or conclusions. In fact, some of the key authors in the field view this as a strength, asking us to view each case as being unique with its own historical trajectory that lacks generalisable lessons (see Baldwin, 1992). Where authors have tried to draw some clearer conclusions their work often contradicts that of other theorists; so, for example, Swank's (2002) suggestion that federalism is correlated with a weakening of support for welfare runs counter to Pierson's (1995, p 473) argument that the links between institutions and policy outcomes are so complex that there is little point in searching for "powerful statistical results by slapping a 'federalism' variable into a quantitative study of OECD countries". Similarly, there are

Box 9.2: Swank's analysis of the impact of institutions on welfare

Swank (2001, 2002) undertook a large-scale quantitative and qualitative study of welfare state activity in 15 OECD countries[a] between 1965 and 1995. His central aims were to explore, first, the 'theory of diminished democracy' (that is, the argument that globalisation is forcing governments to reduce the size of their welfare state irrespective of the political will of the nation) and, second, to explore a counter-argument that the political institutions and ideals of nations have been dominant in shaping welfare policy.

His study concluded that globalisation has had no independent impact upon the welfare state and that responses to globalisation had been fundamentally shaped by the character of each nation's institutions. Indeed, his study identified specific institutional arrangements most likely to be associated with both the retrenchment and the resilience of the welfare state.

The institutional arrangements that he argues have been most effective in protecting the welfare state against globalisation are:

- **inclusive electoral system** (systems of proportional representation that encourage consensus based coalition governments);
- **social corporatism** (strong trade unions and a key role for civil society in the administration of welfare);
- **centralisation of political authority** (where there is an absence of [or where there is weak] federalism);
- **welfare state based on universalism** (where well established programmes with widespread coverage exist).

[a] Australia, Austria, Belgium, Canada, Denmark, Finland, France, Germany, Italy, Japan, Netherlands, Norway, Sweden, UK and US.

those who are critical of the approach's evidence base, which relies primarily on historical case studies that some dismiss as mere storytelling. Moreover, in cases where a more quantitative approach has been adopted, there are suggestions that the validity of the findings are questionable, for the selection of the cases included plays a significant role in sustaining the significance of the models being presented (Kühner, 2003).

However, the biggest problem facing the institutionalists is their (in)ability to explain policy change. In stressing continuity and stability, their approach downplays change and, partially as a result, has some difficulty in explaining the circumstances that lead to change – particularly radical change that displays strong discontinuity with the past. Krasner has tried to overcome this problem by invoking an evolutionary metaphor (1988; see also Baumgartner and Jones, 1993). While the common perception of evolution is that it refers to gradual change, the truth is more complex. Indeed, like institutions, species display remarkable degrees of stability and continuity over time. Changes to species tend to occur rapidly in response to external shocks, such as climatic change or environmental disaster. Gould and Eldredge (1977) refer to this as 'punctuated equilibrium'; in other words, stability interspersed with periods of rapid readjustment and change. For Krasner, what is true of the evolution of species is also true of political institutions. He argues that, all things being equal, political systems will operate at a stable point of equilibrium, with changes being modest and incremental in nature. However, exogenous shocks to the system (such as economic crises, war, technological change) will periodically shatter this equilibrium and require (or, rather, create an opportunity for) more radical change. Other institutionalists invoke alternative metaphors that essentially refer to the same stream of thought such as 'critical junctures' or 'policy windows'. In their discussion of path dependency in pensions systems, for example, Myles and Pierson (2001, p 329) argued "lasting consequences [that is, path dependencies] stem from the success or failure of countries to move through that 'policy window' while it remained open"; in this case, the policy window being the opportunity to expand pension schemes while the increasingly affluent early post-war population still had strong feelings of solidarity following the horrors of the Second World War. While such ideas go some way towards helping to address this problem, they are still a little weak, telling us too little about when such shocks/junctures/windows are likely to occur or how big they have to be in order to trigger change.

Yet, despite its problems, the perspective clearly offers substantial insights. Indeed, we believe the analysis of history and the analysis of institutions ought to play a central role in any proper analysis of policy development or policy trends. The lessons that can be drawn from the historical institutionalists' work are hugely important: that history matters; that institutions foster stability and mobilise bias; that policies display increasing returns and path dependencies; that institutions frame the rules of the game and so fundamentally influence the nature of the policy process and the outcomes it tends to produce. Above all, the perspective is important because it emphasises that politics and the organisation of political life matter. Cynicism towards political life or apathy about constitutional reform are therefore misplaced: both are key in shaping how nations respond to, and, as a result, how citizens experience, key modern-day trends such as globalisation, technological change or demographic change.

Summary

- Institutions play a crucial role at the meso-level of the policy process. They provide a context for micro-level human interactions and filter broad macro-level trends.

- Institutions foster stability and incrementalism. They act as a barrier to change.
- Due to the 'stickiness' of institutions, policies often display 'increasing returns' and possess a strong degree of path dependency.
- Institutions have long-term effects, though these effects are often unpredictable. Policy feedback is a central feature of the policy process as are unintended consequences. History matters.
- Institutions provide the 'rules of the game' for political actors. They fundamentally condition the policy process by distributing opportunities for political action and, in so doing, they mobilise bias.
- Politics and the organisation of political life matter. Analysing varying national institutional arrangements can help us to understand why countries adopt different solutions to similar problems and respond differently to common pressures and challenges.

Questions for discussion

- How far are welfare states 'path dependent'?
- To what extent do institutions set the 'rules of the game'?
- Might constitutional reform help protect the UK welfare state against the threats posed to it by globalisation?

Further reading

Hall, P. and Taylor, R. (1996) 'Political science and the three new institutionalisms', *Political Studies*, vol 44, pp 936-57.

Pierson, P. (ed) (2001) *The new politics of the welfare state*, Oxford: Oxford University Press.

Steinmo, S., Thelen, K. and Longstreth, F. (1992) *Structuring politics: Historical institutionalism in comparative perspective*, Cambridge: Cambridge University Press.

Swank, D. (2002) *Global capital, political institutions and policy change in developed welfare states*, Cambridge: Cambridge University Press.

Policy transfer

Overview
This chapter examines the increase in policy transfer and the opportunities and problems it can create. It reviews the burgeoning literature and considers the implications of policy transfer for the policy-making process.

Key concepts
Policy transfer; lesson drawing; coercive policy transfer; epistemic communities; policy transfer networks.

Introduction

> After Bill Clinton and Tony Blair finish with the elegant dinners and toasts at the G–8 summit this week in England, the real fun begins: the two leaders will lock themselves in a room with a clutch of top officials to talk about government policy for four or five hours. The Sunday meeting at Chequers, the Prime Minister's country mansion north of London, will be the third such bilateral seminar, following one at the White House, when Blair visited in February, and the inaugural 12-hr. "wonkathon" at Chequers in November.... On the agenda for Chequers are social security, welfare, crime, health policy and education, with eight to 10 participants from each side.... "It's a chance to examine the basic principles we have in common, to sharpen our thinking and to talk about common pitfalls," says a participant. (*Time Magazine*, 18 May, 1998)

It might well be argued that a key feature of Tony Blair's premiership has been his predilection for hosting high-level policy seminars with his centre-left counterparts from across the globe. From the well publicised 'wonkathons' with then US president Bill Clinton in the early years of his first term of office through to more recent events such as the Progressive Governance Summit (in which Blair hosted a two-day talk-in with the centre-left leaders of 13 other nations), Blair has been keen to share policy ideas with – and gather them from – other world leaders. Indeed, the official communiqué published by Downing Street at the end of the latter seminar stated that all 14 countries in attendance had "committed to learn from each other", held a collective desire "to increase the activities of our network and widen its reach in order to exchange progressive policy ideas" and that each would "'make particular efforts to draw on the policy experiences of other countries in the network" (see http://www.pm.gov.uk/output/page4146.asp).

In many ways, these statements of intent reflect yet another dimension of the process of globalisation (see Chapter Two). Indeed, the increasing prominence of global policy networks is perhaps one of the more obvious manifestations of globalisation's impact on the policy-making process. Scholars of the policy process have dubbed this sharing of policy ideas **policy transfer** – defined by Dolowitz and Marsh (1996, p 344) as the "process in which knowledge about policies, administrative arrangements, institutions etc. in one time and/or place is used in the development of policies, administrative arrangements and institutions in another time and/or place". Indeed, for Dolowitz and Marsh (2000, p 5), it is now central to both the theory and practice of policy making:

> Given that policy-makers appear to be increasingly relying upon policy transfer, it is something that anyone interested in, or studying, public policy needs to consider.

However, this process of policy transfer is not merely of the explicit, knowing and voluntaristic sort of **lesson drawing** (see Rose, 1991), typified by Blair's policy wonkathons. As we have seen in previous chapters (Chapters Two and Six in particular), another dimension of this globalisation of policy debates has been the rising prominence of supranational bodies such as the World Bank and IMF in national policy debates. While, sometimes, the intervention of such groups is welcomed by key policy makers, there are many occasions on which their relationship with national-level political actors is fraught. These groups often bring with them preconceived ideas about the principles on which policy should operate, and often tie assistance in meeting social problems to policy reform. In less powerful nations – particularly those in urgent need of aid or additional foreign investment – these transnational institutions can almost dictate the nature of policy change. In such cases, the process of disseminating ideas from one place to another is better characterised as being **coercive policy transfer**.

In short, policy transfer is a complex, multifaceted dimension of the policy process. Indeed, the above is just a small flavour of the ways in which transfer can and does take place. In this chapter, we begin to explore policy transfer by looking at the different types of transfer that have been identified by policy analysts and examining some specific instances of policy transfer in the field of welfare policy. We then move on to consider some of the problems that can arise when policy transfer occurs and the ways in which transfer is conditioned and constrained by the context within which it takes place. Finally, we examine some of the problems policy transfer poses for students of the policy process and some of the weaknesses in existing frameworks for the analysis of policy transfer.

Unpacking policy transfer

As with so many of the concepts that have become popular in policy analysis, policy transfer is a loose term that refers to a complex range of phenomena, draws on ideas from across the social sciences and is applied inconsistently. To make matters worse, many theorists also use quite different terms to refer to the phenomenon we are here calling 'policy transfer'. For Dolowitz and Marsh, this is not a particular problem; indeed, they feel it reflects strong interest in this trend across the social sciences. Their solution is to employ policy transfer as a generic, umbrella term that encompasses the many different conceptions of the process by which ideas, institutions or programmes from one time or place are used in another. As Stone (1999, p 52) points out, the list of such conceptions is an extensive one that includes: lesson drawing, policy 'bandwagoning', policy emulation, policy harmonisation, systematically pinching ideas, policy penetration, external inducement, direct coercive transfer, policy diffusion, policy convergence and cross-national policy learning.

The rich variety of terms here gives a hint of the broad nature of 'policy transfer' and the different kinds of processes that Dolowitz and Marsh's term encompasses. Rather than viewing these as competing theories, however, Dolowitz and Marsh instead view them as being different dimensions of policy transfer. Doing so has allowed them to synthesise these approaches into a single framework for the analysis of policy transfer – the so-called **Dolowitz and Marsh model** (Dolowitz and Marsh, 1996, 2000; Dolowitz, 2000). That they have been able to do so reflects the fact that, as Evans and Davies (1999, p 364) point out, these conceptions are "sustained metaphors" rather than fully-fledged theories, which some regard as being problematic and indicative of the 'flabbiness' of the approach as a whole. We will consider such criticisms in due course. First, however, we need to examine the specifics of the Dolowitz and Marsh model and we will do this by exploring each of the key questions that are at the heart of their framework (**Box 10.1**).

Box 10.1: The Dolowitz and Marsh model

The most influential framework for the analysis of policy transfer is the Dolowitz and Marsh model. It centres round the analysis of six key questions (see Dolowitz and Marsh, 2000, p 8):

- Why are organisations/individuals engaging in policy transfer?
- Who is involved in the policy transfer process?
- What is being transferred in this process?
- Where are policies/programmes being transferred from?
- How complete is the transfer?
- What are the barriers to transfer? (With the addition of a 'supplementary' seventh question: Was transfer a success/failure?)

Why engage in policy transfer?

We have already hinted at a number of reasons why policy makers might look to engage in policy transfer. Dolowitz and Marsh suggest that these reasons can be grouped under three headings: voluntary transfer, coercive transfer or a mixture of the two.

At the voluntary end of the scale we have the kind of **lesson drawing** that members of the Progressive Governance Network aim to be involved in: the sharing of ideas about best practice in tackling key policy problems. Politicians often engage in this kind of activity, not least because it can provide a quick route for generating new ideas. In addition, the fact that a policy has been seen to be successful in one country can often give the attempt to implement it in another some additional legitimacy. So, when outlining plans for the introduction of new welfare-to-work policies, Blair made much of the fact that Britain would draw lessons on 'what works' from US experience in this field (see Theodore and Peck, 2000; Peck and Theodore, 2001). In its pure form, voluntary lesson drawing has the potential, therefore, to boost the rationality of the policy-making process, allowing decision makers to consider a wider range of policy options and a broader base of evidence about their impact.

However, this kind of rational approach is far less common than one might imagine, because when policy makers draw lessons they usually do so without considering the full range of policies from which they might learn, or, as Dolowitz and Marsh put it, their actions display bounded rationality rather than perfect rationality. They do so for many reasons, and not simply because their time to conduct a search tends to be limited. In particular, they are limited by external factors. So, choices might have to be restricted to those that are compatible with the dominant orthodoxy (it would be difficult, for instance, to adopt economic policies based on ideas that key financial institutions regard as outdated) or that are acceptable to the international political community. Similarly, choices could be constrained by existing obligations (for example, few countries could adopt US-style nuclear weapons policies because doing so would break treaties they have signed) or because of the need to placate powerful groups within society (for instance, foreign investors may threaten to relocate if higher taxes or labour market restrictions are introduced). In cases such as these, where the search for policy ideas is constrained in some way or another, Dolowitz and Marsh label the transfer as a mixture of voluntary and coercive elements.

Finally, we have transfer as the direct imposition of policy: *coercive* policy transfer. This kind of transfer is more commonly found in developing countries, where external organisations such as the IMF, World Bank, UN or foreign governments or investors use their economic power to impose preferred policies on nations in return for financial or practical assistance (**Box 10.2**). As this indicates, policy transfer is not just about the 'rational' search for ideas – it is also about power too.

Who is involved?

The fact that power is central to the nature of transfer processes means it is important to raise the question of who is involved in it. We can distinguish three broad groupings: insiders, outsiders and global players.

Insiders

First, and most obviously, transfer can involve those on the inside of a nation's political system – **politicians**, **civil servants** or **party officials**. Evans (1999b) describes such an instance in the case of policies for tackling social security fraud. Prompted by concerns among key politicians about the level of fraud[1] and in response to criticisms from the National Audit Office of an approach that was based on detecting fraud rather than preventing it, officials within the (then) Department of Social Security undertook a review of alternative options. Under pressure to produce workable alternatives in a short period of time – just three months – and because of limited expertise in the department itself, this review took the form of a systematic search for ideas that could be transferred from elsewhere. The outcome of this process was a set of new

---

[1] More properly, this should be fraud *and error*. Although contemporary political discourse foregrounds the problem of 'fraud' in social security systems, many overpayments are in fact the result of error on the part of claimants (or, indeed, bureaucrats). The distinction is important for the presentation of losses to the exchequer due to fraud *and* error merely as the result of fraud both erroneously categorises innocent mistakes as criminal activity and overemphasises the extent of the problem of fraud. Policy makers may, of course, find it useful to perpetuate this misunderstanding in order to justify punitive anti-fraud measures. (For more on how discourse helps set the policy agenda, see Chapter Six of this book.)

Box 10.2: Coercive policy transfer: the Costa Rican welfare state

Costa Rica stands out from its Central American neighbours because of its long democratic tradition (dating back to 1889), its pacifist orientations (it abolished its army in 1948) and, above all, its relatively generous and comprehensive welfare state (it has the highest level of Public and Social Expenditure in Latin America). Given all this, by the mid-1970s, many classified Costa Rica as social democratic.

However, where Costa Rica departed from its European counterparts such as Sweden or Denmark was in the strength of its economy. A developing country, with a strong reliance on traditional industries such as coffee and bananas, it was hit hard by a dramatic collapse in coffee prices in the late 1970s. At the same time, its attempts to diversify the economy by boosting industrial activity were hit by huge increases in the price of fuel following the oil crisis and, at the same time, the revolution in neighbouring Nicaragua destabilised the region and, in so doing, damaged key export markets. As a consequence of these external shocks, unemployment doubled, inflation rocketed to 90% and real incomes almost halved.

Facing a near economic meltdown, the Costa Rican government were left with few options and looked to the IMF for financial aid who, in 1981, agreed to lend Costa Rica US$300 million in return for neo-liberal reforms, including the reduction of spending on key elements of welfare policy. When the Costa Rican government began to implement these reforms there was a huge backlash from the public and the president halted the reform programme.

In response to this, the IMF withheld additional payments from the loan agreement and refused to renegotiate the terms of the loan. The Costa Ricans were left with little option but to continue down the neo-liberal reform path, particularly as other sources of aid, most notably the US Agency for International Development (USAID), were only prepared to offer loans or grants if requests for reform were met. Consequently, some key programmes were reduced in scope and public spending dropped during the course of the 1980s. In short, new policies – particularly welfare policies – were coercively transferred from nations such as the US and UK with a neo-liberal bias. This transfer fundamentally impacted on the nature of welfare in the nation; as Wilson argues, "the social democratic model ... if not dead, is at least muted".

However, a note of caution needs to be added to this analysis. While organisations such as the IMF and USAID were certainly at the heart of this change, there were those within Costa Rica who felt such a change was needed in any event; indeed, one of the key political parties blamed much of the 1970s crisis on economic mismanagement and heavy-handed state intervention. Indeed, Wilson (1998) argues that internal forces were key in determining changes.

Sources: Wilson (1998); Biesanz (1999)

policies for fraud prevention that drew on techniques used in the US and Australia and in private sector organisations in the UK that were incorporated into the government's Green Paper on fraud.

Evans' example focuses on a quite specific and fairly technical policy field. However, transfer might also deal with much bigger themes or ideas, particularly when parties or politicians are involved rather than bureaucrats. Peck and Theodore (2001), for example, argue that New Labour drew many key ideas and arguments about welfare reform from Clinton's New Democrats – claims echoed by Deacon (2000) – and suggest that this process was facilitated by explicit links between the two parties. Indeed, they argue (Peck and Theodore, 2001, p 429) that the links between the two parties have been crucial to 'Third Way policy development', which they describe as being "based on a substantially narrow form of 'fast policy transfer' between policy elites". Pierson and Castles (2002) point to the importance of similar links between the UK and Australian Labo(u)r parties in the development of the Third Way, Pierson (2003) highlighting the influence of Australian policies for the funding of higher education on New Labour's introduction of tuition fees for university students. The quality and intensity of links between parties can, of course, be increased when key politicians within them share key ideas and beliefs too; so, Theodore and Peck (2000) highlight the importance of the personal relationships between Reagan and Thatcher and between Clinton and Blair in facilitating policy transfer between the US and UK.

Outsiders

A second group of actors who can be agents of policy transfer are non-governmental organisations (NGOs), such as **think tanks**, **pressure groups** and **corporations**, although Stone – who has written at length about the role of think tanks in policy transfer (see Stone, 2000, 2001) – feels "the non-governmental mode of policy transfer is a relatively neglected dimension" in the literature (2000, p 45). She describes think tank activity as being globalised and writes of think tanks being connected to each other as if part of a "global 'invisible college'" (2000, p 45). The search for new ideas, of course, is the *raison d'etre* of think tanks and given their small size, limited resources and the often tight timescales they work to, it seems natural that think tanks will share ideas with each other and regularly look abroad for innovative policy solutions. Pierson (2003), for example, argues that the Institute for Public Policy Research (IPPR) influenced New Labour's decision to adopt welfare-to-work policies by highlighting the positive dimensions of Australia's Jobs, Employment and Training programme (JET) in their *Commission on social justice* (IPPR, 1994). While he concedes that "the influence of the Commission's report upon Labour in power was more limited than some had expected", he argues that "it was real" (Pierson, 2003, p 88). Tracing the subsequent impact of the report on welfare-to-work, he argues (2003, p 88) that:

> JET re-appears in the 'Road to the Manifesto', the series of documents that foreshadowed the commitments Labour would make in the 1997 general election. By this stage, welfare-to-work was at the forefront of Labour's welfare policy. The strategy paper *Getting Welfare to Work* anticipates a transformed benefit system 'developing on a wider scale the lessons learned from the JET scheme in Australia, and personalising the services available to clients'. JET headed the party's list of 'world's best practice'.

In short, he believes the IPPR played a crucial role in transferring a key welfare policy from Australia to the UK.

Although they are often described as independent policy institutes (see Stone, 2000), think tanks are reliant on others for the funding needed to carry out their activities. For many, this means a reliance on corporate donors and, certainly, this is one indirect way in which corporations may also act as agents of policy transfer. Few suggest that think tanks tailor their arguments to suit their donors – although Barnett (2002) expressed concerns about 'cash for access' – but corporations sponsoring research programmes are clearly more likely to send delegates to research seminars organised by think tanks, build links with those undertaking research and, so, see their ideas published in reports emerging from those programmes. A good example here comes in policies surrounding the use and regulation of digital technologies by government (see Chapter Five). Most of the key think tanks with links to the Blair government have well-established programmes examining these issues (see Hudson, 2002) and, unsurprisingly, corporations who have a business interest in this policy area primarily sponsor these programmes. So, for instance: the IPPR's 'digital society' team receive funding from information and communication technology (ICT) corporations with a stake in e-government such as BT, Hewlett Packard, Microsoft and SchlumbergerSema; Demos' work on the information society has been sponsored by similar corporations, such as EDS and O_2; and the Work Foundation's i-Society programme has been sponsored by Microsoft and PricewaterhouseCoopers. Significantly, many of these corporations also have their own in-house policy teams that publish reports on best practice and innovative techniques for the use of ICTs in government; BT has a well-funded programme called BT Stepchange, and IBM has an Institute of Electronic Government. Similarly, many consulting organisations undertake annual surveys of best practice and innovate application in this field, too. The work of these institutes clearly has an impact in terms of spreading ideas around the globe (for examples of their work, see BT, 2000;

IBM, 2002; Accenture, 2003), particularly if the corporations play a role in helping to manage the introduction or delivery of change.

Coming from the other end of the political spectrum, pressure groups can play the same role as corporations in the process of transfer. They too sponsor think-tank activity (indeed, the Communication Workers' Union sponsor the IPPR's Digital Society programme) and employ in-house researchers to produce reports on key issues. While often lacking the resources of corporations, their perceived independence and lack of profit motive can give them an edge which corporations lack. An excellent example here comes in the case of the *Brent Spar* oil storage platform (see Jordan, 1998; Huxham and Sumner, 1999). The event – described by Lord Melchett of Greenpeace as "a defining moment for the environmental movement" (quoted in Jordan, 1998, p 713) – took place in 1995 and involved a battle between Greenpeace and Shell UK over whether a massive, redundant, oil rig should be dismantled and disposed of in the North Atlantic or, at much greater cost, transported to dry land for dismantling. Shell, having undertaken extensive, scientifically rooted environmental impact analyses, had been granted permission by the UK government to dispose of the installation in British waters. However, Greenpeace staged an occupation of the *Brent Spar* and argued disposal could cause significant environmental damage. They argued that the UK government should adopt the Precautionary Principle[2] that formed the centrepiece of German environmental policy and force Shell to dismantle the rig on dry land because we could not be sure of the environmental consequences of the proposed action. Their campaign gathered significant momentum, with UK voters overwhelmingly against Shell's action and, crucially, citizens in neighbouring countries expressing disquiet too (indeed, in Germany consumers began to boycott Shell garages). This grassroots campaign soon escalated and the issue became a major diplomatic one as other European leaders pressed the then British Prime Minister, John Major, to bring UK policy in line with that of the majority of EU nations by requiring Shell to dismantle the rig on land. Indeed, Chancellor Kohl of Germany revealed to a G7 press conference:

> We told Mr Major it was not the looniness of a few greens, but a Europe-wide, worldwide trend for the protection of the seas. (Quoted in Jordan, 1998, p 624)

In the face of such pressure, the UK government and Shell UK backed down, in "the most public and controversial U-turn in the history of environmental campaigning", according to Huxham and Sumner (1999, p 349). Moreover, this was more than a one-off victory, for it produced a commitment from the

---

[2] Huxham and Sumner (1999, p 353): "The Precautionary Principle arose out of the *Vorsorgeprinzip* (*vorsorge* = foresight, or taking care)".

UK government to refuse all future applications for offshore disposal (Huxham and Sumner, 1999, p 349). In short, by deploying effective campaigning techniques and exploiting public opinion, Greenpeace were able to transfer environmental protection standards from Germany to the UK.

Global players

This example also brings us to our third and final set of agents of transfer, global players: **supranational governmental and non-governmental organisations (NGOs)**; and **policy entrepreneurs, experts** and **consultants**. One of the big problems for think tanks or pressure groups looking to transfer policies is that, ultimately, "to see policy transfer occur, these organisations are dependent on formal political actors" (Stone, 2000, p 66). In the *Brent Spar* case, Greenpeace were clearly assisted by the actions of political leaders such as Chancellor Kohl, who used the meetings of supranational governmental institutions such as the G7 to place pressure on Britain to adopt the proposed policy. We have discussed too (**Box 8.1**) the role of organisations such as the IMF in transferring social and economic policies between nations and, in Chapter Two, the role of the World Health Organisation (WHO) in transferring public health policies between nations in order to tackle global diseases such as SARS or AIDS. We will not dwell too much, then, on the role of supranational governmental organisations and NGOs per se. However, it is worth briefly considering an example of the WHO's work to illustrate the role played by policy experts – in this case medical experts – in policy transfer.

In order to meet its objective of promoting the highest possible standards of health for all peoples (www.who.int), one of the WHO's key roles is to persuade nations to adopt best practice in terms of health care policies. However, determining 'best practice' is a far from straightforward issue and one that needs to be backed by credible, reliable and objective evidence, particularly if nations are to be persuaded to adopt policies that carry direct costs to them or challenge deeply embedded beliefs or behaviours. Even in scientific areas of policy, such as medicine, there can rarely be one 'correct' policy, particularly given the radically varying conditions in which medical services across the globe operate. So, much like policy elsewhere, best practice emerges through debate within policy networks. Crucially, however, in such technical fields, the existence of international **epistemic communities** (Adler and Haas, 1992) – professional, knowledge based networks – adds an extra layer to the policy process and can assist in the policy transfer process.

To illustrate this, we can consider the WHO's efforts to transfer best practice for dealing with sexually transmitted infections (STIs) in poor countries (Lush et al, 2003). Research has documented for many years the higher rates of STIs in developing countries that, in part, are a consequence of underfunded health care systems that lack the resources for laboratory tests for detecting and verifying infections in individuals. In order to overcome some of these limitations, experts working in sub-Saharan Africa in the late 1970s developed so-called 'syndromic management' tools; that is, algorithmic-informed flow charts to help with the identification and treatment of STIs based on symptoms presented by patients. Yet, despite their effectiveness, and the persistently high STI rates, these tools were not adopted on a widespread basis. Part of the problem was, as Lush et al (2003, p 21) suggest, that "in 1990 the policy community concerned about the high prevalence of STIs was still relatively small".

However, with global concern about the rise of HIV/AIDS, funding for organisations such as the WHO and UNAIDS began to increase and both took a keen interest in syndromic management tools. The breakthrough, however, came following the completion by medical researchers and epidemiologists of two random controlled trials (one in Uganda, the other in Tanzania) which demonstrated that the use of syndromic management tools could, by reducing the prevalence of STIs generally, combat the transmission of HIV. This objective, scientific evidence produced by the (global) scientific community persuaded western organisations such as the World Bank, USAID and the UK's Department for International Development to put their weight behind the technique and assisted greatly in the WHO's dissemination of it.

This case study demonstrates very well the role policy transfer can play in policy change. A problem – high STI rates – had existed for some time, as had a policy for improving the situation. The escalation of this problem from a regional one to a global one following the outbreak of HIV/AIDS put the issue onto the agenda of key agents of policy transfer and increased the amount of resources available to address the problem. However, in order to act on the problem, these agents needed objective, reliable evidence from an epistemic community in order to determine best practice. In this case, that community was the international scientific community concerned with medicine and public health and the evidence was gathered to their agreed scientific standards and published and debated in their scientific journals. In short, this international epistemic community acted as a de facto policy transfer network[3].

What is being transferred and how complete is the transfer?

These examples illustrate the huge range of groups that can be involved in the process of policy transfer. At the same time, however, they also show that the substance of the transfer itself can vary widely too. Indeed, Dolowitz and

---

[3] Similar roles can be played by policy experts acting on an individual level (see O'Neil, 2000; and Greener, 2002, on their role in the 1990 NHS reforms in the UK) or by consultants operating on behalf of NGOs (see Dolowitz and Marsh, 2000; or, for a more personal account, Stubbs, 2002).

Marsh (2000, p 12) suggest that "almost anything can be transferred from one political system to another", although they feel it is "important to distinguish between policies, which are seen as broader statements of intention and which generally denote the direction policy-makers wish to take, and programs, which are the specific means of the course of action used to implement policies".

By distinguishing between the transfer of policies and programmes, Dolowitz and Marsh are, in a sense, arguing that transfer activities can be differentiated according to the degree of specificity they possess. At one end, we have relatively general statements of intent: Dolowitz and Marsh highlight **ideologies, ideas and attitudes** and **policy goals**, for example. So, for instance, we discussed earlier claims by Theodore and Peck (2000) and Deacon (2000) that US thinking on welfare-to-work was central to New Labour's policies in this field. While Deacon points to key differences in the nature of the programmes developed in the two nations and to the fact that New Labour drew lessons from nations other than the US too, he is clear in his belief (2000, p 6) that "one of the most striking features of the current debate about welfare reform is the extent to which it has been influenced by ideas and developments in the United States", and highlights in particular that "the language in which these policies are presented and justified has drawn heavily upon that of US politicians and commentators". Indeed, he feels that the transfer of the US discourse by New Labour has resulted in the "Americanisation of the British welfare debate" that has shifted the party's thinking "from the problem of inequality to the problem of dependency" (Deacon, 2000, p 15). In short, it is this transfer of ideologies and attitudes rather than specific programmes that is of most importance to Deacon.

Moving towards a greater level of specificity, Dolowitz and Marsh (2000) suggest that **policy content, policy instruments, policy programmes** and **institutions** can be the subject of transfer too. Dolowitz (1997) himself provides one of the best examples here in his study of the Thatcher government's welfare reforms. Once again the analysis points to the key role US thinking has played in shaping policy in this field[4], Dolowitz suggesting that many of the major aspects of Thatcher's reforms were inspired by the American experience. However, in this instance the influence can clearly be seen in specific programmes and institutions, most notably the introduction of 'job clubs'. Designed to assist those seeking work by boosting motivation and

---

[4] In a more general review of the process of policy transfer, Dolowitz et al (1999) tackle the issue of why the UK borrows so often from the US and why transfer tends to be one way. They argue (1999, p 730) "two factors particularly facilitate transfer between the US and the UK in either direction: the shared language and the shared contemporary commitment to neo-liberalism ... there are two reasons why most of the transfers are US to UK ... the US's role in world affairs, which gives it a sense of superiority making it unlikely to acknowledge that another political system can offer policy models, while the UK sees its models as appropriate in the economic and labour market fields because they are underpinned by the neo-liberal ideology associated with US hegemony".

confidence, improving job search and interview techniques and by providing basic resources for conducting a job search such as writing materials and envelopes, the British 'job clubs' followed almost precisely the American model, from their common name through to their core activities and their requirement of compulsory attendance for four half-days per week. As Dolowitz (1997, p 35) suggests, the transfer of this dimension of policy was highly specific, for "the design, organisation, functions and even the name of British job clubs was transferred from the United States". Indeed, he believes "the transfer was so complete that this is one of the few examples of a government's copying the structure of another system into its own" (1997, p 35).

Aside from the job clubs, Dolowitz also argues that workfare restart programmes for the long-term unemployed and Training and Enterprise Councils (TECs) were transferred from US welfare policy during this period (see Dolowitz, 1997, for details). Significantly, the latter offers an example of another form of policy transfer, that of **negative lesson drawing**. Training and Enterprise Councils, which aimed to draw in private sector expertise in order to boost skill levels in the labour market, were modelled on US Private Industry Councils (PICs). However, the PICs were beset with problems, not least because of their poor accountability and often under-qualified staff. In their plans for the creation of TECs, the Thatcher government tried to overcome these problems and, because of this, Dolowitz (1997, p 37) argues that "this case shows that policymakers can also learn what not to do".

In selectively drawing lessons, however, what both the New Labour and Conservative welfare reform plans show is that the extent of policy transfer can vary too. Indeed, Dolowitz (2000b, p 25) argues that "policy transfer is not an all-or-nothing process". He suggests there are **four degrees of transfer**:

> **copying**, which involves direct and complete transfer; **emulation**, which involves transfer of the ideas behind, but not the details of, the policy programme; **combinations**, which involve mixtures of different policies or programmes; and **inspiration**, where policy in another jurisdiction may inspire a policy change, but where the final outcome bears relatively little relationship or similarity to the original. (Dolowitz, 2000b, p 25; emphases added).

What are the barriers to transfer and how successful was it?

In practice, even a fairly direct attempt at copying a policy may ultimately produce a very different set of policy outcomes to those found in the originating country for the simple reason that no two countries are the same. Indeed, Dolowitz and Marsh (2000) highlight a wide range of barriers to transfer. They point to the problem of **policy complexity** – so, for instance, what may seem like straightforward lessons on the effectiveness of a policy may belie what is, in truth, the complex outcome of a series of interconnected factors. One of the causes of this complexity is **past policies** which, inevitably, interact with the policy being transferred and mean that the country in which the policy is being received has a slightly different set of problems to be resolved than those found in the nation from where the policy is being transferred. Similarly, differing **institutional and structural** settings can be an issue, be this in terms of culture, ideology, bureaucratic practices, technological capabilities or economic wealth. Each nation has differing policy capabilities based upon these factors and faces different policy networks that may well have different values and beliefs. **Language** too can be a barrier to transfer if it prevents a true understanding of the original policy.

Given the existence of these barriers, policy transfer can be a process fraught with difficulties. Indeed, many transfers do go wrong and Dolowitz and Marsh (2000, p 17) admit that "while most studies of policy transfer concentrate upon success there is a need to acknowledge that not all transfer is successful", and suggest that "it is important to examine why some transfer is unsuccessful". They argue that failed transfers can be bracketed under three headings: **uninformed transfer**; **incomplete transfer**; and **inappropriate transfer**. Uninformed transfer occurs when the country drawing lessons has very limited knowledge of the policy they are borrowing and its operation in practice. Incomplete transfer occurs when key parts of the successful policy are not transferred. Inappropriate transfer occurs when too little attention is paid to the differing contexts of the nation from which the policy is being transferred and that which is receiving the policy.

Dolowitz (2000c; see also Dolowitz and Marsh, 2000; Dolowitz, 2001) illustrates these issues with the example of the UK's Child Support Agency (CSA). The CSA, introduced in 1993, aimed to cut back welfare spending by tracking down absent parents (particularly fathers) and compelling them to pay maintenance – calculated by a preset formula – to the parent caring for their child(ren). It presented a significant departure from the status quo in that it replaced the role of the courts in determining maintenance on a case-by-case basis and by introducing a high degree of compulsion in its attempts to reduce state expenditure on lone parents by forcing absent parents to contribute a set proportion of their income to the CSA for transfer to the caring parent[5]. The agency is commonly viewed as a classic example of a policy failure as it was dogged by high profile implementation problems and provoked outrage from parents who felt its heavy-handed approach was unjust. While many have written about the causes of these problems, Dolowitz believes that policy transfer can help explain much of what went wrong, for:

---

[5] Compulsion also existed for the lone parents too who were required to provide information on the identity and whereabouts of the absent parent.

the origins of the agency are to be found in policy transfer from the United States and, to a lesser extent, Australia; and that inappropriate transfer from the US led to important implementation problems. (Dolowitz, 2000c, p 39)

Central parts of the policy were, Dolowitz argues, drawn from the US Child Support Enforcement System (CSES), in particular, the elements of compulsion, the use of a preset formula to determine contributions and, above all, the goal of making absent parents pay. Given the apparent success of the approach in both the US and Australia and the way in which it could dovetail neatly with the then Conservative government's ideology, transfer seemed like an obvious option. However, Dolowitz suggests that the botched policy outcome can be explained with reference to the three types of transfer failure outlined earlier. First, it was an uninformed transfer, for the government had insufficient knowledge of how the CSES operated. The functioning of the CSES varied from state-to-state, but the UK government's attention focused primarily on its operation in Wisconsin. This skewed their understanding of the CSES and, in particular, the way in which it worked alongside, rather than replaced, the courts, for Wisconsin was unusual in eliminating the judiciary from the picture. Second, the transfer was partial for, as suggested earlier, the CSES was only part of the picture in most of the US. Failing to properly understand the package of policies in place in the US meant the CSA operated in a way that only partially reflected the practices of the CSES. Finally, he suggests the transfer was inappropriate as it failed to account for the differing circumstances of the two nations. For one, they have historically quite different welfare traditions – the elements of compulsion and control that characterised the CSA are far more in keeping with the US welfare system than the UK's system. They also had differing economic circumstances at the time too. In particular, Dolowitz argues that the need to reduce Britain's huge Public Sector Borrowing Requirement (PSBR) coloured the introduction of the CSA because it became a vehicle for reducing government expenditure at the macro-level rather than managing family policy at the micro-level[6].

Where does the transferred policy originate from?

In analysing an instance of failed policy transfer, the need to be sensitive to the context within which a policy operates (and, if transferred, will operate) is made clear. In other words, it is vital that those engaged in transfer consider

---

[6] So, for instance, the CSA focused its attention on soft targets that they could easily get money from rather than those who resolutely refused to support their families, something that merely served to heighten the sense of injustice many affected by the CSA felt.

the match between the host and receiving nation; and, for policy analysts, asking 'Where does the transfer originate from?' is, therefore, a key question too – and the final of the six questions which make up the Dolowitz and Marsh model. For the most part, we have assumed in this discussion that transfer occurs between countries, meaning the key factors to which we must be sensitive are those surrounding the cultural, institutional or economic differences between nations. However, Dolowitz and Marsh make it clear that transfer can originate from many different places. In addition to **cross-national transfer**, they argue that transfer can occur **within governments** – so policies might be transferred from one local authority or state government to another for example – and that policies can be transferred from the **past** (see later in this chapter).

Evaluating the Dolowitz and Marsh model

By organising the analysis of policy transfer around the key questions we have just explored, the Dolowitz and Marsh model demonstrates the central role that policy transfer can play in policy change and deepens our understanding of how the process operates and who and what it involves. Moreover, its comprehensive nature – highlighting different dimensions of transfer rather than emphasising one or the other – allows the work of others to be slipped into the framework with ease (indeed, we have drawn on the work of many theorists other than Dolowitz and Marsh in illustrating their model here). However, their framework is not without its critics. Indeed, Evans and Davies (1999, p 365) feel that "although Dolowitz and Marsh have done a great service in organising a fragmented literature into a coherent whole … problems remain".

In trying to offer a comprehensive framework of the process of policy transfer that incorporates so many different types of transfer, which could include almost anything from civil service driven direct copying of a programme from one country to another right through to broad policy ideas being partially inspired by pressure group activity sometime in the past, there is a danger that the credibility of the concept is being stretched a little too far. Indeed, in reading some of the work produced by Dolowitz and Marsh it can be difficult to see where they believe a policy exists that has not been produced as a consequence of policy transfer. As Evans and Davies (1999, p 366) point out, the boundaries surrounding when policy transfer begins and ends need to be drawn more clearly than is the case in the Dolowitz and Marsh model, for "even policy innovations will be bound to rely on prior knowledge to some degree".

This in turn hints at a methodological problem in much of the policy transfer literature. When a broad conceptualisation of transfer exists, proving whether or not transfer has occurred can be problematic. Evans and Davies (1999, p

381) argue that "the existing literature does not provide adequate techniques for demonstrating policy transfer", a claim which we support. Often the approach relies on finding commonalities in the language used by policy makers in different nations or hints in parliamentary debates or interviews that other systems have been considered in drawing up a policy. So, for instance, Dolowitz (1997) claims that the Thatcher government's decision to withdraw benefit from 16- and 17-year-olds was a Beveridge-inspired transfer from the past. He justifies this on the basis that the then Secretary of State for Social Services, John Moore, argued in parliament:

> I have no doubt that our proposals would also be supported by Beveridge if he were alive today. Beveridge wrote that 'for boys and girls there should ideally be no unconditional benefit: their enforced abstention from work should be made an occasion for further training'. (Quoted in Dolowitz, 1997, p 37)

There are many explanations that one might offer for this policy decision: Thatcher's ideological commitment to rolling back the state; the budgetary pressures placed on the government by rising unemployment; the collapse of Keynesianism, to name but a few. One of the least plausible that can be imagined is to ascribe the change to a policy transfer from the past on the basis of Moore's statement, for his speech can and should only be interpreted in one way: a cheeky attempt by a neo-liberal minister to score points against left-wing opponents by using the words of one of their icons against them.

Weaknesses in the evidence used to support claims of transfer are not confined to this case (see **Box 10.3** for another example) and many of the instances cited in this chapter can be critiqued on such grounds. As Evans and Davies (1999, p 382) point out, much of this weakness stems from the failure to ask 'Is there evidence of non-transfer?' – are there alternative explanations for the apparent similarities? Indeed, they argue that, if policy transfer is to be theoretically credible, then rather than seeking to offer an all-embracing framework it must instead "seek to identify and classify remarkable phenomena not otherwise explained" (Evans and Davies, 1999, p 367). They suggest that, in practical terms, this means focusing upon transnational policy transfers and, crucially, "that which takes place consciously and results in policy action" (1999, p 368). This is a much narrower, action-based conception of policy transfer that distinguishes between the unintentional emergence of similar policies – convergence produced by, say, similar responses to similar pressures – and a knowing transfer of policy from one place to another.

In advocating a pared down conception of policy transfer, Evans and Davies also allow us to determine more clearly whether or not transfer has existed. In large part, this is because they place **agents of transfer** at the heart of the model; that is, people who have been involved in the intentional transfer of

Box 10.3: Proving transfer: sources of evidence

Dolowitz (2000b) suggests that the following sources can be trawled for evidence of transfer:

- media
- Internet
- reports and studies
- meetings and visits
- government statements

In practice, those looking to prove transfer tend to piece together a case by using these sources to find: similarities in policy debates and detail between countries; hints or suggestions from politicians that another country's arrangements have been drawn upon; and, evidence of connections (through meetings, visits, secondments) between policy makers in the two countries.

Sometimes, however, the evidence can look a little thin, even in cases where there are clearly strong connections between policies in two nations. In putting together a narrative about policy transfer in the case of the CSA for example, Dolowitz (2000c) places a great emphasis on the similarity of language used in US and UK debates. However, as Pollitt (2001) points out, commonalities in language or rhetoric rarely correlate with common policies, with the borrowing extending no further than the use of the most fashionable buzzwords. Dolowitz also uses quotations from an article in the men's lifestyle magazine *Esquire* to bolster his case, but huge question marks can be placed over the credibility of such sources written, as they are, for the purposes of entertainment without the processes of review or standards of proof required by writing in academic journals or news media.

ideas from one place to another. Proving transfer, they argue, requires the identification of these agents and the exploration of their **intentional** actions. (As we saw earlier, Evans, 1999, proves transfer in the field of social security fraud by identifying specific agents within the civil service and documenting their activities.) However, while many have proclaimed a huge rise in the incidence of policy transfer, applying stricter criteria along these lines means that "proof of policy transfer may be more difficult than is commonly assumed" (Evans and Davies, 1999, p 381).

The Evans and Davies model

None of this is to deny that important changes in the way policy is made are occurring or that instances of policy convergence may in part be linked to the cross-national sharing of ideas. It is, rather, a claim that we need to look beyond simple explanations of policy change and, more specifically, to locate policy transfer in a broader framework that acknowledges the importance of other factors in driving policy change. Arguing along such lines, Evans and Davies (1999) offer a multi-level approach to the analysis of policy transfer: one that emphasises the meso-level nature of the concept of policy transfer and explores its links with macro-level changes and micro-level politics.

First, and building on their claim that we must look for specific agents of transfer, they suggest that transfer involves the establishment of inter-organisational **transfer networks** and that understanding the operation of these networks is vital for understanding the process of policy transfer. Here they draw links with notions of policy networks (see Chapter Eight) and epistemic communities, but argue that policy transfer networks differ from either of these in that they are ephemeral, "ad hoc phenomenon set up with the specific intention of engineering policy change" and so, ordinarily, "they exist only for the time that a transfer is occurring" (Evans and Davies, 1999, p 376). They argue that "by implication, policy transfer networks matter because without them other policies might be adopted" (1999, p 376). In other words, it is within these networks that we find the purposive, intentional actions of transfer agents, for individuals within the networks perform the search for ideas, make the key decisions about which policies might be suitable for transfer and so on. Tracing the actions of such networks, therefore, is useful not only for proving that transfer has occurred, but can tell us much about the nature of transfer too by establishing who is involved in the network and why.

Crucially, these networks do not act in isolation from their environment, and Evans and Davies stress the importance of understanding the links between these **meso-level transfer networks** and the broad macro-level contexts within which they operate. In particular, they are keen to link policy transfer with the kind of phenomena we examined in Part One of this book: globalisation, technological change, economic change, and the emergence of a competition state. It matters, they argue, why networks have been established, for often transfer is initiated in response to macro-level changes or pressures: to find solutions to new problems caused by globalisation, to explore how other nations are exploiting new technologies or in response to poor economic performance because of the improved running of competing economies. Failure to examine such links between the macro- and meso-levels can result in a skewed analysis that places too much emphasis on policy transfer in driving policy change and too little on the broader forces underpinning or driving this change. Again, however, this is not to understate the importance of policy transfer, for the linkages between meso and macro can operate the other way around too. Indeed, Evans and Davies are keen to stress the role transfer has played in the process of globalisation, not least through the creation of new 'opportunity structures' that hasten and facilitate the spread of ideas.

To put it another way, they believe that there is a continual, iterative relationship between policy transfer networks and the context within which they operate. While transfer can produce policy changes that impact on broad macro-level contexts, those macro-level contexts can equally force policy changes that transfer networks bring into being. Here, there is something of a common theme connecting the latest debates about policy transfer with those about the other meso-level notions examined in this book such as institutions or policy networks. Evans and Davies stress the importance of viewing transfer as a 'theoretical bridge' that allows us to understand the links between individual action and broad macro-level changes. To underline this they argue that policy transfer analysis needs to be rooted in a **structuration approach** (Giddens, 1984; Wendt, 1987; see also Chapters Seven to Nine of this book) that "conceptualizes agents and structures as mutually constitutive yet ontologically distinct entities. Each is an effect of the other. They are 'co-determined'" (Evans and Davies, 1999, p 371).

Conclusions

Here, we have only been able to offer a brief overview of the emerging arguments about what constitutes policy transfer, when it occurs, how it occurs, why it occurs and how it ought to be analysed. We have shown that while there is broad agreement that transfer is an important process on the increase, there are disagreements about what precisely constitutes transfer and when we can be sure it has occurred.

However, while there are undoubtedly some weaknesses in the approach as it stands, a focus on policy transfer certainly has some merits. Not least, it demonstrates the importance of adopting a more global approach to the practice of policy analysis (see Parsons, 1995) and emphasises the plurality of actors that can become involved in the policy-making process, albeit in often subtle or indirect ways. Moreover, the approach has a real strength in terms of offering an explanation of **policy change** rather than policy stability (Greener, 2002), a characteristic that marks it apart from the other meso-level approaches considered in this text.

However, we agree with Evans and Davies that caution needs to be applied when analysing potential instances of transfer and that the term ought to be used to refer to purposive, deliberative action in which the actions of individuals – through transfer networks – lead to identifiable instances of lesson drawing or coercive transfer. Moreover, their claims that the approach needs to be located in a context that acknowledges the relationship between transfer networks and the broader macro-level context in which they operate is one we endorse too, for there is a very real danger of ascribing too much weight to policy transfer in cases of policy change if such contexts are ignored.

Indeed, as key exponents of the approach, even Dolowitz and Marsh (2000, p 21) agree it has limits, for they do not claim that "policy transfer is the sole explanation of any, let alone most, policy development". Instead, their view is that "an increasing amount of policy development, and particularly policy change, in contemporary polities is affected by policy transfer" (2000, p 21). It seems sensible to conclude then, as they do, that "As such, when we are analyzing policy change we always need to ask the question: Is policy transfer involved?", so long as we avoid jumping to premature conclusions about the extent of policy transfer by coupling this with the proviso from Evans and Davies (1999, p 382): to also ask "Is there evidence of non-transfer?"

Summary

- Policy transfer is the "process in which knowledge about policies, administrative arrangements, institutions etc. in one time and/or place is used in the development of policies, administrative arrangements and institutions in another time and/or place" (Dolowitz and Marsh, 1996, p 344).
- There is general agreement that policy transfer is on the increase and that policy makers regularly draw lessons from abroad.
- Policy transfer is not always a voluntary activity – transfer is often coercive in nature.
- Policy transfer can involve a wide range of political actors. Those outside of government can play an important role in the process and epistemic communities are often influential.
- There is disagreement about what constitutes transfer. Evans and Davies (1999) suggest it is best viewed as purposive, intentional action that involves ephemeral transfer networks.
- Policy transfer needs to placed in a framework that acknowledges its relationship with macro- and micro-level forces. A structuration approach can help achieve this.

Questions for discussion

- Why has the extent of policy transfer type activity increased in recent years?
- Are notions of policy transfer too broad to provide meaningful theories of policy change?
- How does policy transfer interact with the macro-level changes such as globalisation or shifting political economies described in Part One of this book?

Further reading

Dolowitz, D. (ed) (2000a) *Policy transfer and British social policy: Learning from the USA?*, Buckingham: Open University Press, pp 9-37.

Dolowitz, D.P. and Marsh, D. (1996) 'Who learns what from whom: a review of the policy transfer literature', *Political Studies*, vol 44, pp 343-57.

Dolowitz, D.P. and Marsh, D. (2000) 'Learning from abroad: the role of policy transfer in contemporary policy-making', *Governance-An International Journal of Policy and Administration*, vol 13, pp 5-24.

Evans, M. and Davies, J. (1999) 'Understanding policy transfer: a multi-level, multi- disciplinary perspective', *Public Administration*, vol 77, pp 361-85.

Stone, D. (1999) 'Learning lessons and transferring policy across time, space and disciplines', *Politics*, vol 19, pp 51-9.

Part 3: Micro-level analysis

eleven

Decision making and personality

Overview

Decision making is a fundamental aspect of all human existence and is central to the policy process. One of the main explanations in the social sciences for this is rational choice theory, which is based on the assumption of people behaving in their own self-interest and weighing the cost and benefits of taking particular actions. In the real world, knowledge and choices tend to be limited: there is a 'bounded rationality'. Beyond this concern with rationality are explanations of decision making that characterise it as a much more chaotic and messy process that develops incrementally. This chapter considers the pros and cons of this debate before exploring the role of personality and the influence that political elites have in shaping policy. A key social science debate arising from this is the extent to which people are shaped by institutions and structures or themselves shape the institutions (*agency* versus *structure*). Institutions are shown to be not merely structures but are an 'assumptive world' of values.

Key concepts

Rational choice; bounded rationality; incrementalism; oligarchy; structuration.

Introduction

Making decisions is an everyday, minute-by-minute activity of human beings. Most other animals are guided by instinct and necessity. Only humans and a few close primates are capable of complex assessment of options. We can even imagine choices that are not realistic or available to us. No other animals can do that. Decision making is a higher-order, intellectual activity and almost everything that happens to us in our daily lives assumes a capability to make more or less rational decisions. Indeed, an important branch of the decision-making literature focuses on what can broadly be described as the psychology of human motivation to make choices. Albeit surrounded by advisers, what was going though Tony Blair's mind when he committed British troops to the battlefield, which he has done five times in his premiership to date, including twice against Iraq? He must have known people would die and be maimed, the huge financial costs involved and the availability of other options to solve the problems. According to Lasswell, probably the greatest of the 'founding fathers' of the policy analysis approach, the answer rests in the type of values that he has been conditioned to accept and to which he is psychologically attuned. Much of Laswell's early writing concerned the psychology of decision making and how the existence of core values leads to different policy outcomes. We will return to this approach later in the chapter.

It must be immediately clear that in this general sense decision making is a ubiquitous feature of the policy process. At every stage in the process – from deciding to decide through to how a policy should be operationalised, implemented and evaluated – individuals and groups are making decisions. What should be done next? What weight of evidence supports one rather than another option? How much do we know about the consequences of any choice that is made? Might it be the case that increasing and extending the top-up fees for higher education will deter students from less well-off backgrounds? Will the Foundation Hospitals policy increase service standards across the NHS or create a two-tier health service? Weighing up options, calculating the political risks and finally deciding what to do is the bread and butter of political life and decision making reverberates through its institutional structures; the armed forces, universities and hospitals. And, as we will see in Chapter Twelve, at the 'street-level', managers, soldiers, teachers, nurses all individually have to decide how to respond in the 'real world'.

Decision making is essentially about these responses and how to explain how complex decisions are made and what in the end happens. The prime minister through to the staff nurse, each and every one has to decide what to do and it is the myriad decisions made that is the real stuff of the policy process. This is why we are discussing decision making in the micro-level section of the book where the focus is on individuals and the detailed, day-to-day management of the policy process. Yet again it must be emphasised that these divisions of the policy analysis literature are to a large extent artificial constructs that help to contain and manage the vast scope of this subject matter. It is important to keep hold of the wider picture, remembering that policy analysis is an *approach*, a way of thinking about the 'real world', not an answer to its mysteries. With this in mind, the chapter considers the idea of rationality in the decision-making process, the way in which values are embedded in institutions and how actors on the policy stage are influenced by their surroundings. This returns us to a fuller consideration of the 'agency' and 'structure' debate touched on in a number of earlier chapters of this book.

Rational choice and decision making

The idea of rationality occurs at almost every stage of the policy process. We will come across it in the next chapter in relation to the idea of the conditions for perfect implementation, which is premised on the notion that there are clear-cut solutions to social problems. What is needed for successful implementation is an intelligent policy, a clear management structure and a compliant street-level workforce to deliver the services. Rationality has a long pedigree in the social sciences. The most widely explored and highly contested version appears in the debate around so-called **rational choice theory** (see Ward, 2003, for an overview).

Rational choice theory is derived from early accounts of economic behaviour, especially as described in the work of the 18th-century Scottish economist Adam Smith and in 19th-century utilitarianism associated with the work of the English philosopher Jeremy Bentham. Although derived from different premises, the common point of their thinking is that the basic unit of society is the self-seeking individual motivated by their need and desire to maximise their own advantage. The essence of the position is that people act rationally in pursuit of their own wants and needs. As Elster neatly summarises, "The elementary unit of social life is the individual human action" (Elster, 1989, p 13). One branch of rational choice theory argues that human beings possess a psychological imperative to pursue their own interest. The sociologist George Homans, for example, argued that behaviour is programmed by the human desire for approval (or the threat of punishment) in much the same way that animal behaviour can be shaped by the giving or withdrawal of food. People are conditioned to behave through society's structures of rewards and punishments. Homans saw the receipt of social approval as the glue that binds society together (along with monetary reward). Social exchange and economic exchange are the basis of most behaviour (Homans, 1961).

However, most rational choice authors do not find the need for such an extreme positivist version of social behaviour. Following the logic of economic exchange, the orthodox argument is that there are rewards and costs in any transaction and that people are bound to follow a course of action that is most profitable to them. Translated into the social domain, this means that wider society is structured around social exchanges which maximise status, social rewards and 'utility' (the use that a person gains from a service, a relationship, a product). Of course, not everyone can maximise their 'wants' all the time so that an essential part of rational choice theory is that individuals must calculate for themselves the most effective course of action and should try to anticipate the consequences of what they do. In reality, people's bargaining power is likely to vary considerably so that they may be dependent on one or two key relationships. Other people will have a strong 'market' position and so be better placed to secure their objectives and yet others may be engaged in networks in which the exchange relationships are quite complex.

Criticisms of rational choice theory

The main problem with rational choice theory is that if people are so self-centred and bounded by social and economic exchanges, how is it possible to account for collective action? This was precisely the issue on the mind of probably the greatest English political philosopher, Thomas Hobbes (1651), who, writing in the 17th century (around the time of the English Civil Wars), argued the need for 'government' in order to rescue society from falling into anarchy. In other words, if everyone is so self-centred, how is it possible for society to exist at all? How is it possible in the context of the policy process for political institutions to function? This is the most difficult question for rational choice theorists because, while it can be explained why someone might on a calculation of rationality join, say, a trade union, imagining there will be personal gain, this does not explain why they join when they might reap the benefits without belonging or needing to join. Wage increases do not go only to the union members. The rational choice argument that explains this is that the decision to join or not will depend on institutional circumstances. If the union operates a 'closed-shop' agreement (now very rare) so that the company only deals with a particular union, then it is quite rational to join the union because it may be the only way to access the wage rise or improvement in working conditions. However, this does not alter the fact that many organisations do not have such a monopoly but still have large and active memberships.

Another issue that rational choice theory has difficulty explaining is the philanthropic or altruistic instinct that is such a common feature of daily life. People generally behave thoughtfully towards others: young people give up their bus seat for an elderly person, volunteers donate their blood, a kind word of thanks is spoken (see, for example, Titmuss, 1970). Rational choice theorists argue that this is simply the result of social conditioning and is in any case quite arbitrary: most people do not donate blood. If people have been socialised to behave in a certain way, they might think they are acting rationally when in fact, strictly speaking, they may not be. Scott (1999, p 76) argues, "If people want to help others and get a sense of satisfaction from doing so, then giving help is an act of self-interest". This, however, is a tautology; that is, a circular argument. Rather more plausibly, it can be argued that, in certain circumstances, cooperating with others is the most rational decision. Indeed, it has been argued that human beings have a genetic predisposition to cooperation (although as we will see later in this chapter, there is a strong case, argued famously by Richard Dawkins (1976), that the real genetic instinct is to be selfish) but whether or not genetics can explain altruistic or selfish behaviour, rational choice theorists find it hard to explain away such things as people's sense of duty or the strong (irrational) instinct towards social justice that is common in society but may be a zero-sum option for the selfish individual.

Nevertheless, despite our scepticism of these aspects of rational choice theory, it is more than plausible that in most policy-making scenarios there will be transaction costs for the actors involved. Even 'strong' prime ministers need the support of his/her close cabinet colleagues when he/she is engaged in an issue in which they have sunk a lot of political capital, on which they have decided to stake their authority. Tony Blair is at the time of writing engaged in a campaign, against a majority of his own MPs, to increase university top-up fees. In terms of domestic policy, he has bid up the stakes on this issue to the point where he has been compelled to put his own personal authority on the line. It is a high-risk strategy. Issues do not normally reach this level of risk because even the prime minister's time, energy and resources are limited. The political costs to him of pushing though this issue are massive in terms of future pay-offs. As we will show later in this chapter, 'personality matters' – in other words, the personal qualities and energy of cabinet ministers and especially prime ministers have significant effects on policy outcomes – but it should never be forgotten that there are institutional constraints and trade-offs on what can be achieved. Tony Blair is unquestionably limited by his pact with Chancellor of the Exchequer, Gordon Brown, concerning which of them should be prime minister, and this is a significant constraint on his authority over domestic policy. The point here is that at any level in the political system there are bound to be transaction costs which must be risked for a policy to reach the serious political agenda and make progress (Dunleavy, 2003, p 352). Understood in this institutional context, rational choice theory – involving the assessment of opportunity and transaction costs to the individual – has an important contribution to make in understanding the policy process.

Bounded rationality

A central figure in the debate about rationality in the policy-making process is Herbert Simon (see especially 1960, 1982) whose publications across nearly half a century have had a major influence. Simon began by arguing that rational choice theorists often overlook the reality of what happens in organisations because of their extreme focus on the individual and/or Freudian-inspired psychoanalysis. He argued that people are basically rational but constrained by incomplete knowledge and a limited capacity to deal with complex issues. Away from the high-stakes and high-risk environment of the core executive, focused on the prime minister, more mundane actors tend to be habitual in behaviour, causing institutions to change slowly and tend to inertia, choosing 'safe' options and limiting wider ambition. It has often been observed in the institutionalist literature that political institutions are 'sticky'. According to Simon, this results from people's **bounded rationality**: that people's knowledge is incomplete and limited and that outcomes tend to reflect an organisation's value system which, taken together, does not necessarily produce the most effective or beneficial results in the long run. Recognising this gap, Simon set out to improve performance through the use of new technologies, especially computers and training programmes (Simon, 1960).

The best-known challenge to Simon's optimistic outlook – that decision making could be controlled and improved – was made by Charles Lindblom (see especially 1959, 1979). Starting out as an economist, Lindblom gradually, over several decades, came to write in the language and concepts of political science. During this transition, he moved from a conservative, 'classical' pluralist outlook to a much more radical critique of the modern American political system, arguing that far too much control of the policy agenda had slipped into the hands of big business (see also Chapter Seven). Linblom argued that the basic character of the political process is 'muddle'. The Simonian idea of the application of rationality in the design of new policy – think tanks, improved management, involvement of policy 'experts' – is destined to frustration and failure, according to Linblom. His idea of 'the science of muddling through' asserted that strategy could be guided only by trial and error, by opting for limited objectives and using thoughtful research and evaluation (Lindblom, 1959). Although not necessarily the main point of Lindblom's contribution, it is his idea that policy is essentially an incremental process characterised by muddle for which he is best known. In other words, given all the constraints, the lack of rationality and the existing policy environment, the best that can be hoped for in the policy process is gradual, step-by-step change. Policy making is not in this sense a hopeless mess but should be approached realistically in the knowledge that there is unlikely to be a rational 'solution'. According to Lindblom, limited aims and options are far more likely to succeed than grand designs (Lindblom, 1979).

In his later writing, Lindblom argued that this is the inevitable consequence of the unequal distribution of power, especially the economic strength of big business to manipulate the policy agenda. His step-by-step approach should thus be read not as a conservative endorsement of the *status quo* but simply as a realistic appraisal of what is and is not possible to achieve through the political system. As he said, it is not clear, indeed it is quite unnecessary, that a "radical diagnosis must lead to a radical prescription" (Lindblom, 1988, p 15).

The role of personality

As we saw earlier, some rational choice theorists argue that human beings are programmed to be selfish. The new science of genetics has thrown a renewed focus onto the age-old problem of the individual in society, what Hobbes in the 17th century called 'the war of each against all'. The idea that human beings, indeed all the animal kingdom, is genetically programmed to be selfish, as argued for example by the molecular biologist Richard Dawkins (1976) in his notorious book *The selfish gene*, has raised the spectre that antisocial, criminal or sexually deviant behaviour can be genetically modified. As we shall see, such a view is implausible and says more about the nature of society in recent decades than it does about the tremendous benefits to humankind of the new knowledge of the genetic structure of life. At the micro-level of policy analysis, it is, however, clearly necessary to discuss the role of personality and individuals in shaping policy and in the policy-making process. The individual personalities of the great leaders through to those of the street-level bureaucrat matters a great deal in what happens. As Parsons (1995, p 370) suggested:

> Far too much analysis of the policy process – and of particular moments of decision – has excluded the personal and the role of actual people and personalities … without such consideration the analysis of policy-making can be (rightly) accused of lacking any sense of reality.

Harold Lasswell, the founding father of the policy analysis approach, placed great emphasis on the role of subconscious behaviour and the role of personality in shaping policy outcomes. His books *Psychopathology and politics* (1930) and his later work *Power and personality* (1948) explored ideas about why particular personalities develop political ambitions and how private motives and personality traits interact with institutional structures. He argued that understanding the background, personal feelings and emotions of political actors was vital to explaining how they confronted problems and developed policy. He even probed into Freudian psychoanalysis for explanations of why some people sought to exercise political power. For example, he suggested that some powerful leaders, such as Hitler, were compensating for loss of self-esteem in earlier life and damaged egos. One of his aims in developing what he called 'the policy sciences' was precisely to help decision makers understand their own limitations, prejudices and values so that they could make better and more rational choices, although it is doubtful whether he could have helped Hitler (who was known to be clinically mentally ill).

It does seem clear that policy outcomes reflect not only the macro- and micro-level influences but also the personality and temperament of the decision makers, their attitudes and belief systems (values) and how they perceive their role in the wider context of the policy environment. This ensemble of factors is what Vickers (1965) called the 'appreciative system'. In his book *The art of judgement*, Vickers follows quite closely Simon's ideas, especially on the bounded nature of rationality, but argues that decision making is not in reality about achieving targets or 'best practice' (see Chapter Thirteen of this book) but is best thought of as an amalgam of facts and values in which human frailties and insights are inevitably a major part. Vickers was a realist: he fought in both world wars, trained as a lawyer and became the legal adviser to a number of important public bodies, notably the National Coal Board and later on the Medical Research Council. He was thus a man used to dealing with 'reality' and came to believe that people's beliefs and values are inevitably intertwined with 'facts':

> [F]acts are relevant only in relation to some judgements of value and judgements of value are operative only in relation to some configuration of fact. (Vickers, 1965, p 40)

Especially he knew that it was human agency, under pressure on the front line of war or in public policy, that was crucial to what happened. In any situation chosen outcomes inevitably reflected the character and temperament of the personalities involved, their attitudes and values and how they perceived their role in the policy environment. Vickers was very sceptical of so-called 'scientific' approaches to management and decision making – ideas such as cost–benefit analysis and programme budgeting. He saw decision making as a complex, multi-tiered activity involving the interaction of values and 'reality judgements'. As such, he was much more concerned about communication between participants, developing the art of making judgements, rather than the mechanistic formulae of the systems analysts.

A number of political scientists have used Vickers' ideas as the basis for developing models that relate the influence of personalities to the wider context and policy environment. Greenstein (1969, 1992), for example, gives a central place to the personality of key actors in shaping policy outcomes. Human agency is at the centre of how politicians and decision makers shape the policy agenda and how they understand their own place inside institutional structures. A 'strong' political leader such as Margaret Thatcher clearly used the force of her personality and her personal values to inform and shape the policy agendas of the 1980s. 'Thatcherism' is synonymous with monetarist economics and authoritarian populism, which embraced attempts to dismantle the Beveridge welfare state, contract out delivery and end the 'dependency culture' (see Gough, 1983; also Chapters Three and Five of this book). More recently, having lost out to New Labour at two General Elections, the Conservative Party's determination to unite around a new, strong leader led to the humiliation of Iain Duncan-Smith, who after two years as his party's first directly elected leader, was replaced in favour of Michael Howard, a more robust and experienced politician who had held a number of ministerial posts including that of home secretary in the John Major government. 'IDS' disastrously promoted himself as the 'quiet man' of British politics and, despite his attempt to 'turn up the volume', his leadership qualities were fatally flawed.

The charismatic leader

The need for **charismatic leadership** has a long provenance in political science. The great German sociologist Max Weber (1864-1920) discussed the idea as one of his three types of authority (the other two being *traditional* and *rational-legal*). His central question was to discover how modern western society broke with tradition. He believed that it was the evolution of rational action, in the context of rational-legal states, which marked the break from the past. In this process, political leaders and institutions in general, so he argued, attempt to secure the compliance of the people by virtue of their legitimate control of political institutions. Their authority is obeyed because it is believed that they have a right to make policy or issue commands. One method for achieving this was the idea of a charismatic leader, someone of outstanding leadership ability able to inspire devotion from his followers and whose legitimacy flows from his/her strength of personality. This idea was most famously discussed by Robert Michels (1911), who knew Weber, in his analysis of the (socialist) German Social Democratic Party before the First World War. It is inevitable, according to him, that political elites will compete for power either with or without the consent of the people and that this is the inescapable character of all political life. The danger of the 'oligarchical' nature of modern bureaucracies, by which power comes to be concentrated in the hands of a few powerful people, had been recognised initially by Weber. Michels' study of the SDP, a Marxist party that in theory should exemplify democratic principles above all others, showed that the leadership gradually assumed more and more power itself by manipulating the agendas of meetings, managing the wider operation of the party and its political programme, and by the members' own psychological need for a strong leader. A central feature of Michels' **Iron Law of Oligarchy** was the need for a party organisation to have a charismatic leader, which derived as much from the need of the mass membership as it did from the power-hungry political elite. In the words of Michels' (1911, p 365) famous political dictum, "who says organisation says oligarchy".

   The mass's need for successful leadership points to the significance in politics of subconscious, psychological issues and a number of writers, including Lasswell, have used Jungian psychoanalytical theory to explain the behaviour of politicians. Jung, who was a disciple of Freud, believed that not only was there a personal unconscious mind but also a 'collective unconscious' which was constructed out of a number of archetypes. The collective unconscious can be likened to an inheritance common to all people; for example, everyone has a mother but according to Jung we also have within ourselves a sense of motherhood (an archetype), whether or not the relationship with our birth mother was good. According to Jung, if a mother failed to satisfy the demands of the archetype, the person may seek maternal comfort elsewhere; in the church – especially through the Virgin Mary – or in identification with 'the motherland'. Jung thus derives people's behaviour from unlearned, universal energy and works back to the individual psyche.

The best-known study of the impact of Jungian ideas on political leaders is Louis Stewart's analysis of US presidents and British prime ministers in which he tried to explain why some people become political leaders (Stewart, 1992). Stewart argued that there are leadership types depending on the child's birth order: youngest children are said to be more rebellious, middle children more accommodating and the eldest the carrier and preserver of tradition. He showed that first-born children are in fact heavily over-represented among political leaders, the reason being, so he argued, that they embody the essence of all these roles. However, some psychologists argue that the propensity of political leaders to be first-born children is the product of the more intense nature of the upbringing given to them (more is spent on them and they have a greater weight of parental expectation resting on them). Other psychologists argue that it is the interaction of the first-born with their younger siblings that is the real cause of their leadership qualities because they are better prepared for power struggles, having been 'leaders' within the family (Andeweg and Van Den Berg, 2003).

Jung's way of thinking should not be confused with the micro-focused approach to personality of molecular geneticists that became very fashionable in the 1970s and 1980s in the run-up to the mapping of the human genome. Richard Dawkins' (1976) idea of the **selfish gene**, for example, has enjoyed popular currency (his book was a best-seller) because it was an apparently simple way to explain behaviour. Dawkins argued in his notorious book that all natural selection can ultimately be traced back to the genetic imprint of DNA, and that there is an 'intelligence' inside DNA which compels it to seek its own selfish replication:

> ... the gene reaches out through the individual body wall and manipulates objects in the world outside, some of them inanimate, some of them other living beings, some of them a long way away. With only a little imagination we can see the gene as sitting at the centre of a radiating web of extended phenotypic power. (Dawkins, 1976, p 265)

In fact these somewhat mystical and bizarre ideas say more about the contemporary state of society in the latter decades of the 20th century, in which individualism and the values of the aggressive free market found a powerful voice in Thatcherite politics. Serious geneticists, social philosophers, psychoanalysts and political scientists, while accepting the significance of the individual 'subject' as the source of all society and social ideas, could never accept such a crude, deterministic proposition that human beings are genetically pre-programmed. Nevertheless, it is widely and popularly believed that genes are responsible for such phenomena as homosexuality, criminal behaviour and even the welfare state dependency of some single mothers. Dawkins (1976, p 126) himself argued that, "Individual humans who have more children than they are capable of rearing are probably too ignorant in most cases to be accused of conscious malevolent exploitation". To reduce social problems to the level of genetics is an extremely dangerous and misleading assertion because, as we have shown throughout this book, policy essentially resides in the political institutions of society and it is ludicrous to think that wider environmental factors and political culture can be reduced merely to strands of DNA. And as we have seen earlier, there is a close relationship between this and individual consciousness and even subconsciousness. Scientific research into genetic modification to combat, for example, diseases such as Huntington's disorder or muscular dystrophy have, of course, great potential, but the same could not be said about the control of sexuality or criminality, even if a genetic propensity was discovered. Crime is a social problem and has to be solved socially.

The assumptive world and institutional values

Finally, to reiterate the key theme of this chapter, it is important to recognise that the **assumptive world** – the world of people's beliefs and values – has a key role in shaping the **value systems of institutions**. An organisation is not simply composed of its structures, its tiers of organisation, management systems and functional departments, but is itself socially constructed, involving for example the purpose of the organisation, its image to the outside world and how strongly the leadership and management can impose their ideas about the policy agenda. The ability of powerful leaders to shape the political agenda and institutional values is clearly seen in March et al (2000) study of the role of cabinet ministers in modern British government. They showed that in certain circumstances the personality and political ambition of ministers is crucial to the general direction taken by departments of state. They cite the example of Michael Howard, who was renowned as an anti-liberal home secretary with a very specific agenda: "I deliberately set out to change the system so that I gave the police a fairer chance of bringing criminals to book and also by encouraging the courts to imprison those criminals responsible for a disproportionate amount of crime" (Michael Howard, cited in Marsh et al, 2000, p 308). He thus set out to undermine the much more liberal-minded approach then current in the Home Office, which had resulted from the influence of Roy Jenkins in the 1960s. March et al conclude from their study of several key ministries of state that cabinet ministers are powerful and key players, being potentially agents of significant change. Ministers have multiple roles both inside and outside the department: they have to be party activists, operate across the core executive as well as inside their ministry, in which full-time civil servants tend to defend a long-term departmental 'line' on core policy. They also have a crucial role in developing their own careers; to survive, win promotion or even to become prime minister. Their conclusion that ministers have become more proactive since the 1980s is an important finding in the wider analysis of how central government functions. For our purpose, this study shows the significance of personality in shaping policy but from within the structures and roles by which all cabinet ministers are constrained. It is unusual to find a study that captures this balance between structure and agency so clearly.

The issue of how to relate together the influence of the attitudes and ideas of freely determined individuals and the extent to which what they do is in fact shaped by social and political institutional structures is one of the most complicated issues in all the social sciences. It was precisely to address and answer this question that the British sociologist Anthony Giddens arrived at his concept of 'structuration' (**Box 11.1**).

Box 11.1: Structuration theory

Giddens contended that modern social life is increasingly saturated by the new communication media including the Internet which creates a stretching of time and space beyond anything previously known or possible. Structuration theory attempted to bridge the gap between the potential of individuals to reach beyond the confines of their everyday life in this new stage of modernisation and the day-by-day structures that inevitably confine people – who in reality can only be in one place at one time. The routine of daily life its structures, opportunities and constraints interact with the subjective experience of individuals in what Giddens called a 'duality of structures'. Structuration refers to the study of the relationship between the new unbounded possibility of people reaching across time and distance and their being rooted (what Giddens calls being 'embedded') in daily routines. It is in 'social practice' not structures, political or social, that social systems are constituted and reproduced:

> The basic domain of study of the social sciences, according to the theory of structuration, is neither the experience of the individual actor, nor the existence of any form of social totality, but social practices ordered across space and time. Human social activities, like some self-reproducing items in nature, are recursive. That is to say, they are not brought into being by social actors but are continually recreated by them via the very means whereby they express themselves *as* actors. In and through their activities agents reproduce the conditions that make these activities possible (Giddens, 1984, p 2).

In other words, it is the continual activity of day-to-day routine that in the end builds into larger institutional structures and is a continuous iterative process.

The core of Giddens' argument is that structure exists because of social action. In the domain of political life, the same logic applies. Political actors and political structures exist in a perpetually recreating 'duality'. For example, the idea that the great departments of state are constituted, made up from, previous structuration processes reflecting the values of strong (and weak) ministers and interaction with their civil service, is a key lesson for policy analysts. Organisations such as these are not simply 'structures', but themselves harbour key value systems that inform and direct the policy agenda. These complex ideas are very close to those of the political scientists building on the new institutional literature and concerned with how human agency and institutional structures interact and spin off each other.

Greenstein's (1992) model of decision making for example, following on from Vickers, maps out the interaction between macro-level influences and the micro-level (such as the character and social background of the actors, their temperaments, personal characteristics, opinions, ideological beliefs and personal values). Decisions are the product of the interaction between the wider environment, institutional frameworks and the personalities involved. A university is a complex organisation but its pursuit of knowledge and its critical investigation of social and physical reality is a unifying principle and stands alongside the cherished value of academic freedom. The armed forces have an equally clear focus on the values of discipline and hierarchy in attaining their goal of an efficient fighting force. The assumptive world of organisations is therefore a matter of chance but reflects long-run values and its 'real' purpose. Institutional values can be likened to the oxygen that flows through the bloodstream of the body, without which the body would quickly perish. This is similar to the idea of the 'epistemic community' theorised by Ernst Haas (1990; see Chapter Ten of this book) in which a community of like-minded professionals unite around a common set of political values, the aim being to translate their values into the public domain and ultimately policy. The key point is that such an epistemic community is bonded by its common adherence to a core set of values. This idea should remind us of the discussion earlier in the book about policy networks and help to connect the key meso-level concept of networks with micro-level decision making discussed in this chapter. They are part and parcel of the policy analysis approach and we should not fall into the trap of thinking that these middle range concepts are somehow separate entities.

Conclusions

Decision making without a human face loses touch with reality. That is the key lesson of this chapter. The rationalist idea that people can be organised and managed to achieve 'best practice' is a pipe dream and flounders because the policy process is a messy business involving human fallibilities and foibles.

Policy rarely begins with a *tabula rasa* but is much more sensibly characterised, in Lindblom's (1979) words, as a process of **disjointed incrementalism**. Inside this story, the presence of key personalities and actors is crucial to what happens. Political elites play a particularly powerful role in shaping the direction of policy and Michels' aphorism that 'who says organisation says oligarchy' is a key lesson of political science and a salutary warning not just for political parties of the Left. Here, without being able to discuss his idea in detail, we should acknowledge the seminal influence in much of what has been written in this chapter, indeed throughout the book, of the ideas of Max Weber, particularly his ideas on the nature of 'causality'; of what it is that shapes society and social development: the influence of socio-cultural factors, as well as the economic.

The determinism of populist geneticists such as Dawkins, hoping to 'explain' everything in the deceptively simple idea that genes are independent agents that programme people, pale in the face of the weight of the accumulated knowledge of the social sciences. The much more complicated reality of the interaction between institutions and human agency and personality, discussed by political scientists such as Vickers and Greenstein (among others) and explained in Giddens' idea of structuration, give us a much more plausible 'cold shower' of realism. Institutions and policy agendas are ultimately nothing without the messy, fallible and sometimes inspiring influence of human agency. Personality matters.

Summary

- Decision making is a higher order, intellectual activity and almost everything that happens to us in our daily lives assumes a capability to make more or less rational decisions.
- Rational choice theory is derived from the premises that the basic unit of society is the self-seeking individual motivated by their need and desire to maximize their own advantage. The main problem with this view is how to account for collective action.
- Herbert Simon's idea of 'bounded rationality' argues that policy outcomes reflect the value system of organisations but does not necessarily produce the most effective or beneficial result in the long run. Recognising this gap Simon set out to improve performance through the use of new technologies, especially computers, and training programmes.
- Against the Simonian idea of rationality, Lindblom argued that the basic character of the political process is 'muddle'. His idea of 'the science of muddling through' asserted that strategy could be guided only by trial and error and that policy making is essentially an incremental process. According to Lindblom, limited aims and options are far more likely to succeed than

grand designs and even radical change, which he supported, needed to be implemented step by step.

- Laswell argued that policy outcomes reflect not only the wider context but also the personality and temperament of the decision makers, their attitudes and belief systems (values) and how they perceive their role in the wider context of the policy environment. Vickers was also very sceptical of so-called 'scientific' approaches to management showing that in reality decision makers needed to learn 'the art of judgment'.
- The necessity and inevitability of strong leadership has been a recurring theme in the social sciences and was first conceptualised by Weber in his idea of charismatic leadership. The inevitability of power elites was a central feature of Michels' Iron Law of Oligarchy and partly arises from the mass's psychological need for a leader they can look up to.
- Ideas derived from psychoanalysis, especially the work of the Swiss psychologist Jung, can help explain the motivation for people to become leaders. Laswell used this theme and approach in his discussion of the influence of personality on the political process.
- Giddens' idea of structuration theory attempted to bridge the gap between the potential of individuals to reach beyond the confines of their everyday life in the modern world and the day-by-day structures that inevitably confine people – who in reality can only be in one place at one time. The routine of daily life its structures, opportunities and constraints interact with the subjective experience of individuals in what Giddens called a 'duality of structures'. In this way, he discovered how we can solve the issue of whether it is institutions that shape and determine how people behave or whether individuals themselves create political and social structures.

Questions for discussion

- To what extent is policy the result of the ideas of individual politicians?
- Why is decision making a central concept of policy analysis?
- Why did Michels argue that power in organisations inevitably floats to the top?

Further reading

Andeweg, R.B. and Van Den Berg, S.B. (2003) 'Linking birth order to political leadership: the impact of parents or sibling interaction?', *Political Psychology*, vol 24, no 3, pp 605-21.

Kingdon, J.W. (1984) *Agendas, alternatives and public policies*, Boston, MA: Little Brown.

Lindblom, C.E. (1979) 'Still muddling through', *Public Administration Review*, vol 39, no 6, pp 517-25.

Vickers, G. (1965) *The art of judgement: A study of policymaking* (2nd edn 1983), London: Chapman and Hall.

Implementation and delivery

Overview

The final moment in the policy process comes when the service is delivered to customers or clients. What happens here is crucial to whether the policy as designed by policy makers is delivered or whether teachers, nurses, social workers – so-called 'street-level bureaucrats' – change the policy by what they do, or do not do. 'Top-down' theorists argue that there can be perfect implementation if street-level workers are compliant; 'bottom-up' theorists, however, claim that it is inevitable that front-line staff will have an impact, indeed the major impact, on what happens. More recently, network theorists have pointed out that the top-down/bottom-up paradigm has been superseded by a new agenda which considers the operation and management of networks. At the micro-level of analysis, implementation is a key moment and has a significant impact on policy outcomes.

Key concepts

Perfect implementation; street-level bureaucrat; top-down–bottom-up theory; Taylorism; network management.

Introduction

Throughout this book, reference has been made to the key moment in the policy process when a public service or programme is finally implemented in practice: new housing is finally built, real homes are found for the homeless, qualified teachers and nurses swell the numbers of their existing colleagues, the new battleship is launched. In the past, following the metaphor of the policy cycle, this all seemed unproblematic – a problem was identified, a decision was made to do something about it, a policy was designed and finally came the time to deliver.

However, policy analysts have questioned this model of policy making. The grounds for this are, first, that the idea that there are policy makers 'up there' who simply issue commands to those below and a successful outcome is guaranteed – the classic notion of a 'top-down', Weberian bureaucracy – has been shown to be naive. Second, there is a clear assumption of rationality in such a view. An intelligent, efficient, and properly resourced system, so it was argued, will by default deliver the end product demanded by policy makers. It was simply assumed that civil servants, housing officers, teachers or whoever were broadly speaking following directives given to them by their managers who in turn followed orders that came down from the policy level, or centre (parliament, government). Over the last two or three decades, this view has been challenged in a series of studies that demonstrated not only the lack of rationality in much of the decision-making process but also that 'street-level bureaucrats', in the words of the American political scientist Lipsky (1979), exerted considerable, even decisive, influence over what happened on the ground. Implementation was identified as a process, not an end product; and those people involved on the front line can and do have a major impact on the outcome, whatever the policy makers think or demand.

More recently still, the new governance debate and the emergence of the idea of policy networks as the engine room of the modern polity has thrown the implementation level into renewed and sharper perspective (see Chapters Six and Eight). Policy, any policy, is unlikely to be delivered by only one organisation and inevitably involves the complex interaction of policy networks with diffuse power centres. As we saw in Chapter Six, the old-fashioned unitary state has given way to a differentiated polity characterised by significant areas of autonomy from the centre and operating through policy communities and networks (Rhodes, 1996a). A major part of this new superstructure involves the separation of 'steering' from 'rowing' (Osborne and Gaebler, 1992). As a result, the nature of the implementation process is bound to have changed, the implication of this being that if there has been a shift towards a largely unaccountable networked polity, the influence of the 'street level' may well have grown in significance. More than this, it is also very probable that the layout of the 'streets' on the metaphorical policy-making map has changed significantly due to the rise of the networked polity. This is not to say that the separation of policy making from delivery is a simple split between top and bottom, as argued in the old-fashioned studies, but draws attention to the fact that a great deal of the steering of policy is now in the hands of 'implementers'. However much Tony Blair or Gordon Brown wish to control what happens on the ground they know that delivery in the modern state necessarily belongs to the partnership of the private, public and voluntary sectors.

This chapter is about *rowing*, about what happens to policy at the point of delivery. It sketches out the main themes of the implementation literature using a number of models as a means of summarising this now quite extensive body of work. We begin by considering the contrast between top-down and bottom-up theorists.

The top-down school

Disillusioned by the failure of social reform in the 1960s and 1970s social scientists began to question the orthodox, 'constitutional' view that policy was decided by politicians and implemented by public administrators. For example, the failure of the War on Poverty in the US showed that street-level workers and bureaucrats were unable to deliver more harmonious and stable inner-city communities and, moreover, the outcomes of these programmes were quite unlike those the policy makers had envisaged. Policy was quite often prone to outright failure from the point of view of legislators and often created unintended and perverse consequences.

A classic case of this in Britain was the failure of the notorious 1957 Rent Act to revive the fortunes of the private-rented sector. This sector of the housing market, which at the time was where well over 50% of people lived, was in decline due to the continuation of wartime limits on the rent landlords could charge. It had been thought by the Conservative government that liberalisation of the rental market would stimulate the market but what actually happened was an acceleration in its decline. This was literally a street-level problem, in this case connected to changed conditions in the wider housing market and new limits on tenants' security of tenure, so that rather than re-letting their rooms and houses most landlords when they got the chance tended to sell their houses to private buyers (**Box 12.1**).

In the policy analysis literature, the most influential and frequently cited study that raised the issue of the problems of policy delivery, was by two American political scientists, Pressman and Wildavsky (1973). Their analysis of an Economic Development Agency in Oakland, California found that the implementation of an urban regeneration project was inhibited by lack of coordination between the various agencies involved in it. They showed the necessity to establish clear lines of communication, provision of adequate funding and to ensure effective management of the scheme. Their findings triggered a debate about the conditions necessary for successful implementation of policy, throwing the focus on what happened in practice at the point of delivery. Theirs was essentially a top-down analysis based on the idea that the policy process was rational and therefore amenable to intelligent management. A series of studies followed on from this focusing on the question of how to improve delivery, the assumption being that if it was faulty in some way it was the result of deficiencies in how the project was put into practice. Gunn

Box 12.1: The 1957 Rent Act: a study in policy failure

During both world wars in the 20th century, the government controlled the housing market and stopped landlords increasing their rents. This was at a time when most people in the country lived in private rented housing. In 1945, 59% of households rented their home from a private landlord. Prices, however, rose sharply during and after the war, by 105% between 1939 and 1951, causing problems for landlords who could not get an economic return from their properties while rents were controlled. The 1957 Rent Act was a radical measure intended to revive the fortunes of the private rented sector (PRS) and encourage landlords back into the market. Across most of the market rents were decontrolled meaning that landlords could charge a market rent and get easier possession of their property. Rent increases were quite sharp and for many tenants, in the absence of housing benefit, this was a difficult period.

In fact, because house prices were beginning to go up, but particularly that the profitability of investing to let privately had fallen, most landlords because they could obtain vacant possession of their houses and flats more easily than before decided to sell them, and quite often to the sitting tenant. This meant that the 1957 Rent Act far from reviving the PRS actually *increased* the speed with which it had previously been declining. This is a spectacular example of 'policy failure', when implementation went seriously wrong.

(1978), for example, made a list of 'best practice' conditions, which would result in, so he argued, successful implementation:

- the need for sufficient time and resources to be available;
- that there were no major external constraints that would hold up the programme;
- a small and well-defined chain of command in the management systems;
- a single implementing authority;
- clear understanding of the desired outcome;
- agreement among all those involved on the aims of the project;
- perfect communication.

Dunsire (1990) started from the opposite point of view by listing the conditions in which policy implementation failed and drawing attention to human frailty in subverting best-laid plans. If things went wrong, according to Dunsire, it was because the personnel involved did not do what they were told or managers made mistakes in designing the programme. At any rate, breakdown in the delivery of policy, or worse, failure to implement according to top-downers is due to human fallibility and emotion and what is needed to put this right is stricter enforcement and tighter appraisal of the administrative machine. For Dunsire, the problem was a failure of rationality. This position is very close to the ideas of F.W. Taylor whose famous book *Scientific management* put forward the idea that the organisation of institutions should be approached as a form of engineering (Taylor, 1911). People are cogs in a machine and need only be properly motivated (or disciplined) for a smooth operation (note that Taylor himself was an engineer by profession). Later, 'Taylorism' became very influential as a management method aimed at reducing bureaucracy and controlling those who remained, especially civil servants involved in spending public money.

According to Elmore (1978, 1979), systems management requires a strong top-down structure but it is also clear that in complex organisations it is necessary for there to be devolution of authority down the system in a process called 'suboptimisation', giving significant areas of discretion to people working on particular tasks inside the overall structure and who broadly accept the organisation's goals. The granting of discretion in the organisation does, however, raise major issues because it requires boundaries to be defined around the areas of discretion, monitoring the performance of suboptimal units and dealing with 'spillover' effects and mistakes. The sense in which there is flexibility in systems management is limited to the achievement of goals set by top managers (Elmore, 1978). The point here is not that people lower down the system have free will but that their will needs to be psychologically attuned to perform in accordance with the central decision makers' aims. Failure to implement properly is a failure to identify weaknesses and lapses in the performance of subordinates.

Elmore goes on to point out that there are very few case studies in the systems management literature of its application to social programmes. This, he suggests, is a result partly of the complicated distribution of powers between central and local governments each of which has its own politically defined jurisdictions but is more a question of the extent to which systems management is a normative model, that is, whether it describes reality as it is or as it *ought* to be. Street-level bureaucrats have their own minds and their scope for the use of discretion is much wider than in more technical projects. As Parsons (1995) points out it is this that accounts for why it was possible in the middle of the 20th century to put men on the moon but for society still to be unable to house the homeless.

All these approaches have basically been written from within the classical Weberian paradigm, which sought to order society via a bureaucratic hierarchy. For Weber, bureaucracy was not a pejorative term for all the ills and failings of public services (the modern 'blame culture') but was a necessary correction to types of authority based on medieval ideas of rule by divinely inspired monarchs or inherited privilege. Much better according to Weber to have an authority that was impersonal, predictable and efficient. His was *the* quintessentially top-down view of the policy process and how complicated societies should be disciplined and organised (Weber, 1949). In modern-day systems management turning a blind eye to actual human behaviour does, however, rather miss the point that the human condition is nothing if not fallible and, apart from this, there is always going to be a wider context to the policy process which more often than not builds up from what went beforehand (see Chapters Nine and Eleven of this book). At the very least, a variety of agencies and actors will be involved in delivering even the simplest policy (Chapter Six).

The bottom-up school

It is, by contrast, precisely a central feature of the bottom-up school that human agency in reality determines how a policy is implemented, how effective it is and whether or not it achieves what the designers of the policy intended. Some bottom-uppers argue that in fact policy is all about what happens at the moment of delivery and it is in effect this point in the policy cycle that defines policy. One of the first studies to demonstrate this effect was Johnson's (1972) evaluation of the role of employment officers in California. Changes in the front-line delivery of employment advice, including the abolition of reception desks made little difference in practice to how the clients were treated. Indeed, at the discretion of local officers counters were reintroduced. Johnson's point was simply that experiments imposed from above had very little effect on the day-to-day interaction of the employment officers and their clients. The best-known work that challenged the top-down view was that of Lipsky (1971, 1979) who took the debate one step further by arguing that policy (in inner-cities) was not in reality the product of policy makers but was the outcome of the activity of 'street-level bureaucrats', those people at the front line in service delivery. His most detailed study (with Wetherly) was an evaluation of plans to end discrimination against disabled children in US state schools involving every school producing an action plan of how such children were to be integrated into local schools, the aim being to overcome their stigmatisation. However, due to the lack of resources and a significant increase in administrative load, local administrators and teachers invented their own rules for identifying the most difficult cases including euphemistic re-labelling. The upshot of this was that, through these new routines and informal procedures, the broad intention of the new law was subverted. Front-line staff thus developed their own 'coping strategies'. The question therefore arose as to whose policy was in fact being implemented; not apparently the policy as designed by the policy makers but what the street-level workers would tolerate or adapt into existing practice (Wetherly and Lipsky, 1977).

Lipsky observed a paradox in which street-level professionals, operating inside complex bureaucracies felt "themselves to be doing the best they can under adverse circumstances" (Lipsky, 1979, p xii) but also having a significant degree of discretion in how they treated their clients. Hill (1997) argued that Lipsky appeared to be inconsistent when he portrayed street-level bureaucrats as either spearheading service delivery or as begrudging cogs in a complex bureaucratic machine. The answer he argued seemed to be that resource constraints compelled front-line workers to operate defensive practices to their own benefit or simply to keep basic services going. Street-level bureaucrats thus create operating routines that simplify their workload and also define their areas of special professional competence. The tendency, therefore, is to stereotype clients because this leads to much easier and quicker solutions. Informal rules and procedures based on the discretion of front-line staff gradually come to shape what in fact is delivered to the public (Hill, 1997). Most bottom-up analysts support a version of the argument that due to lack of resources, uncertainties about their own job security and often under pressure of overload street-level bureaucrats feel alienated and undervalued. It was also apparent, as Lipsky argued, that superiors often had difficulty controlling their front-line workers. Indeed, research in the 1990s into New Public Management (NPM), which claimed to be able to enforce greater compliance and limit these delivery problems, (see **Box 6.1** in Chapter Six for a critique of NPM), showed that NPM was much less effective in changing street-level cultures than was at first imagined (Hood, 1995).

Bottom-up approaches to implementation accept, therefore, that it is inevitable that professional and street-level bureaucrats have a major impact on policy outcomes. Policy and practice are not that different and in reality the delivery stage has considerable, if not in some cases a decisive, impact on outcomes – which may be quite different from the intention of the designers of the policy. In reality, policy making is still in progress at the moment of delivery. Indeed, it can plausibly be argued that there is no real distinction between policy and implementation. Policy can in the most extreme version of the bottom-up perspective best be defined as what happens during implementation. Elmore, for example, devised the idea of 'backward mapping', in which policy rather than being thought of as an imposition from the top is best understood in terms of its outcomes and impact on people. Thus, top-down theory is basically a deceit, a myth with no basis in the real world (Elmore, 1979).

Models of implementation

One solution to the incompatibilities of the top-down and bottom-up approaches was devised by Elmore (1978, 1979) who argued that in the real world it is necessary to be flexible and sensitive to both the interests of policy makers, managers and the street-level operatives. Different issues and circumstances require different frames of reference. Elmore thus proposed four models of implementation, which he thought of as providing insight into the complexities of the policy process. No one model could provide the answer to every situation. His four models are summarised in *Table 12.1*.

Table 12.1: *Elmore's models of social programme implementation*

	Systems management	Bureaucratic process	Organisational development	Conflict and bargaining
Central principle	Rationality	Discretion; routine	Autonomy; control by workforce	Exercise of power; competition
Distribution of power	Centralised	Dispersed; fragmented	Equality of responsibility	Unstable and dispersed
Decision-making process	Suboptimality	Incrementalism	Working groups with strong interpersonal relations	Bargaining for conflict resolution
Implementation process	Monitoring; compliance	Change established working practice	Consensus-building	Resolution of differing interests

Source: Based on Elmore (1978)

Systems management equates with the strong top-down structures of the rationalist school, but, according to Elmore, requires a strong top-down structure, but also acknowledges that in complex organisations it is necessary for the devolution of authority down the system in a process called 'suboptimisation', giving significant areas of discretion to people working on particular tasks inside the overall goals. The granting of discretion in the organisation does, however, raise major issues because it requires the boundaries to be defined around the areas of discretion, monitoring the performance of suboptimal units and dealing with 'spillover' effects and mistakes. Indeed, the sense in which there is flexibility in systems management is limited only to the achievement of goals set by top managers. The point here is not that people lower down the system have free will but that their will needs to be psychologically attuned to perform in accordance with the central decision makers' aims. Failure to implement properly is a failure to identify weaknesses and lapses in the performance of subordinates. Suboptimisation is not, therefore, an invitation to free thinking but of thought control. As in Orwell's *Nineteen eighty four*, 'Big Brother' is watching you (Orwell, 1949).

Bureaucratic process relates to the bottom-up perspective and throws attention onto street-level workers and the degree of discretion they have in implementing programmes. Unlike systems management, which tries to control subordinates, this approach accords a considerable amount of discretion to operatives and draws attention to the moment of delivery. As Elmore observes, "From the client's perspective, the street-level bureaucrat *is* the government" (Elmore, 1978, p 199). The bureaucratic process model also draws attention to the existence of 'operating routines', the day-to-day processes that shape how people work but which also act as barriers to change, creating institutional inertia. Understanding what actually happens at this level in the policy process is crucial but not readily amenable to change because of the demands of the job, which often rely on building up long-term relationships with 'clients'.

Organisational development throws the emphasis in implementation onto consensus building between managers and street-level workers. Here the point is that because both sides are highly educated, there needs to be feedback and communication across the organisation with decision making emanating from a mature trust between the various levels in the system. The aim is to move away from thinking in terms of 'top' and 'bottom' and more in terms of the organisational development and maximising the effectiveness of the services' delivery. Implementation failures result, according to this view, not from poor management control or bureaucratic routine, but from the lack of consensus and a sense of commitment at all levels in the agency. This model draws attention to the limits that external bodies have over changing the strategy or programme of an agency. Governments might wish to move policy in a new direction but it will need to win over hearts and minds in the delivery agencies if it is to be successful.

Conflict and bargaining draws attention to a problem with all the other models, that of power. What happens when an organisation refuses to change or the workforce will not comply with new policy directives? What happens when routine and consensus fail? In reality there is always likely to be conflict around the design and purpose of social policy. There is no single, definitive 'policy' that everyone supports. Instead, policy is always the outcome of a process of conflict between differing interests and a process of bargaining to resolve disputes. Agencies do not necessarily have to change their view but they do have to be prepared to adjust their view to accommodate other interests. Success or failure in policy implementation is therefore relative. Neither does it arise from a common agreement on purposes and policy direction, which is also a feature of the other three models (a result of management control, bureaucratic process or consensus building). In this model, conflict and bargaining provides temporary solutions but no overall agreement on long-term aims.

Implementation and policy networks

Various attempts have been made to overcome the polarisation of the top-down and bottom-up schools and to go beyond Elmore's idea that there is no one 'solution' to implementation. The most notable attempt was in the work of Sabatier. With Mazmanian (1979) he drew on the major lessons of both schools in an attempted synthesis. Once again this took the form of a prescription of six conditions necessary to achieve effective implementation. In fact, it read rather like the top-down commandments: the need for clarity in defining objectives, if needs be, a legally enforceable procedure for obtaining compliance by street-level workers; insider support from the centre of political power; and a clear conceptual basis to the means of promoting change. But in later work, Sabatier (1986a) developed a more elaborate synthesis, which recognised both the existence of complex policy networks (the need for inter-organisational coordination) and also the top-down prescription for how best to achieve perfect implementation.

This approach built on Sabatier's idea that the policy process should be conceptualised as a series of policy networks (he called them 'sub-systems') composed of all the agencies and actors with an interest in the particular policy field: politicians, civil servants, interest groups, academic think tanks and research units, the media, as well as the street-level professionals involved at the point of delivery. These sub-systems were referred to by Sabatier (for example, 1988) as 'advocacy coalitions' and are characterised by having a strong core of central beliefs and values which most of the coalition partners adhere to. The looser elements of the coalition according to this idea are more vulnerable to changing ideas and new policy directions. The key is, however, that the main core is less vulnerable to the whims of public opinion and provide the backbone of what is essentially an elite driven policy process. Change occurs when feedback into the coalition from the wider economy, strong public opinion and spillover from other sub-systems compel it. Policy sub-systems are perpetually engaged in a process of testing and learning about the wider policy environment and whether there is a need to change policy direction or even to give up core beliefs (Sabatier, 1988).

This is a useful way into thinking through the impact of policy networks on the implementation process. The advocacy coalition model takes on board the perspective of the bottom-up school especially in considering the wider inter-organisational and networked character of the policy process and attempts to harmonise this with the essentially elitist position, which is still the essence of Sabatier's position. The problem, however, with attempting a synthesis is that there cannot be a reconciliation of the fundamental values that lie at the core of different approaches. As we have stressed throughout this book, much of the art of policy analysis revolves around the identification of value systems, the problem being that these are often not made explicit or even recognised by some authors as being part of their thought process. But at the deepest level of analysis, it is value-systems that are the foundations on which the superstructure of ideas and institutions are ultimately built. Here, for example, the bottom-up focus on the street-level dimension of the policy process is built round values concerned with empowerment and the relationship between users of services and professionals at the point of delivery. The idea that there is little – indeed in some bottom-up versions, *no* – distinction between policy making and policy implementation is radically different from the core values of top-downers. In their case, the emphasis is on hierarchy, discipline and compliance to the wishes of the policy-making elite. Reflecting on the attempt by Sabatier and Mazmanian to synthesise the top-down and bottom-up theorists Parsons (1995, p 487) sums up this point, "In their desire to construct a comprehensive model, the authors ignore the possibility that what they are trying to combine are, in a Kuhnian sense, incommensurate paradigms".

Parsons goes on to say that a better way to consider implementation is precisely what Elmore proposed in his models – that there is no single model that is appropriate to every eventuality but rather a palette of ideas from which to choose – and later on in his ideas of 'backward mapping' that outcomes should be measured by their impact on individuals rather than predetermined criteria (Elmore, 1979).

Success or failure in policy outcomes depends very much on the point of view of the observer and participants. The rationalist retort to this is that such wishy-washy, indecisive thinking satisfies no one and provides no basis for improving the implementation process. Nevertheless, at the deepest level of debate, the value systems that lie at the heart of all the implementation models make it difficult to avoid the conclusion that no one model has the answer to the Holy Grail of perfect implementation. For policy analysts, the real world is far too complex and 'networked' for there to be an ultimate solution to the puzzle of implementation and delivery. We have to live in the messy and imperfect world of humankind and contend with the Mammon of political power.

Networks in practice

As we saw in Chapters Six and Eight, policy networks are a key meso-level concept standing, as they do, at the heart of the contemporary system of governance (Rhodes, 1997; Marsh and Smith, 2000). Their role in mediating interests and patterning policy is increasingly recognised in the literature as a core explanatory paradigm. Their role is particularly significant at the moments just before and during policy implementation. It follows from this that we need to understand more not just about the fact of their existence or how we define them but how in practice they operate as delivery agencies. In other words, we need to think about the idea of the *management* of policy networks.

Important research in this direction has been conducted in the Netherlands by Kickert and his colleagues at Erasmus University (Kickert et al, 1997).

As a starting point for understanding **network management**, they show that "the network approach builds on the bottom-up criticism [of the top-down model], but offers a more realistic alternative for the [top-down] model" (Klickert et al, 1997, p 9). Having shown this connection to bottom-up theory they then go on to contrast the approach to policy making that flows from juxtaposing the network perspective against the top-down–bottom-up dichotomy. In essence, what they were trying to show was that network theory offers a qualitatively different paradigm for explaining how policy making functions. *Table 12.2* summarises the key differences between the models.

Their model – much like that developed by Rhodes et al (see Chapters Six and Eight) and not unlike Sabatier's 'advocacy coalitions' – "considers public policy making and governance to take place in networks consisting of various actors (individuals, coalitions, bureaux, organisations) none of which possess the power to determine the strategies of other actors", and, crucially, offers strategies for governance that might be used to steer or direct these networks (Kickert et al, 1997, p 9). However, their research advances these earlier approaches because they begin to think through how, at a practical level, networks operate in the delivery of policy. So, they compare the management styles required for organising networks to those found in top-down, systems management, what they call the **classical management style** (see *Table 12.3*). They suggest that the latter relies on a system controller who sets goals, leads implementation and monitors progress (with a view to enforcing these goals), and that this top-down approach "cannot be used in a network situation" because "a single central authority, a hierarchical ordering and a single organisational goal do not exist". Instead, the focus should be on "coordinating the strategies of actors with different goals and preferences with regard to a certain problem or policy measure within an existing network of interorganisational relations" (Kickert et al, 1997, p 10-11).

Kickert and Koppenjan (1997, p 43) build on this, suggesting that network management is a form of steering that may be seen as "promoting the mutual adjustment of the behaviour of actors with diverse objectives and ambitions with regard to tackling problems within a given framework of interorganisational relationships". Klijn (1997, p 33) argues that the network management perspective "underlines the highly interactive nature of policy processes [and] leads to a different view of governance [where] governmental organisations are no longer the central steering actor in policy processes and management activities assume a different role ... directed to a greater extent at improving and sustaining interaction between the different actors involved and uniting the goals and approaches of the various actors". This thinking clearly builds on Rhodes' (1996a, 1997) notion of policy networks as self-

Table 12.2: *Top-down, bottom-up and network perspectives compared*

Perspectives	Top-down	Bottom-up	Network
Dimensions			
Object of analyses	Relation between central ruler and target groups	Relation between central ruler and local actors	Network of actors
Perspective	Central ruler	Local actors	Interaction between actors
Characterisation of relations	Authoritative	Centralised versus autonomous	Interdependent
Characterisation of policy processes	Neutral implementation of ex ante formulated policy	Political processes of interest representation and informal use of guidelines and resources	Interaction process in which information, goals and resources are exchanged
Criterion of success	Attainment of the goals of formal policy	Local discretionary power and obtaining resources in favour of local actors	Realisation of collective action
Causes of failure	Ambiguous goals; too many actors; lack of information and control	Rigid policies; lack of resources; non-participation of local actors	Lack of incentives for collective action or existing blockages
Recommendations for governance	Coordination and centralisation	Retreat of central rule in favour of local actors	Management of policy networks: improving conditions under which actors interact

Source: Adapted from Kickert et al (1997, p 10)

Table 12.3: *Classical and network management compared*

Perspectives	'Classical' perspective	Network perspective
Dimensions		
Organisational setting	Single authority structure	Divided authority structure
Goal structure	Activities are guided by clear goals and well defined problems	Various and changing definitions of problems and goals
Role of manager	System controller	Mediator, process manager, network builder
Management tasks	Planning and guiding organisational processes	Guiding interactions and providing opportunities
Management activities	Planning, designing, leading	Selecting actors and resources, influencing network conditions and handling strategic complexity

Source: Adapted from Kickert et al (1997, p 12)

organising, interdependent frameworks for action that lack a sovereign authority. Phrasing these thoughts in more practical terms, Kickert and Koppenjan (1997) suggest that two forms of network management exist: **game management** (managing interactions within networks) and **network structuring** (building or changing the institutional arrangements that make up the network).

Turning firstly to game management, they argue that actors engaged in network management have a number of options open to them here. First, and most fundamentally, they can engage in *network activation* strategies. Primarily this involves "initiating interaction processes or games in order to solve particular problems or to achieve goals" (Kickert and Koppenjan, 1997, p 47) and could involve the 'selective activation' of certain parts of a network best placed to tackle a particular problem (or, indeed, the 'deactivation' of elements acting as a barrier to change). At a simpler level, a strategy could revolve around *arranging interaction* which might involve an attempt to "formalise the agreements and rules which regulate interaction" (Kickert and Koppenjan, 1997, p 48) or *facilitating interaction* by "creating conditions for the favourable development of strategic consensus building in interaction processes" (Kickert and Koppenjan, 1997, p 49). Finally, if networks become 'blocked', management strategies might include *brokerage* – which they describe as 'guided mediation' that attempts to match problems, solutions and actors – or, in a worst case scenario, *mediation and arbitration*, which could involve attempts to promote consensus or even the introduction of a third party mediator.

While Kickert et al appear to have well developed ideas about 'game management' strategies, they seem less sure of how 'network structuring' strategies might be deployed. Indeed, they sound a note of caution here, suggesting that "if it proves *impossible* to solve problems within the existing

---

Box 12.2: Network management in the NHS

Hudson and Hardy (2001) provide an excellent illustration of the New Labour government's attempt at managing networks in the NHS. They detected a move towards 'network working' as part of the government's health service reforms, though they noted that the limits of the approach were yet to be identified and the mechanisms it entails were still in development. While in England, there was still a cautious approach to change that resulted in a tendency towards 'top-down' measures of control such as national targets, guidelines and frameworks, they found that in Scotland – partly because of broader shifts in governance there – reform was "more explicitly rooted in a network mode which reflects the shift from a system of 'government' to one of 'governance' characterised by self-organising, inter-organisational networks" (Hudson and Hardy, 2001, p 333).

This shift to 'network working' was reflected in comments made by health care managers and professionals interviewed by Hudson and Hardy for their study. For instance, a Scottish GP argued that the Health Board's role was that of "networker; [they are] the people that push things into the system and bring the appropriate people together", something Hudson and Hardy (2001, p 331) felt reflected the limited power but significant influence of the boards. A member of a Scottish Health Board commented: "It's a network, we are all in a network.... But making partnership work, that's hard work, it is difficult. It is often seen as soft, but it is really hard" (2001, p 331). Another GP underlined the real nature of change, arguing, "It is important that we try and reassure people that we are not trying to substitute one command and control system for another. This is different; we are looking at these integrated networks and looking at links, extended teams, real teams" (2001, p 332).

What the reforms in both Scotland and England have in common, however, is the attempt to move away from both hierarchies and markets and, instead, to bringing in new, more collaborative forms of partnership working that, as their starting point, acknowledge that health care interventions are delivered by a complex network of actors. Rather than trying to control these networks in a top-down way through hierarchical control via Whitehall or to allow individual GPs (acting on their patients' behalf) to drive them in a more bottom-up way through their consumer power in quasi-markets, the new approach looks to harness, steer, and activate these networks in a more creative manner.

network, one *might* consider modifying the network" (Kickert and Koppenjan, 1997, p 51, emphases added). On the whole, they regard it as unwise to attempt much more than a 'tinkering' with network structures; in particular, they highlight the danger that pre-existing social capital might be destroyed by overly aggressive attempts at network structuring. They argue that changes should normally be focused on the key variables that are likely to cause blockage: the distribution of power and the costs of maintaining the network. In particular, they suggest removing veto points that may result from an excessive imbalance of power within the network and reducing the costs, in a general sense, of actors being involved in the network by streamlining the network as far as possible.

Finally, if these options fail, 'reframing' *may* be an appropriate option, by which they mean introducing radical change that challenges actors' frames of reference, deliberately disrupting the equilibrium of the network in the hope that a period of flux will be followed by the network being re-established at a more desirable 'point of equilibrium'. There are, of course, no guarantees that this situation will produce a more desirable network structure.

What all this leaves us with is a world view where, following Rhodes (1996, 1997), a new form of network-based governance has emerged, but where a new and less well-understood form of management is emerging to complement this shift, namely network management. It is a 'weak' form of steering where complexity produces many uncertainties for government in terms of policy outcomes for it involves a relaxation of central control and an acceptance that dependency on other actors makes the top-down model redundant anyway. Indeed, Kickert et al (1997, p 167) suggest governance strategies must build in – *embrace* – these uncertainties and accept that the best that can be hoped for is "an indirect form of steering which tries to influence the strategic actions of other actors".

However, their perspective is far from distopian. As they put it:

> We believe that the existence of networks cannot be denied. It is far better to face this fact and try to analyse how they work, looking for ways to improve them rather than trying to ignore or abolish them. Networks are here to stay and policy science must face the challenge. It is possible that policy networks are dysfunctional, but they are not dysfunctional by definition. A lot depends on the way they function, that is to say, on the quality of interaction processes within networks. (Kickert et al, 1997, p 171)

Conclusions

This review of the implementation literature shows how the debate on this key moment in the policy process has advanced in recent years. Perhaps most significantly we have shown it is not possible to make a synthesis between top-down and bottom-up models. Sabatier, who is a key author in this debate, has not really produced a synthesis, more a hybrid which retains a large element from the parent material, the classic tests of the top-downers, of the need to develop conditions for creating and sustaining compliance among street-level implementers. Furthermore the review has shown that the bottom-up language of empowerment and top-down insistence on compliance are values that lead inexorably to different ways of thinking about the policy process. The top-down metaphor of discrete policy stages (or points in a cycle) operating through a bureaucratic hierarchy is at odds with the bottom-up version in which the engine room of the policy process comprises inter-organisational networks and markets. When push comes to shove in Sabatier's synthesis it is the values and interests of the powerful political core that are most significant. Street-level actors retain a powerful ability, through their negotiative power, to fix very different policy outcomes to those intended by their masters even though they themselves are frequently in conflict with each other, so that there rarely is an unambiguous result. Rather more fundamentally, it may simply be that human rather than technological problems are more complex and less easy to solve.

Finally, while acknowledging the pedigree of policy network analysis within the bottom-up school the fact that the 'differentiated polity' is *defined* in terms of networks, not just as the structure but also as the agency, as the engine that drives the policy machine, there is a case for saying along with Kickert and his colleagues that the top-down–bottom-up paradigm has been superseded by a focus on the *management* of networks. As yet the evidence on this remains sketchy but in this context the metaphor of steering becomes blurred. The contemporary state is not completely rudderless but how steering occurs is still somewhat of a mystery and can be explained only by new empirical research. What is absolutely clear is that there has been a powerful drift – a strong tide, rather – that has swept the implementation level (and, as a result, policy network analysis) to the very heart of the policy process.

Summary

- Implementation is a key moment in the policy cycle and those involved in the delivery of services at the front line ('street-level bureaucrats') have a significant role in shaping policy outcomes.
- Breakdown in the delivery of policy, or worse, failure to implement according to the top-down school is due to human fallibility and emotion and what is needed to put this right is stricter enforcement and tighter appraisal of the administrative machine.

- Most bottom-up analysts support a version of the argument that, due to lack of resources, uncertainties about their own job security and often under pressure of overload, street-level bureaucrats feel alienated and undervalued.
- Various attempts have been made to overcome the polarisation of the top-down and bottom-up schools, notably Sabatier's attempt at a synthesis. It is difficult, however, to match up concepts with incompatible value systems (in this case compliance versus empowerment).
- Policy networks do not fit either the top-down or bottom-up model because the emphasis is on intergovernmental relations. The policy process is essentially interactive.
- The management of networks is a much less well-understood process. It involves a 'weak' form of steering where complexity produces many uncertainties for government in terms of policy outcomes because it involves a relaxation of central control and an acceptance of dependency on other actors. This makes the top-down model redundant.

Questions for discussion

- To what extent are street-level bureaucracts delivering their own policy rather than that of policy makers?
- Is it possible to arrive at a synthesis between the top-down and bottom-up models of decision making?
- Why have decision makers found it easier to put a man on the moon than to provide housing for homeless people?

Further reading

Hill, M. (1997) *The policy process in the modern state* (3rd edn), London: Prentice Hall/Harvester Wheatsheaf.

Kickert, W.J.M. and Koppenjan, J.F.M. (1997) 'Public management and network management: an overview', in W.J.M. Kickert, E.H. Klijn. and J.F.M. Koppenjan (eds) *Managing complex networks: Strategies for the public sector*, London: Sage Publications, pp 35-61.

Lipsky, M. (1979) *Street level bureaucracy*, New York, NY: Russell Sage Foundation.

Pressman, J. and Wildavsky, A. (1973) *Implementation: How great expectations in Washington are dashed in Oakland; or Why it's amazing that federal programs work at all, this being a saga of the economic development administration as told by two sympathetic observers who seek to build morals on a foundation ruined by hopes* (2nd edn 1984), Berkeley, CA: University of California Press.

thirteen

Evaluation and evidence

Overview

According to the classic 'stagist' view of the policy process, policy should operate as a cycle, agenda setting being followed by the implementation of a decision, the effectiveness of which is systematically evaluated so that evidence on strengths and weaknesses can be fed back in order to shape the future policy agenda. In reality, evaluation and evidence play a far messier and less systematic role in the policy process. This chapter examines the true role of evaluation and evidence in the policy process, examining the many different ways in which policy is evaluated, the problems that occur in trying to evaluate the effectiveness of policies and the barriers to a more evidence based approach to policy making.

Key concepts

Summative evaluation; formative evaluation; the evaluative state; the measurement culture; evidence based policy; systematic reviews; realistic evaluation.

Introduction

> I beg to move: That this House notes the abject failure of the Government to meet its targets for delivery on public services; believes the current public service agreement regime to be deeply flawed; is concerned in particular that the volume of targets and their rigid and centralised structure have stifled local initiative, diminished professional responsibility, distorted priorities and diverted time and attention away from the task of improving public services; regrets that the Government has used targets as a substitute for real reform.... (Michael Howard, House of Commons Hansard Debates, 7 July 2003, col 763)

> ... there is nothing a government hates more than to be well-informed; for it makes the process of arriving at decisions much more complicated and difficult. (John Maynard Keynes, quoted in Solesbury, 2001, p 7)

We begin the final core chapter of our book with the quotation from Michael Howard, not because we wish to endorse his view on the Blair government's progress, but because it captures many of the dilemmas raised in debates about how and why we can or should evaluate the effectiveness of government policies. As the welfare state and, indeed, citizenship itself has become more consumerised (Needham, 2003), governments, particularly in Anglo-Saxon nations, have looked to demonstrate the value of public services by setting measurable standards, targets and objectives for public service organisations. Indeed, as the Howard quotation hinted, the relative success or failure of government services or policies is now often judged in terms of their progress in meeting such pre-established targets. However, many are sceptical of the value of such an approach, questioning whether we can set meaningful targets for complex public services and raising concerns about the potentially negative impacts of ranking and rating or naming and shaming our hospitals, schools, councils and universities. Significantly, Howard raises such questions in the above passage and uses the data provided by these measures, standards and targets to justify his claim that the government is failing. This hints at the difficult role evidence plays in the policy process for many politicians bringing with it, as Keynes suggested, challenges to current ways of thinking and often exposing inadequacies in existing government policies.

However, despite such dangers, the Blair government have invested considerable faith in the value of a more informed approach to policy making, viewing it as central to improving the quality of public services. Indeed, in its *Modernising government* White Paper (Cabinet Office, 1999, p 20), the government committed itself to making better use of evidence and research and "learning the lessons of successes and failures by carrying out more evaluation of policies and programmes". For some, this pragmatic approach to policy making is central to New Labour's Third Way philosophy, the emphasis being on **what works** or **evidence based policy** (EBP) rather than a rigid ideology (Davies et al, 2000; Solesbury, 2001; Sanderson, 2002). Temple (2000, p 313) even goes so far as to suggest that: "Something genuinely *new* is happening in British politics. The agenda is not ideologically driven, but output driven".

Taken at face value, it is difficult to dispute the validity of such an approach: basing policy making on evidence, measuring the success and failure of policy interventions and trying to determine 'what works' all seem eminently sensible objectives – making them a reality is, however, far easier said than done. As we have shown in earlier chapters of this book, policies operate in complex systems and are subject to a wide range of influences. Given this, unravelling the forces that impact on a particular policy and the circumstances that might influence whether or not it is a success or failure is a far from straightforward task (Sanderson, 2000). Moreover, whether a policy is a success or failure may very much depend upon where you stand; that is, a value judgement rather than objective statement of fact (Pawson, 2002a). Similarly, there are difficult issues surrounding how much evidence might be required before a policy ought to be enacted and, likewise, whether policy interventions should be delayed until sufficient evidence has been gathered and analysed concerning the extent of a problem and the most effective policy response (Smith et al, 2001). Consequently, in searching for robust policy evaluation tools policy makers and policy analysts have had to confront searching questions about the nature of policy, research evidence and knowledge (Sanderson, 2000; Pawson, 2002b).

Evaluation: the classic/rational view

Before delving into some of these more complex recent debates, it is worth taking a step back, however, and looking at earlier work on the topic, for, while recent policy trends have heightened interest in issues surrounding policy evaluation, it has long been an established topic within the policy analysis literature. Indeed, the classic stagist view of the policy process as a **policy cycle** – a simplified approach we reject in this text – regarded evaluation as central to the policy-making process, marking both the beginning and end of the cycle, the effectiveness of policies being formally evaluated post-implementation and the findings of the evaluation feeding into policy reform in order to improve effectiveness (**Figure 13.1**).

This is significant, for it tells us much about the classic view of policy evaluation: a rational input of evidence into the policy process in order to increase the rationality of the (policy) output. This chimes well with the Blair government's commitment to "regard policy making as a continuous, learning process, not as a series of one-off initiatives [and so] improve our use of evidence and research so that we understand better the problems we are trying to address" (Cabinet Office, 1999, p 17). It also helps us to understand the difference between policy research undertaken for evaluation purposes and more general policy research undertaken by academics with an interest in social and public policies, for the former is intended for decision making, embedded in a real-world policy setting and, ultimately, judgemental (Parsons, 1995). While this distinction should not be drawn too sharply – much evaluation research is actually undertaken by academics commissioned by governmental agencies (see, for example, Hasluck, 2000) and much academic research draws judgements on the efficacy of government policies (see, for example, Haubrich, 2001) – it does provide us with a starting point for thinking about how evaluation research

Figure 13.1: Evaluation and the policy cycle

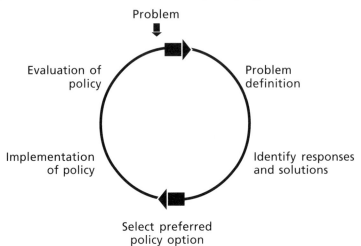

might be defined (see also Geva-May and Pal, 1999). Adopting this perspective, the following features of the **classic** or **rational view** of evaluation research are particularly worth emphasising:

- It tends to be **retrospective** rather than prospective – that is, it is conducted after a policy has been implemented.
- It tends to have a **narrow focus**, examining a specific policy or programme rather than looking more generally at a policy sector for instance.
- It tends to be concerned with **causal issues** – practical questions such as what impact policy x had on problem y or how far programme a progressed in reaching target b.
- It offers **summative judgements** on the success or failure of specific policies or programmes.
- It tends to draw on a more limited range of research techniques. The desire for clear, explicit and objective evidence about what works means the dominant approaches imitate or replicate those found in the hard sciences. In particular, **quantitative approaches** dominate, with **experimental research** (**Box 13.1**) regarded as the 'gold standard'.

In short, this view of evaluation research heavily mimics the rational paradigm of the hard sciences. As Bate and Robert (2003, p 250) argue, "traditional approaches to evaluation involving measurement, description and judgement have been dominated by the scientific method" and draw heavily on a **positivist** world view that emphasises the measurement of observable 'facts'. Indeed, some go so far as to suggest that in order to meet the goal of producing rational, neutral and objective work "in principle, evaluation should not make

Box 13.1: Experimental policy evaluation

Experimental evaluations that mimic methods utilised in the hard sciences are at the core of the rational model of policy evaluation. In this approach 'experiments' are set up to assess the impact of a policy, usually by undertaking comparisons of a new policy with an established one by, for instance:

- studying the extent of problem *x* before and after the introduction of policy *y*;
- studying the extent of problem *x* in places with different policies (for example, a pilot site with a new policy against an area with standard policies);
- randomly allocating citizens to two different programmes and comparing the progress of people within each group.

The latter form – **randomised allocation evaluation** – is generally seen as the gold standard within the classic model. An excellent example of this approach in practice can be found in connection with the evaluation of some fairly recent radical welfare reforms in Florida, US.

In 1994, Florida introduced the Family Transition Program (FTP) to replace the established Aid for Families with Dependent Children (AFDC), the key source of income for many welfare claimants (particularly single mothers). While there were a number of important differences between the two programmes, the key changes were threefold:

- more intensive contact with advisors trained to help welfare recipients get access to training, employment and non-financial health and social services;
- more conditions attached to assistance and financial penalties for failure to meet them (for example, children not having up-to-date immunisations or having a poor school attendance record);
- strict time limits on the availability of cash benefits – generally no more than 24 months in any 60-month period.

In order to evaluate the impact of this policy change – of more than local significance given it anticipated national reforms being steered through Congress – a four-year-long randomised allocation evaluation was commissioned. What this meant in practice was that welfare recipients were randomly allocated into one of two groups (those subject to the conditions and entitlements of FTP and those subject to the old rules and entitlements of AFDC) and their progress tracked for four years. Using various official statistical sources and through surveys of the client group, data was gathered on a wide array of factors such as impact on employment, income, childcare arrangements, school performance, childhood behaviour, parenting styles and emotional well-being.

Although space precludes a full discussion of the findings, the following key points emerged concerning those on FTP rather than AFDC:

- Those at low risk of long-term welfare dependency (LR) saw substantial increases in their employment (5%) and income ($3,868) on FTP.
- Those at high risk of long-term welfare dependency (HR) saw more modest increases in employment and income (the latter roughly equal to the income lost from withdrawal of cash benefits).
- Family Transition Programme recipients relied more heavily on others for childcare than AFDC recipients – an effect particularly pronounced for the HR group.
- There was little impact on school performance for children in HR families.
- Children in LR families performed and behaved more poorly at school and were more likely to be known to the police.

While this is only a snapshot of the findings, they demonstrate the important nature of policy relevant findings that can emerge from an experimental evaluation. In this case, while opponents of the policy felt it would hit the poorest hardest and exponents that it would improve the well-being and reward the efforts of 'hard working', low-income families the evidence showed that both, in some ways, were wrong. While the very poorest did not gain, their position did not significantly worsen either (although this should not be taken to mean their lot was a decent one under FTP; in fact, far from it). Instead, the group whose well-being was hit hardest was that of families in need of temporary help when employment breaks down. In short, and in non-financial terms at least, the evaluation showed that the policy had precisely the opposite impact of that intended: little effect on long-term welfare recipients and a great impact on those at low risk of welfare dependency but in need of support from time to time.

Sources: Bloom et al (2000); Morris et al (2003)

recommendations based on the answers obtained but merely present the data" (Geva-May and Pal, 1999, p 261).

Box 13.1 provides a case study of the rational approach to policy evaluation in action based upon experimental research – in essence an attempt to replicate the randomised controlled trials found in medical research. Interestingly, the Blair government have shown more interest in such approaches than their predecessors, particularly with respect to the use of policy pilots; indeed, Sanderson (2002, p 9) describes the scale of piloting in welfare state services as "significant" (see Middleton et al, 2003; and Cabinet Office, 2003a, for examples) and, as this book was going to press, the largest random allocation policy experiment ever mounted in Britain was being launched in order to test different approaches to getting people into work (see Cabinet Office, 2003b). While there are undoubted benefits in using this approach – in the FTP example a number of important findings that ran contrary to expectations were generated – at the same time, there are severe limitations in the approach.

First, as with any piece of social research, there are significant problems concerning the **collection**, **accuracy** and **validity of data** used in experimental evaluations. In our case study, the researchers compiled a huge data set to support their work. However, they noted problems with some of the data concerning employment and income: the figures given by welfare recipients themselves did not match with those found in the state government's tax records for instance. This is significant, for these were two of the more straightforward measures – statements of fact in clear, linear measures (hours and US dollars) – but problems arose nonetheless. Many of the other measures were more problematic dealing with subjective phenomena (for example, happiness) or relying on questionnaire data or observations that could not be checked against official records. While the researchers were perfectly aware of these problems and worked hard to minimise inaccuracies the point is that the data standards employed in the hard sciences cannot always be replicated in social research and poor data can produced flawed research findings.

A similar problem comes in terms of the **validity of the analysis** that underpins the experiment. Even if perfect data was available researchers need to decide which questions to explore and select a strategy for analysing the data. In our example the researchers examined FTP's impacts in both economic and social terms. However, had they looked only in economic terms the evaluation would have painted a very different picture: one of families on the margins of welfare seeing a significant increase in their income and those dependent on welfare getting into work and seeing their income remain stable despite benefit cuts. It was in examining the social consequences of FTP that the major downsides of the policy were exposed. Similarly, the analytic strategy deployed in the FTP evaluation relied heavily on an approach that split welfare recipients into different categories according to their 'risk' of being dependent on welfare. The decision to do this had a major impact on the study (and was central to the findings) but was neither obvious nor based on well-established groupings. It is highly likely that a different group of researchers would have analysed the data in a different manner. In other words, analytic strategies impact on findings and can bias studies in one direction or another. So, while the mission of evaluation research is "technical integrity and research objectivity" (Geva-May and Pal, 1999, p 260) in practice "value-neutral research is not possible" (Palumbo, 1987, p 32, in Geva-May and Pal, 1999, p 260).

Political barriers to the rational model

We could highlight similar problems, such as whether or not the evaluation of a policy in isolation can capture the true complexity of social policy interventions (a point we will return to later in this chapter), but all of these are technical problems. This is not to say that they are unimportant (quite the opposite), but, rather, to draw a distinction between issues of technique and a broader set of practical problems we now wish to turn to. For the rational model to have any meaning two sets of conditions need to met. First, it must be possible to conduct a rational, objective, 'scientific' evaluation of a given policy – and we have already shown there are problems here. Second, and, in our opinion, more importantly, it must also be possible to feed rational evaluation evidence into the rational policy cycle in order to improve policy by correcting deficiencies identified by evaluators. This condition is almost wholly unrealistic as, in practice, decision makers are rarely inclined to conduct policy making according to the rational, evidence rich, scientific approach that forms the classic model.

First, there are important **ethical and moral objections** to random allocation policy experiments. Many decision makers and front-line workers –and, indeed, many citizens – are uncomfortable with the idea of using people as the objects of social experiments. This is particularly so (as with much social policy) if the subjects of the experiment are the poorest or most marginalised in society and the effect of the experiment is to deny some of them access to important services or resources that policy makers feel might help them (Cabinet Office, 2003a). Certainly Sanderson (2002, p 12) subscribes to this viewpoint, observing – in connection with the Blair government's welfare reforms – "In national initiatives, such as the New Deal programmes, the use of control groups is … not practical primarily due to ethical objections to denying some eligible people the benefits of the initiative".

At a more practical level, there can also be quite severe conflicts between the needs of a scientific model of evaluation and the interests of politicians with respect to the most appropriate **time frame** for policy evaluations. In the case study we provide above, four years was allowed for the evaluation, but, from a scientific perspective, Sabatier (1986b) has suggested a time frame of at least ten years is required in order to allow a policy's implications to be properly teased out. In the case of a major policy reform such as Florida's FTP, it is easy to see Sabatier's point of view: if we wanted to analyse the full impact of the changing childcare patterns, increased petty crime and lower school performances, it seems to have produced in children we would probably want to see how this impacts on (say) well-being, employment patterns, family forms, personal health and crime patterns in the longer term as these children become adults. While it is perfectly feasible for the researchers to resurvey or revisit those who participated in the original survey or simply track their progress for a longer period, in practice even an experiment as long as the one in our case study is unusual; indeed, as Pawson (2002, p 157) puts it, "evaluation research is tortured by time constraints". That this is so is unsurprising given that politicians face regular elections and need to demonstrate progress to electors before going to the polls. They cannot afford to look to the long term by giving policies a decade to bed down before gathering evidence (their careers are likely to be over by then!). Instead they want quick answers about whether or not a policy is working as they look to make a short-term impact on the problems at hand (see Cabinet Office, 2003a).

Indeed, this hints at a further problem with the rational model: that of **whether or not politicians will respond** to findings. As Leicester (1999, p 6) suggests, the need for politicians to build support for their actions often works against the input of scientific evidence into the policy process as "seeking for consensus among all interested parties and the public is ultimately a form of *political* policy-making in which politics is the art of what is possible, rather than what is rational or what might work best". One of the themes we have stressed throughout this text is the complex, non-linear form that policy making takes and the multiple, often conflicting and unpredictable forces that impact on it; the policy process is not straightforward and rational, and it is largely because of this that:

> To date, research evidence on what works has been just one, relatively minor, ingredient in the process from which policy decisions emerge. In practice there are enormous forces of inertia which operate to preserve the *status quo*, influenced not only by party ideology, but also by the policy preferences of the bureaucracy and professional groupings, and by the demands of the public and client-based pressure groups. (Davies et al, 1999, p 3)

Again, this is only to be expected: governments are elected on the basis of manifestoes which detail policies they will pursue and politicians come into office with clear ideas (even ideologies) they want to pursue. In short, they will often already think they know the answers to the problems they are grappling with and can, for obvious reasons, be sensitive to the threats of scientific evaluations that might tell them they have got it wrong. Given this, when evaluations do occur, in practice they are often toned down or their status downplayed. For example, the Blair government often tag pilot sites with names such as 'trailblazers' or 'pathfinders', suggesting they are examples for others to follow at a later date rather than experiments testing the validity of the approach (see Sanderson, 2002), while Thatcher often rolled out policies nationally without bothering to wait for the results of pilot-site evaluations (see Packwood et al, 1991, for an example).

Formative evaluation

In response to some of these limitations of the rational model, much as with debates over the most effective strategy for implementing policies (see Chapter Twelve), a more bottom-up approach to evaluation has emerged in which there has been:

> a shift away from the (still) dominant paradigm of a scientific, experimental approach to a position where the participants [that

is, street-level bureaucrats] have begun to take a more active role in shaping the research: the notion of research with and for the people rather than on them. (Bate and Robert, 2003, p 251)

This alternative approach to policy evaluation stands very much in opposition to the rational model: indeed, Julnes et al (1998) suggest we have witnessed something of a **paradigm war** in evaluation research. On the one hand, we have the classic rational approach, based upon retrospective, quantitatively driven summative evaluations. On the other, we have a more **formative approach** to evaluation, that looks to guide policy **as it develops**, draw on a wider, **more qualitative** evidence base and that is "characterised by the active participation of major stakeholders in the research process" (Bate and Robert, 2003, p 251).

The key differences between the rational (summative) and formative models are summarised in **Table 13.1**. At the heart of the 'paradigm war' is a debate about the nature of knowledge and the most appropriate role for the researcher in generating it. Whereas the summative model is founded upon positivism, the formative model is based upon **constructivism**: it views "knowledge of

Table 13.1: Summative versus formative evaluation

	Summative evaluation	Formative evaluation
Nature	Non-interventionist	Interventionist/improve as you go
Asks	What happened? How you did	Why it happened? How are you doing?
Evaluator	Independent	Participant and co-researcher
Temporality	Retrospective	Prospective
Focus	Cost effectiveness	Process
Purpose	'Dials'	'Can openers'
Outcomes desired	Evaluation for judgement	Evaluation for improvement
Consequence	Evidence for accountability	Evidence for improvement
Key questions	Does it work? Was it worth the investment?	What are we achieving? Can it be improved?

Source: Adapted from Bate and Robert (2003, p 252)

the social world [as] socially constructed and culturally and historically contingent" (Bate and Robert, 2003, p 251). What this means in practical terms is that researchers look not only to gather data about the impacts of a policy but, crucially, also look to gather data about the **processes** that have produced these impacts: not just what happened, but how it happened and which factors or processes produced success or failure. In order to do this, they broaden their methodological toolkit and embrace qualitative techniques that allow them to gain a more detailed picture of the policy as it is implemented – not least by involving participants in the research in order to gather their views. Such an approach is qualitatively different both for the researchers and those involved in delivering policy and involves starkly different relationships between the researchers and the researched: given formative research is based on a world view in which knowledge is less certain or less absolute the focus is not so much on providing an external judgement on performance as helping to improve policy through learning and the sharing of knowledge and experience. In short, it becomes evaluation *with* street-level bureaucrats rather than *of* them (Bate and Robert, 2003).

Proponents of the formative approach argue it is more likely to have an impact on policy than summative evaluation, not least because feedback and findings appear *as* (rather than *after*) the policy is being rolled out. In addition, many suggest the collaborative approach can 'energise' participants and increase their reflexivity (Pollitt, 1999; Bate and Robert, 2003). Although the literature could be stronger in terms of evidence of the positive impact of formative evaluation techniques, Brown and Kiernan (2001) conclude, from a review of the literature and their own experience of conducting evaluation programmes, that formative evaluations produce significant gains against summative evaluations in terms of improving the implementation and delivery of policy programmes. At the same time, however, Pollitt (1999) points to limits of the approach, suggesting that it can only deliver gains in situations where core values are shared by key stakeholders, a collaborative working environment exists or can be fostered and when key decision makers are prepared to engage with a complex and diffuse set of research findings rather than looking for a definitive, summative judgement from the evaluation. In addition, there are dangers too that the close working relationship developed between researcher and researched can damage the objectivity or critical distance of the evaluation process.

However, perhaps the greatest weakness in the formative approach is that, in practice, it is unlikely to produce little more than a fine-tuning of the policy – a tinkering at the margins. While Bate and Robert (2003) stress the advantageous timing of formative evaluations against their summative counterparts, the fact is that even with a formative evaluation the key decisions about the overall shape and direction of policy have already been made, so the problems of political resistance to subsequent change if an evaluation throws up key problems still exists. Indeed, in their review of formative evaluations, Brown and Kiernan (2001) suggested the clearest impact came in terms of increasing the knowledge and awareness of participants rather than policy detail.

The rise of the evaluative state

Somewhat ironically perhaps, while politicians have been reluctant to expose the outputs of their actions to explicit summative evaluations, they have been increasingly keen to measure, monitor and evaluate the performance of those working within public services. Heavily linked to the rise of the New Public Management (NPM) (see Pollitt, 1993; Kettl, 2000; Pollitt and Bouckaert, 2000), the use of performance indicators and performance measures has proliferated in public services across the globe in the past two decades (Carter et al, 1992; Sanderson, 2001). While this trend follows the prescriptions of formative evaluation in examining processes on the ground level and in largely looking to improve the implementation of policy rather than offering retrospective summative judgements, it builds on the rational model insofar as the preference has been for top-down quantitative measures. It is to this that Michael Howard refers when bemoaning the stifling environment of targets, audits and inspections that are very much a feature of contemporary public services.

Yet, while Howard makes his critique to attack the current New Labour government, the shift towards NPM began under the Thatcher government, and more than a decade ago Henkel (1991) coined the term **evaluative state** to describe the widespread presence of performance measurement and evaluation processes within the public services. It is in large part due to the shift from government to governance in which government 'steers rather than rows' (see Chapter Six of this book; also: Osborne and Gaebler, 1992; Rhodes, 1996) that we have witnessed the proliferation of performance measures within public services, because such a mode of service delivery means "responsibility for operational management is devolved but within a framework of accountability for results" (Sanderson, 2001, p 298). In practice, this means that, in order to ensure services are being 'rowed' in the right direction, "performance is scrutinised at different levels through a variety of means: in terms of outputs through systems of performance measures and indicators; in terms of managerial systems and processes through inspections and quality audits; and in terms of contract performance through monitoring of standards" (Sanderson, 2001, p 298).

Such is the proliferation of performance measures in the UK that there are literally thousands of public targets, indicators and measures (never mind the less formal internal ones), so here we can do little more than give a flavour of the 'evaluative state' by illustrating some of the mechanisms outlined above.

Box 13.2 lists the key elements of what the House of Commons Public Administration Committee (2003) has called the **measurement culture**. Some are familiar parts of public discourse, the league tables ranking the quality of schools and universities, for instance, or the prominent performance indicators such as crime rates or the number of school pupils passing key examinations. Others are well established features within public services but, perhaps, a little less well known, such as standards – that is, the expectation that those needing a hospital appointment should wait no longer than six months for example. All of these began life under the Thatcher and Major Conservative governments; indeed, setting published standards for public services was one of John Major's key ideas, being at the heart of his Citizen's Charter (Pollitt, 1994), and have been continued, often in modified form, by the Blair government.

At the core of the current 'measurement culture', however, are a number of key elements that are essentially New Labour innovations. First, measurable policy targets have been a defining feature of the New Labour government even before it was elected: at the heart of its 1997 General Election campaign was the pioneering 'pledge card' which set out five key policy targets[1] they promised to meet if elected, including directly measurable commitments to cut NHS waiting lists by 100,000 and get 250,000 young people off benefits and into work. Numerous targets have been established since then: to eliminate child poverty by 2019; raise health care spending to the EU average by 2006; make all public services available electronically by 2005, for instance. Key targets are written into the second of the key tools developed by New Labour: Public Service Agreements (PSAs) which are, in essence, contracts between the Treasury and government departments specifying what will be delivered in return for public money and agreed on a biennial basis as part of the Comprehensive Spending Review (see later in this chapter; Parry, 2003). The number of targets contained within the PSAs is huge: the 1998 Comprehensive Spending Review alone set some 366 targets (House of Commons Public Administration Committee, 2003, annex, Table 1.1), and many are quite specific; for instance, the Department for Work and Pensions' 2002 PSA commitments include paying Pension Credit to at least three million pensioner households by 2006 and to reduce losses from fraud and error for Income Support and Jobseeker's Allowance by 33% by March 2004 and 50% by 2006 (HM Treasury, 2002b, p 31; see also HM Treasury, 1998, 2000, 2002a).

Although this 'measurement culture' is undoubtedly the most prominent manifestation of policy evaluation, in practice we should distinguish it from the sort of activities at the heart of the summative model, for the emphasis is primarily on **continuous evaluation of performance within a policy**

---

[1] The five pledges in full were to: cut class sizes for five, six and seven year olds; fast-track punishment for young offenders; cut waiting lists by 100,000; 250,000 young people off benefits and into work; no income tax increase.

Box 13.2: The language of the measurement culture: a glossary

Inputs: the resources used by an organisation.

Outputs: the services, goods or products provided by the organisation with the inputs.

Outcomes: the benefits or value generated by the organisation's activities.

Performance indicators (PIs): quantifiable measures used to monitor performance and report on it to the public.

Management information: usually includes both numerical and non-numerical ways of monitoring and understanding performance.

Performance management: used in a wide variety of ways and usually at least includes:

- identifying objectives;
- allocating them to individuals or teams; and
- monitoring progress.

Targets: usually desired or promised levels of performance based on performance indicators. They may specify a minimum level of performance, or define aspirations for improvement.

League tables: intended to enable comparisons of performance between different service providers to be made.

Public Service Agreements (PSAs): first introduced in the 1998 Comprehensive Spending Review as an integral part of the Government's spending plans. Each major department has a PSA, setting out the department's objectives and the targets for achieving these.

Service Delivery Agreements (SDAs): introduced in the 2000 Spending Review, set out lower level output targets and milestones underpinning delivery of the PSA.

Standards: may be used for a variety of purposes, including indicating to the public the minimum standard of service they can expect from a public body, or to a service provider the standard which should be achieved (and against which they may be assessed for compliance). Targets can be based upon standards – for example to achieve a minimum standard consistently, or to improve over time so that the standard is achieved.

Benchmark: normally involves a detailed analysis of comparative performance to help identify what underlies differences between two similar bodies.

Source: Reproduced from House of Commons Public Accounts Committee (2003)

Box 13.3: The institutions of the UK's measurement culture

While much evaluation is still conducted on an ad hoc basis – in connection with specific policies, programmes, initiatives or reviews – a wide range of permanent institutions underpin the measurement culture. Some examples include:

The National Audit Office (NAO)

An independent body headed by the Comptroller and Auditor General that scrutinises public spending on behalf of parliament. It audits the accounts of all government departments and agencies and reports to parliament on the economy, efficiency and effectiveness with which these bodies have used public money (www.nao.gov.uk).

The Audit Commission

An independent watchdog set up to ensure public money is spent economically, efficiently and effectively in local government, housing, health and criminal justice service (www.auditcommission.gov.uk).

Commission for Health Improvement (CHI)

An independent, inspection body for the NHS. It inspects NHS organisations in England and Wales and highlights areas of best practice and poor performance (www.chi.nhs.uk).

Office for Standards in Education (OFSTED)

A non-ministerial government department whose main aim is to help improve the quality and standards of education and childcare through independent inspection and regulation and the provision of advice to the Secretary of State for Education (www.ofsted.gov.uk/).

Social Services Inspectorate (SSI)

Is part of the Department of Health and is responsible for inspecting local authority social services departments and assessing their performance (www.doh.gov.uk/ssi/index.htm).

framework rather than retrospective evaluation of the policy framework itself. Sanderson (2002, p 3) suggests there is a qualitative difference between the two activities, experimental policy evaluation involving the generation of **knowledge** about what works while performance measurement merely involves the generation of **information** about what is happening. In short, the latter is of a much lower order and, consequently, less threatening to the government's agenda and politicians' interests.

At the same time, however, there is much that unites the two also: in particular, both have quantitative and positivist leanings. Consequently, they share many common problems too such as whether or not appropriate measures have been selected, whether they can truly capture the complexity of public services and how far the indicators remain relevant when divorced from their local context. Critics suggest that there is a tendency to focus on factors that are easy to measure rather than those which really matter, for indicators to be treated as 'dials' rather than 'can openers' (the object of investigation rather than its starting point) and, to echo Michael Howard, to undermine the discretion and power of front-line workers by imposing rigid frameworks in a top-down manner (see Carter et al, 1992).

Evidence based policy (EBP)

While the 'measurement culture' is a clear attempt to inject more evidence and information into policy and, more particularly, practice within public services, its focus on process and the measurement of performance within services (rather than of competing policy frameworks) ultimately limits its impact on the overall shape of policy. As with formative evaluation, its effect tends to be one of tinkering at the margins: fine-tuning policies whose core objectives have already been established.

Significantly, the most recent turn in evaluation research looks to use evidence in a very different way by feeding it into the policy process *before* fundamental decisions are made. Its rationale deriving from "a stunningly obvious point about the timing of research vis-à-vis policy: *in order to inform policy, the research must come before the policy*" (Pawson, 2002a, p 158) (see **Figure 13.2**). Dubbed **evidence based policy (EBP)**, the approach has "emerged as central to policy making and governance in Britain and many other Anglophone countries" (David, 2002, p 1).

With EBP, "like all of the best ideas, the big idea here is a simple one – that research should attempt to pass on collective wisdom about the successes and failures of previous initiatives in particular policy dimensions" (Pawson, 2002a, p 160). The approach takes its cues from **systematic reviews** in medicine (see CRD, 2001; Boaz et al, 2002), which, rather than reinventing the wheel by carrying out fresh empirical research to test the efficacy of particular medical interventions, instead looks to systematically review existing research – logging, summarising and synthesising their findings – in order to pool the evidence base and produce more robust conclusions. The same logic is at play within the EBP movement, which looks to use the huge volume of research on past policies to inform decision makers' thinking at the policy-making stage (Solesbury, 2001).

However, social policy interventions are not strictly analogous with medical interventions: while ten human bodies can be pretty much expected to respond in the same way to a particular drug or treatment, ten different countries, policy sectors or historical eras could quite conceivably produce ten different results when using the same policy tool (in other words, policies are socially and historically contingent). Moreover, and perhaps because of this, medical and policy researchers conduct and report their work in very different ways,

Figure 13.2: **The research/policy sequence**

1. Evaluation research (standard mode)

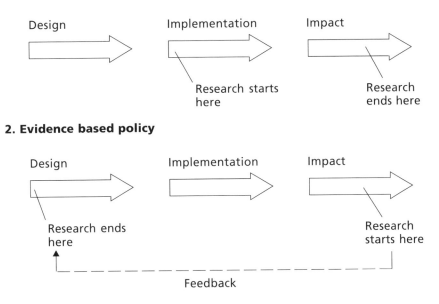

2. Evidence based policy

Source: Adapted from Pawson (2002a)

the standardised scientific logic of the former making it easier to summarise and synthesise than the more discursive, theoretically based approach found in the social sciences. Given this, the paradigm war in evaluation research reappears in current debates over how we might operationalise EBP, with a quantitative, positivist school looking to closely follow the techniques employed in evidence based medicine and a qualitatively driven school preferring to adopt a more discursive, narrative-driven approach. To illustrate this distinction, it is worth briefly describing the different methods the two schools of thought employ.

The quantitative school adopt an approach Pawson (2002a, p 161) terms **numerical meta-analysis** and is "based on a three-step model: 'classify', 'tally' and 'compare'". Those undertaking a review of, say, policies for improving the take-up of social security benefits would, having conducted an extensive search of both published and unpublished research on policies in this sphere, look to **classify** the (often thousands of) studies according to the type of policy intervention used in each instance (for example, a radio-led publicity campaign, mass mailing, benefit advice surgeries, and so on). Having done this, the researchers would then begin the **tallying** process: recording the net effect of the policy in each study and then calculating the mean effect across the studies for each particular category identified in the classification stage.

Finally, the researcher would, using the mean effect scores, **compare** the different mechanisms to determine which approach is the most effective; so, for argument's sake, it might be found that radio campaigns boost take-up by a mean of 10%, advice surgeries by 15% and mail drops by 20%, the evidence thus showing that the latter is the most effective policy approach in this area.

By contrast, the qualitative approach, which Pawson (2002a) calls **narrative review**, eschews the tallying process at the heart of its rival. While also involving the compilation of a database summarising the key dimensions of a wide number of studies, the data collected in the qualitative approach is text-based rather than numerical: written summaries rather than 'headcounts'. In addition, the substantive nature of the data differs too, being about processes and what happened at the street level rather than outcomes. Finally, in terms of picking out 'best buys', practice varies: some researchers simply let the studies speak for themselves, presenting a tabular summary of existing evidence; others pick out what they regard as exemplary programmes within those reviewed; and others go for a hybrid approach, picking elements from different programmes that might come together to form a model of best practice (see Pawson, 2002a).

It could be argued that one of the key advantages of EBP is that it is less threatening to policy makers and practitioners than either summative or formative evaluations, for it uses research evidence to inform policy without making direct judgements about specific policies or programmes. In short, it does not threaten careers or reputations. Significantly, the Blair government have launched a number of "highly visible initiatives ... substantially funded to provide the sort of credible evidence that evidence-based policy requires" (Packwood, 2002, p 268). Many follow from a report – *Adding it up* – published by the Cabinet Office's Performance and Innovation Unit in 2000 (Performance and Innovation Unit, 2000b) and include an Adding It Up Implementation Group, an Evidence Based Policy Fund and a new Prime Minister's Strategy Unit which includes a Policy Resource Centre and a new Government Chief Social Researcher's Office (GCSRO) (see www.addingitup.gov.uk; www.pm.gov.uk/output/Page77.asp). Crucially, departmental PSAs are used as a lever for getting departments on board the EBP train: the Evidence Based Policy Fund feeds directly into the setting of PSAs and departmental strategic objectives and a web site, Evidence Policy Choice (www.addingitup.gov.uk/epc/epc_overview1.cfm), tracks and documents the link between the two. On top of this, much of the GCSRO's work has centred on making better use of existing evidence and boosting research and evaluation skills within government[2].

---

[2] It is also worth adding, that the Economic and Social Research Council have invested considerable resources within the social science research community in establishing a Centre for Evidence Based Policy and Practice and a broader network connecting to it. See www.evidencenetwork.org.

Realist considerations

As Solesbury (2001, p 7) puts it, "There is, then, something about public policy and practice in Britain at present that has prompted a renewed concern with evidence". He goes on, however, to argue that while most social scientists "probably welcome this" we should not "be too simple minded in our enthusiasm.... We must not forget that there is more to policy and practice than the disinterested pursuit of truth and wisdom" (2001, p 7). Once again, hopes of using evidence to boost the 'rationality' of the policy-making process need to be tempered by the realist concern with what actually happens in practice: as Packwood (2001, p 270) suggests, "it would be more accurate to refer to an evidence-informed approach, as policy is determined according to more than research evidence alone, including financial, economic and strategic factors, and practitioner knowledge". On a similar note, Young et al (2001, p 217-8) argue for an **enlightenment approach** to EBP that holds the more limited ambition of 'illuminating' the landscape for policy makers rather than determining their decisions; they do so, in part, because "the rush of enthusiasm for evidence-based policy making overlooks the fact that a great deal of research has already been carried out on a wide range of social problems, providing policy makers with pointers that they rarely follow".

However, the realist perspective does not suggest there is no future for EBP or evaluation research more generally. Indeed, many realists (such as Pawson and Tilley, 1997; Julnes et al, 1998; Sanderson, 2000, 2002; Pawson, 2002a, 2002b) offer a constructive way forward that takes as its starting point the complex, non-linear nature of the policy process. Adopting such a perspective, Sanderson (2000, p 447) argues:

> evaluation in the context of complex policy systems must cope with the 'embeddedness' of such systems within a wider range of social processes. Individual components of policy interventions cannot be evaluated effectively if they are 'lifted' out of this context; it is necessary to identify and understand the influence of the key contextual factors and also the 'historical' nature of the task.

In order to do this, Sanderson (2002, p 4) argues that "evaluation should be 'theory-based' and focused on explaining and understanding how policies achieve their effects". He claims that one of the real weaknesses of evaluation research is that, having been seen as a 'technique', the debate about how it should proceed has been dominated by concerns with method – as reflected in the quantitative–qualitative 'paradigm wars'. The result has been to obscure the important role theories should play in policy evaluations, for it is only through theory that we can seek to understand and explain what makes policies 'work'. Pawson (2002b, p 342) puts the case forcibly:

> Realism adopts a 'generative' understanding of causation. What this tries to break is the lazy linguistic habit of basing evaluation on the question of whether 'programmes work'. In fact, it is not programmes that work but the resources they offer to enable their subjects to make them work.

More specifically, what Pawson and Tilley (1997) argue is that successful outcomes (O) are not the straightforward product of a policy or programme but, rather, result from underlying policy mechanisms (M) and their interaction with the context in which they operate (C): or, as they express it: **outcomes = mechanisms + context**. In order to understand 'what works', therefore, we need to develop theories about how M_1 and C_1 interact to produce O_1. So, to return to our example of a benefit take-up campaign, there would be little point in evaluating a particular campaign – let us say, mass mailing of leaflets explaining entitlements – simply by measuring the number of new claimants. While this would tell us about M (the mailing) and something about O (the number of people encouraged to claim), without exploring C our understanding of what worked would be minimal. Indeed, C is as critical as M: in this case, the numbers claiming would be influenced not just by the campaign itself but other factors such as how generous the benefit is, whether or not potential claimants feel a social stigma is attached to the benefit, how easy it is to claim and so on. Consequently, the task of the evaluator, from a realistic perspective, is not to 'measure' outcomes but to test theories about which combinations of M+C lead to desirable outcomes. So doing, they suggest, increases the rigour of evaluations, not least by allowing researchers to build complexity into their work – to account for the impact of institutions, networks or changing economic circumstances on policy outcomes. Moreover, such an approach need not divorce evaluation from its practice-based roots. As Sanderson (2002, p 18) points out, "social programmes are based upon explicit or implicit theories about how and why programmes will work and the task of [realistic] evaluation is to surface those theories, identify the key assumptions and test their validity". Equally, as Pawson and Tilley (1997) suggest, there is much to be gained by fusing this approach with knowledge and concepts garnered from academic work too.

Although Pawson and Tilley developed their perspective in connection with evaluation in the general sense, Pawson (2002b) has more recently proposed a realist approach to evidence based policy too. Building on the O=M+C model, he argues that a 'realist synthesis' of EBP would, first, look to compare families of policy mechanisms rather than families of policy programmes given the assumption that it is the mechanisms (M) that are the key agents in producing change. Second, the approach to data collection would be different too, looking not for 'what works' but, rather, "what works for whom in what circumstance" (2002b, p 342): in other words to gather information on C as well as O.

Finally, "the approach to *generalisation* is also different. The policy community is not offered a 'best buy' (approach 'x' or case 'y' seems to be the most successful) but a tailored, 'transferable theory' (this programme theory works in these respects, for these subjects, in these kinds of situations)" (2002b, p 342); or, to put it differently, the evidence is used to test a series of theories combining different O=M+C theories and the most robust are put forward.

Ultimately, the bottom line is Pawson's realist synthesis of EBP "eschews the idea of replicating best buys and exemplary cases" because "social interventions are so complex that there is little hope of reproducing them lock, stock and barrel and, even if one could, they are so context sensitive that the 'same' assemblage may then go on to misfire" (Pawson, 2002b, p 349). Here there are strong parallels with debates in the policy transfer literature (see Chapter Ten) concerning how far it is practicable or desirable to transfer successful policies from one place to another, and particularly with claims that transfer often fails because of a lack of sensitivity to differing contexts. Interestingly, Mossberger and Wolman (2003; following Rose, 1991) argue that policy transfer is a form of **prospective policy evaluation** and suggest the success rate of policy transfers could be increased if evaluation techniques were deployed in selecting candidates for transfer. More importantly, however, it is because of the context sensitivity of policy that realists advocate an enlightenment model to EBP: when there are no absolute answers it is important for social scientists to "remain modest in our claims to improve the conduct of public affairs" (Solesbury, 2001, p 9).

Conclusions

Here we have been able to offer little more than a very brief review of the many different approaches that fall under the broad heading of 'evaluation' along with some equally brief illustrations of how these issues are playing out in practice; in so doing we have necessarily simplified key elements of many of the approaches and, following Pawson (2002b), should stress that, in practice, the different approaches or paradigms are less rigid than the ideal types we have outlined here; indeed, methodological pluralism is very much the norm in contemporary evaluation research (Pawson and Tilley, 1997; Sanderson, 2002; Bate and Robert, 2003). While wary of presenting 'straw men' versions of opposing perspectives, our view, nevertheless, is that the realist approach and associated enlightenment perspective are the most robust articulations of how evaluation should proceed and what we can hope to achieve in boosting the use of evidence in policy making.

We adopt this position in large part because the realistic perspective concurs with the multi-level perspective of the policy process we have presented in this text: one that sees multiple influences operating at different levels and in which policy making is a non-linear phenomenon where actual outcomes are often unintended consequences. At the same time, it also sees evaluation and evidence as only ever playing one, small part in shaping policy outcomes, again consistent with our view that policy is shaped at multiple-levels by multiple forces. None of this is to dismiss the importance of using evidence to inform policy or the need for rigorous policy evaluations: both are vital. Instead, as Sanderson (2002, p 8) puts it, "it implies that there are no 'foundationalist' guarantees but nevertheless that our knowledge of the social world can help us '... in our attempts to steer the juggernaut' [Giddens, 1990, p 154]". In short, evidence can play a crucial role in increasing our **reflexivity**.

However, while some, such as David (2002) and Temple (2000), have proclaimed that the recent upsurge of interest in evaluation and EBP marks the emergence of a new, more enlightened approach to making policy, we should, perhaps, be wary of reading *too* much into recent developments. Pollitt (1998) says we should ask whether politicians *really* want more policy knowledge to inform their judgements than in the past and, if so, why? Part of the answer, he suggests, is that the declining popularity of politicians has reduced their legitimacy and the tightening of budgets has increased the intensity of political battles – both necessitating greater ammunition in battles for policy change and so the need for evidence to underpin decisions. However, he (1998, p 219) worries too that:

> because of its legitimacy-conferring properties, evaluation will be used by politicians in a mainly symbolic role. Thus, *being seen to have set in hand or demanded evaluations would become more important than what is done with the results of those exercises.* In this scenario, evaluation becomes a badge of modernity, a token of 'good management' ... evaluations being used as shiny decorations rather than serious tools.

Summary

- The evaluation of government policies is increasingly routine and systematic.
- Different approaches to policy evaluation exist – some theorists talk of 'paradigm wars' existing.
- The last 20 years has seen a significant rise in the use of quantitative performance indicators to evaluate the effectiveness of public services as part of the move towards the 'New Public Management' and the emergence of governance.
- New Labour regard evidence based policy as central to the modernisation of government. Some theorists see the Third Way as the triumph of pragmatism ('what works') over ideology.

- In recent years the notion of evidence based policy (EBP) – the attempt to systematically review past experience to inform future policy – has risen in prominence; the paradigm wars are replicated in EBP.
- Pawson and Tilley advocate a 'realistic' or 'realist' approach to evaluation, which acknowledges the complexity of the policy process and socially and historically contingent nature of policy knowledge. They advocate a theory driven approach to evaluation that explores outcome, mechanism and context combinations.
- Realists adopt an enlightenment perspective which sees a limited role for evidence in the policy process – to illuminate options for decision makers rather than to dictate solutions to them.
- We should ask why politicians are showing an increased interest in evaluation and EBP: there is a danger that their legitimising functions are being used in a purely symbolic fashion.

Questions for discussion

- What role does evaluation play in the policy-making process?
- How far have the New Labour governments moved towards a model of 'evidence-based policy making'?
- Why have politicians shown an increased interest in evaluation and evidence in recent years?

Further reading

Cabinet Office (1999) *Modernising government*, London: Cabinet Office.

Pawson, R. and Tilley, N. (1997) *Realistic evaluation*, London: Sage Publications.

Sanderson, I. (2002) 'Evaluation, policy learning and evidence-based policy making', *Public Administration*, vol 80, pp 1-22.

Solesbury, W. (2001) *Evidence based policy: Whence it came and where it's going*, Working Paper 1, ESRC UK Centre for Evidence-based Policy and Practice.

Temple, M. (2000) 'New Labour's Third Way: pragmatism and governance', *British Journal of Politics and International Relations*, vol 2, pp 302-25.

Electronic resource

Adding It Up (www.addingitup.gov.uk)

Conclusions: policy analysis and welfare states

Introduction

This final chapter departs from our macro-, meso- and micro-level structure because we wish to end the book by summing up and justifying our general approach before outlining what is perhaps the most important message from this book: the necessity for social policy as a sub-field of the social sciences to take much more seriously the knowledge base offered by political science, without which its multidisciplinary status is endangered. Without a sure and firm interdisciplinary foundation, the subject has been rocked by unnerving doubts about its claim to be a distinctive body of knowledge, indeed about its very survival as a subject taught in British universities. We believe that part of the explanation for this is that not enough attention has been paid to the 'policy' part of social policy, especially in an era when the role of the welfare state has been dramatically reconfigured. Not everyone believes that there has been much change, and some scholars argue that the Beveridge welfare state is more or less still with us and is largely intact. Such a reading of the situation, we believe, is dangerously to underestimate the realities as we have outlined them in these pages, especially the role of welfare policy in the creation of the competition state; in short, that the welfare state is no longer a redistributive, insurance-based, universal package of policies and programmes designed to overcome the Five Giants. Instead, its fundamental effort has been and continues to be reorientated to gearing up the British economy to compete in the global economy. As we have constantly reiterated in the book, this is not the same as saying there do not remain strong elements of the old order in the current system: it is precisely our case that institutional structures are 'sticky';

that is, they are persistent because social and economic interests reside in them, ideas and new developments are filtered through their networks and change is fundamentally incremental.

It is the aim of the good policy analyst to tease out the old from the new and provide, therefore, an open-minded and balanced understanding of the contemporary welfare state.

The Big Mac metaphor

The approach adopted in this book has been built round the three layers or tiers of influence that shape the development and nature of the policy process. Although we do not want to push the metaphor too far (one of us is a vegetarian!), we have spoken about it as a 'Big Mac' approach; in other words, three layers through which students of social and public policy need to bite to get the full flavour of what is shaping policy and delivery. To reiterate the approach:

> The macro-level ('macro' being derived from a Greek word *makros*, meaning long, extensive) encompasses the broad parameters that shape policy. We have identified globalisation as a key issue here, especially the power of the global marketplace in compelling nation states to conform to its influence and disciplines.

> The meso-level concerns the practice of the policy-making process itself and the institutions engaged in designing and seeing policy through to its delivery. This, crucially, is embedded in what we have identified as the key conceptual tool of this level, of policy networks; the agencies and bodies that initiate, filter and shape policy outcomes.

> The micro-level focuses down onto two themes. First, perhaps the key moment of the policy process, when 'the policy' is at the front line of delivery, when consumers and agencies engage. The second theme is the opposite pole of the macro-level, focusing on the influence of individuals and powerful personalities and elites in shaping outcomes.

As we have stressed throughout this book, these three levels are not always easy to discern, and it is certain that the boundaries between them are not discrete. But our reading of the literature and evaluation of contemporary reality is that this approach is much more fruitful and conceptually 'open' than the orthodox policy analysis approach with its emphasis on the policy cycle. The policy cycle is a useful metaphor but, in our view, is increasingly detached from reality, which is far more messy, unpredictable, complex and multilayered than the 'stagist' approach is able to comprehend. Policy rarely begins from a *tabula rasa*. It almost never has a beginning that is unconnected with policy that has gone before and does not unfold in a neat series of steps, from 'deciding to decide', through to policy design by 'policy makers' and delivery by 'administrators', who are simply functionaries of managers and policy makers. It is difficult to find examples in the literature of policy that has proceeded from beginning to end in this way (the end finally coming in the stage of 'evaluation'). Those that there are, are almost always unwittingly shrouded in top-down, systems-management theory in which the focus is on the issue of how to design 'perfect implementation'. In other words, the emphasis in these papers is on the branch of the subject identified by Lasswell as 'knowledge for' the managers of people. It is an inherently top-down perspective, which, in our view, sits uneasily with real-world policy processes.

Our approach

Our approach may be criticised for being eclectic in its willingness to be open to the conceptual repertoire. We would argue, however, that this is part and parcel of a critical approach to policy analysis, which is necessarily multilayered. Our approach is multi-theoretical. Where we are rather less sanguine is insisting on the historically and socially contingent nature of policy. This is perhaps the key lesson to emanate from the 'new institutionalist' literature (and which we echo very much). The institutionalist schools encompass a wide variety of perspectives, but all share the basic premise that political institutions are central to the nature of policy change and are the agencies that establish and operate the rules of the game. How these bodies interact and are configured in any one country is central to policy making and political outcomes. Institutions incorporate culturally shaped social norms including, indeed especially including, those shaped by social class configurations and the influence of social and economic elites. Institutionalist approaches provide analytical bite and knowledge of the sources and distribution of political power as it operates within and through political agencies and structures.

Most powerful of all is the historical institutionalist strand of this literature because it provides a rich palette of concepts that enable understanding of change over time. How have we arrived at the current state of play? How, in the case of the British welfare state, are we to make sense of its present reconfiguration without a fundamental grasp of its long historical progress? Perhaps the main lesson from all the institutional literature is precisely how 'sticky' and persistent existing institutional structures can be. Pensions policy based around long-term savings spread over literally a lifetime cannot easily or quickly be re-engineered. The stickiness of housing policy due to the physical nature of housing – built of bricks and mortar and designed to last 60 years or more – is legendary.

Even more than this, seeing the big picture can only be accomplished by recognising moments of crisis and change or those times when stability and consolidation is the watchword. Middle-range concepts such as **punctuated equilibrium** (patterns of stability and change), **veto points** (which head off or filter out unacceptable policy change), **critical junctures** (moments of crisis) or of **path dependency**, or institutional **lock-in** (factors that shape the direction of policy change) provide key insights into the reality of policy change and above all of how new ideas challenge existing paradigms, struggling against them, implanting new ideas into the institutional structures where they are filtered and screened out or absorbed. Change is the result of this process of institutional testing, and what happens, whether there is a fundamental paradigm shift, or more usually, a metamorphosis of policy and matching institutional adjustments, is a product of these processes.

The comparative dimension

These ideas also point to another product of the historical institutionalist school and which is fundamental to our approach in this book: that is, policy is inherently and indelibly comparative. The whole point of arguing for the significance of institutions in shaping social and political change and using concepts such as path dependency is to show how different countries evolve different solutions and pathways through the process of modernisation and change. One of the greatest dangers of un-theorised research or analysis is ethnocentrism, imagining from the limited view of one's own case that all other countries or cases are similar or at least can be understood using shared frames of reference. The comparative welfare state literature is replete with juxtapositional studies in which countries have allegedly been compared, where in fact they contain parallel discussions with comparison reserved for a concluding (and usually very short) chapter. Even though this book is essentially built around the British case and is not designed to be a 'comparative' textbook, its engagement with concepts such as globalisation, policy transfer, path dependency and so on means that it is inherently comparative. Britain cannot be understood as an isolated island in the Atlantic Ocean, because the forces that are shaping the future of its social and public policies, especially the economic power of the worldwide marketplace, are deployed across the globe. Our point is that the routes taken (that is, the *pathways*) in each nation state are both forced by this agenda but are by the same token locked into its institutional and cultural/historical legacy. Catholic conforming societies and Protestant-influenced nations have different welfare state settlements and different patterns of housing tenure. In other words, the legacy of the 15th-century Reformation echoes down through the centuries, and to fully understand our society, let alone others, requires engagement with this long history.

In short, we cannot understand or even half comprehend our own case without reference to others. Imagining the Beveridge welfare state to be an archetype, an idea sometimes openly suggested and often intuitively present in the literature, against which all others, or at least comparable industrial nations, should be judged, is highly misleading. The paradigm of the British welfare state does not easily fit most other cases in the western cultural tradition let alone that of the emerging Pacific Rim and the wider Asian experience. Trying to use 'our' experience and the resulting conceptual framework to evaluate other traditions stands a high chance of distorting reality because explanations have to be forced, rather like trying to wear a left shoe on a right foot. It can be done but it pinches, chafes and is unsustainable for very long. A very good case of this is the way in which British comparative housing scholars have used the British home-owning society, with its separate public and private rental sectors, as a norm against which to analyse other countries. Unfortunately, most European nations do not have such a neat division between the rental sectors; neither do they have such an emphasis on home ownership. Trying to understand German or Swedish housing in terms of British tenure structure inevitably generates flawed and misleading analysis, especially in their treatment of rental housing (Lowe, 2004).

In short, both this book and our general approach to policy analysis are inherently comparative. This is the only way to understand the contingent nature of social and public policy. Institutional structures are the product of different cultures, histories and ideas and how nation states chart their pathways through the 21st-century world will be patterned by the past. As we showed in Chapter Two, this means that globalisation, despite the powerful agency of the worldwide economy, is not creating a conforming, convergent response but deepening and divergence. How different countries find their way through this new world order is highly dependent on the historical settlement of their political institutions. As we have said, at several places in the book, *politics matters*; now, we want to affirm that **comparative politics matters**.

Implications of our approach

In our wish to be clear, it is sometimes easy to overlook the most basic elements of our approach, or to fall into the trap, which we criticise others for, of being implicit or unclear in the use of concepts. Some aspects of our position outlined above require more clarification.

Conceptual basis

Our choice of three levels of analysis – macro, meso and micro – is not arbitrary; rather, it derives from how we basically read the social science literature, especially that part of it concerned with welfare states. We outlined in Chapter One the characteristics of each level and their respective pros and cons. In our approach, macro-level theories and influences – globalisation, demographic change, economic restructuring – provide the broad parameters against which the policy process engages. Being aware of the problems of general theory is important to how they are handled. Their convergence dynamic, their tendency towards inductive logic in relation to evidence, their attempt to create universalist, all-embracing explanations are the main problems. Such concepts are powerful; they are 'red-hot', and engaging innocently with them is fraught with danger and the possibility of being burnt! Properly grounded policy analysis needs to draw from the evidence base of grand theory and related concepts but not fall uncritically into their logic.

The same is the case with research and scholarship at the other extreme, the micro-level. Here we are presented with a different set of difficulties arising not from the *over-conceptualised* nature of the literature but the reverse. Micro-level research by its very nature focuses down onto individual cases and often tries to explain social phenomena through descriptive categories. A great deal of social policy research is of this type, heavily empirical and dealing with the lowest common denominator of 'facts'. The danger of micro-level analysis, therefore, is the classic dilemma of not being able to see the wood for the trees. The main lesson for us in research and policy analysis that concentrates on individual cases – or, as Chapter Eleven did, considers the impact of individuals on the policy process – is the loss of theoretical focus. Properly understood, for example in the case of charismatic leadership, there is a great deal to be learned about the reality of the policy process and the actions that individuals take inside institutional settings. We have rehearsed the argument about 'structure and agency' in the text and do not need to repeat it here. The point is that individuals and personality matters a great deal to the outcomes of the policy process and in shaping the development of political cultures. It is the theorisation of the individual or the individual case that is crucial. Unwitting emphasis on facts and data (the latest version of which is known as evidence based policy making) in the absence of social theory (or using it implicitly) is a significant danger for the relevance of this sort of work and how it can contribute to the wider social sciences.

Without ourselves being entirely convinced about it, we have also posed the delivery stage of the policy process as a micro-level process. It has a certain resonance in that the moment when lessons are taught, keys to new housing are handed over, patients await their operations, and so on, is when implementation of policy ostensibly takes place. This is a very personal time in which agency professionals, Lipsky's street-level bureaucrats, and their clients or 'customers' access the services they need. As the surgeon makes her incision, there is in a sense nothing between her and her patient. Our understanding of this must, of course, be linked to the meso-level, the institutional structures and the broader parameters which shape the policy process.

Theories of the middle range

Meso-level concepts, built up from what Merton (1957) called 'theories of the middle range', are a very strong influence in the thinking behind this book. Over the last 15 years, work drawn from this level, especially, as we have indicated, that of the institutionalist schools, has been very productive in showing the institutional bases of social change. The logic has been for an emphasis on cultural contexts using historical and qualitative data. More recently still, the work of scholars such as Esping-Andersen (1990), Castles (1998) and Swank (2002) has moved the literature a stage further by developing work that uses large sets of empirical data but, crucially, in a rich theoretical context. In all these cases, this work has pointed towards dynamics of change that are much more divergent than convergent and where the attempt has been to evaluate the basis on which societies differ or are similar. The development of typologies has been a major step forward (Esping-Andersen's 'three worlds of welfare capitalism' or Castles' 'families of nations') in integrating historically and culturally sensitive studies with hard data. There is of course ample scope for criticism of these studies but their multi-theoretical approach has moved welfare state research significantly forward. A new type of literature has emerged.

Policy analysis in political science

The place of policy analysis and the influence of the wider political sciences should not be overlooked in this appraisal. Some of the best work, particularly under the influence of Theda Skocpol (1992; Skocpol and Amenta, 1986), has recognised the need 'to bring the state back in'. In political science, the role of the state itself had for many decades been neglected, relegated to mere description as in the case of the old-fashioned public administration tradition or rather 'overdetermined' in the somewhat mechanistic Marxist critique (state power is determined by the ruling class). It became clear, however, that the state could no longer be thought of as a 'black box' through which social power is exercised.

Our point is that, on the one hand, in the words of Karl Popper (1957), there is a danger in generalist theory of a 'poverty of historicism' – it is deterministic and ahistorical. Equally, and on the other hand, there is a danger in micro-level data gathering research of a 'poverty of empiricism', which is atheoretical and descriptive without purpose, unable to integrate with the wider social sciences and uncritically ethnocentric. Theory of the middle range (our meso-level of analysis), however, is both able to assess the claims of the universalist theory and detailed empirical research from a properly conceptual basis. But more significantly, it understands the contingent factors that shape society and social progress by giving full credence to the networks and institutions that are central to the policy process. Without the meso-level of analysis, we are blinkered from understanding how policy works. It is for this reason that we have emphasised this level in the text.

It is our belief that, on a more practical level, knowledge based around meso-level theories is much better placed to understand how to improve policy making and delivery. While often seen as abstract and lacking in practical relevance, we believe that in developing richer 'knowledge of' the policy process, meso-level approaches highlight the limitations of many of the more practically oriented 'knowledge for' schools of thought. This is because the old-style administrative tradition and the contemporary new public management approach draws from the overly simplified, rationalist, top-down school. We have shown in the text that the concepts related to this, notably the policy cycle, provide a very one-dimensional view of reality. Meso-theory and its connection to the macro- and micro-levels injects a much more soundly based, cold shower of realism. The policy process is not neatly packaged and rarely approaches meeting the conditions for perfect implementation often written about in the 'stagist' literature. It is a messy, sometimes incoherent, business, the stickiness of institutions constrains the development of new agendas and the grubbiness that often seems to typify the policy process, especially the role of politicians if the media is to be believed, puts the whole process in a bad light. We argue, nevertheless, that this is a much more realistic view of the policy process. Indeed, it may be that politics as it is generally understood has built up a heavily overinflated expectation of what it is and what it can deliver and by lowering expectations and revealing its real world policy analysts might serve to increase its legitimacy. Be that as it may, our purpose has been to demonstrate that, by using theories of the middle range, our understanding of the policy process is much more realistic than that offered in the rationalist literature.

Bringing politics back into social policy

We have argued that it is very difficult to understand the development of the modern welfare state without considering the nature of the policy-making process and the capacity of the nation state to create and deliver public policies. The rearticulation of the British state over the last 30 years has been dramatic and the creation of the hollowed-out, post-industrial, competition state has been a major consequence of this. It is important to note, however, that much of this analysis has been brought into social policy by political scientists –

often those working in American and European universities where the analysis of (public) policy is closely aligned with political science. The mainstream of social policy research in the UK has chosen to tread the well-worn pathways of empirical, policy-related research often eschewing such theoretical debates. Social policy in our view has been and remains a seriously under-theorised subject, and is in danger of losing its rightful place in key social scientific debates as a result. The reason we pull no punches on this is because we believe that this should not be allowed to happen. Social policy has much to contribute but it will do no such thing if it persists in pretending that it is a social science discipline in its own right. It is not: it is a **multidisciplinary field of inquiry**. This is not an 'academic' question, but is fundamental to the survival of the subject. Our very clear message from this book is that, by re-engaging with political science, social policy as an academic subject can take a major step back to its true interdisciplinary nature. To paraphrase Skocpol it is time to 'bring politics back in'.

One of the reasons for the unbalancing of social policy's disciplinary foundations has been an overexposure to sociology. Recent attempts to 'rethink' social policy (see, for example, Lewis et al, 2000) by injecting a stronger theoretical focus into the subject have drawn heavily on concepts developed in the sociological literature. At an anecdotal level, the number of universities in which sociology and social policy are housed in a single department[1] also illustrates the close ties between the subjects. For many, this is not an issue; indeed, Golding (2000, p 181) laments "the accidental organisational and disciplinary rift between sociology and social policy which emerged in post-war British social science". Sociology is of course a key influence and especially important for its conceptual knowledge of social structure: the class basis of society, gender inequalities, race and ethnicity and more recently in defining the nature and consequences of 'virtual reality'. However, the sociological agenda has squeezed the other disciplines to the margins of the subject. The operation of the state in patterning society and the role in this of political institutions is the terrain of political science. Of course, this is not to reify the disciplines and there are many areas of overlap between them but the knowledge base of political science is massive and its disciplinary insights around the nature and consequences of political power are vital to modern social policy. The subject needs to rebuild its conceptual aptitude based around a much more balanced *interdisciplinary* foundation.

A second, closely related flaw in social policy arises from the temptation to retreat into ever more complex empirical research in which all social phenomena are reduced to a lowest common denominator of 'facts',

---

[1] For instance, at the universities of Durham, Kent, Leeds, Liverpool, Newcastle and Nottingham. By contrast, we are unaware of any departments of Politics and Social Policy in the UK, although Goldsmiths and Dundee did have such departments until relatively recently.

unconnected to the wider social sciences. Attention then shifts towards method rather than theory as researchers develop ever more elaborate mechanisms for investigating policy facts. We have discussed this issue in this book and do not need to repeat the case. However, this also arises from the under-theorised state of the subject. Without a conceptual basis in the disciplines there is a temptation to fall back on a type of research that reduces all social phenomena to 'facts'. While social policy research can rightly point to its methodological sophistication – and can probably claim a lead over other strands of social science research in this respect – it should not lose sight of the historically and socially contingent nature of policy. As we argued in the previous chapter, developing knowledge of individual policies is not enough: we need also to theorise the processes that surround policies too.

In short, we believe that social policy's unique contribution to knowledge is in jeopardy if it does not re-engage with social theory and particularly rediscover its interdisciplinary foundations. A first step in this process would be to bring back the disciplinary knowledge from the political sciences. A first product of this would be an awareness that the British state has changed almost beyond recognition in the last three decades and that the role of the welfare state is radically different from only a very few years ago. It is time to put back the 'policy' into social policy. It is our firm hope that this book makes a contribution to this aim and that the series as a whole serves to strengthen and develop the much needed and valuable insights into 21st-century Britain that the social policy perspective, its concepts and methods offer. *Understanding the policy process is vital to understanding welfare.*

References

Accenture (2003) *eGovernment leadership: Engaging the customer*, London: Accenture.

Addison, P. (1994) *The road to 1945: British politics and the Second World War*, London: Pimlico.

Adler, E. and Haas, P. (1992) 'Conclusion: epistemic communities, world order, and the creation of a reflective research program', *International Organization*, vol 46, pp 367-90.

Alford, R. (1975) *Health care politics: Ideological and interest group barriers to reform*, Chicago, IL: University of Chicago Press.

Álvarez, I. and Kilbourn, B. (2002) 'Mapping the information society literature: topics, perspectives, and root metaphors', *First Monday*, vol 7 (http://firstmonday.org/issues/issue7_1/alvarez/index.html).

Anderson, R. (1996) *Security in clinical information systems*, Cambridge: Cambridge University Press.

Andeweg, R.B. and Van Den Berg, S.B. (2003) 'Linking birth order to political leadership: the impact of parents or sibling interaction?', *Political Psychology*, vol 24, no 3, pp 605-21.

Angell, I. (2000) *The new Barbarian Manifesto*, London: Kogan Page.

Armingeon, K. and Beyler, M. (eds) (2003) *The OECD and European welfare states*, Cheltenham: Edward Elgar.

Bachrach, P. and Baratz, M. (1962) 'Two faces of power', *The American Political Science Review*, vol 56, pp 947-52.

Bachrach, P. and Baratz, M. (1963) 'Decisions and nondecision: an analytic framework', *The American Political Science Review*, vol 57, pp 632-42.

Bachrach, P.S. and Baratz, M.S. (1970) *Power and poverty, theory and practice*, New York, NY: Oxford University Press.

Baldwin, P. (1989) 'The Scandinavian origins of the social interpretation of the welfare state', *Comparative Studies in Society and History*, vol 31, pp 3-24.

Baldwin, P. (1990) *The politics of social solidarity: Class bases of the European welfare state, 1875-1975*, Cambridge: Cambridge University Press.

Baldwin, P. (1992) 'The welfare state for historians. a review article', *Comparative Studies in Society and History*, vol 34, pp 695-707.

Barnett, A. (2003) 'Labour face "cash for access" claims over think-tanks', *The Observer*, 30 June.

Bate, P. and Robert, G. (2003) 'Where next for policy evaluation? Insights from researching National Health Service modernisation', *Policy & Politics*, vol 31, pp 249-62.

Baumgartner, F. and Jones, B. (1993) *Agendas and instability in American politics*, Chicago, IL: Chicago University Press.

BBCi (1999a) 'Protests overshadow WTO talks' (http://news.bbc.co.uk/1/hi/world/
    americas/542622.stm).

BBCi (1999b) 'Police admit riot failings' (http://news.bbc.co.uk/1/hi/uk/405601.stm).

BBCi (1999c) 'City violence premeditated Straw' (http://news.bbc.co.uk/1/hi/
    uk_politics/374625.stm).

BBCi (2001b) '"Epoch-making" poster was clever fake' (http://news.bbc.co.uk/1/hi/uk/
    1222326.stm).

Bell, D. (1974) *The coming of post-industrial society*, London: Heinemann.

Bell, D. (1979) 'The social framework of the information society', in M. Dertouzos and
    J. Moses (eds) *The computer age: A twenty year view*, Cambridge, MA: MIT Press,
    pp 163-211.

Benson, J.K. (1982) 'A framework for policy analysis', in D. Rogers and D. Whetten
    (eds) *Interorganisational coordination: Theory, research and implementation*, Ames,
    IA: Iowa State University Press, pp 137-76.

Beveridge, W. (1942) *Social insurance and allied services*, London: HMSO.

Beveridge, W. (1944) *Full employment in a free society*, London: George Allen &
    Unwin.

Beyler, M. (2003) 'Globalization, Europeanization and domestic welfare state reforms',
    Global Social Policy, vol 3, no 2, pp 153-72.

Biesanz, M. (1999) *The Ticos: Culture and social change in Costa Rica*, Boulder, CO:
    Lynne Reinner.

Bijker, W. (1995) *Of bicycles, Bakelites, and bulbs: Toward a theory of sociotechnical
    change*, Cambridge, MA: MIT Press.

Blair, T. (1998a) 'Foreword' in Cabinet Office (ed) *Our information age: The
    government's vision*, London: Cabinet Office.

Blair, T. (1998b) *The Third Way: New politics for the new century*, London: Fabian
    Society.

Blair, T. (1999) Beveridge Lecture, Toynbee Hall, London, 18 March.

Blair, T. and Schroeder, G. (1999) *Europe: The Third Way/Die Neue Mitee*, London:
    Labour Party.

Bloom, D., Kemple, J., Morris, P., Scrivener, S., Verma, N. and Hendra, R. (2000) *The
    Family Transition Program: Final Report on Florida's initial time-limited welfare
    program*, New York, NY: Manpower Demonstration Research Corporation.

Boaz, A., Ashby, D. and Young, K. (2002) *Systematic reviews: What have they got to
    offer evidence based policy and practice?*, Working Paper 2, London: ESRC UK
    Centre for Evidence-based Policy and Practice.

Börzel, T.A. (2003) 'Organizing Babylon – on the different conceptions of policy
    networks', *Public Administration*, vol 76, pp 253-73.

Brown, J. and Kiernan, N. (2001) 'Assessing the subsequent effect of a formative
    evaluation on a program', *Evaluation and Program Planning*, vol 24, pp 129-43.

BT (2000) *eGovernment: Ready or not?*, London: BT.

Buckley, R. and Tsenkova, S. (2004) 'Housing reforms and market performance', in S. Lowe and S. Tsenkova (eds) *Housing change in East and Central Europe: Integration or fragmentation?*, Aldershot: Ashgate, pp 3-20.

Burnett, J. (1986) *A social history of housing* (2nd edn), London: Methuen.

Burrows, R. and Loader, B. (1994) *Towards a post-Fordist welfare state?*, London: Routledge.

Cabinet Office (1998) *Our information age: The government's vision*, London: Cabinet Office.

Cabinet Office (1999) *Modernising government*, London: Cabinet Office.

Cabinet Office (2000) *e-Government: A strategic framework for public services in the information age*, London: Cabinet Office.

Cabinet Office (2003a) *Trying it out: The role of 'pilots' in policy-making*, London: Cabinet Office/PM's Strategy Unit.

Cabinet Office (2003b) *What can and cannot be learnt from the employment retention and advancement demonstration?*, London: Cabinet Office/PM's Strategy Unit.

Carter, N., Klein, R. and Day, P. (1992) *How organisations measure success: The use of performance indicators in government*, London: Routledge.

Castles, F.G. (1998) *Comparative public policy: Patterns of post-war transformation*, Cheltenham: Edward Elgar.

Castles, F.G. (2001) *Do institutions matter? One question, two approaches*, Inaugural Lecture, University of Edinburgh.

Castells, M. (1977) *The urban question*, London: Edward Arnold.

Castells, M. (1996) *The rise of the network society: The information age: Economy, society and culture, Vol I*, Oxford: Blackwell.

Castells, M. (1997a) *The power of identity, the information age: Economy, society and culture, Vol II*, Oxford: Blackwell.

Castells, M. (1997b) *The end of the millennium, the information age: Economy, society and culture, Vol III*, Oxford: Blackwell

Castells, M. (2000a) 'Materials for an exploratory theory of the network society', *British Journal of Sociology*, vol 51, pp 5-24.

Castells, M. (2000b) *The rise of the network society: The information age: Economy, society and culture, Vol 1* (2nd edn), Oxford: Blackwell.

Castells, M. and Himanen, P. (2002) *The information society and the welfare state: The Finnish model*, Oxford: Oxford University Press.

Cawson, A. (1982) *Corporatism and welfare*, London: Heinemann.

Cerny, P. and Evans, M. (1999) *New Labour, globalization, and the competition state*, Working Paper No 70, Harvard, NY: Center for European Studies, Harvard University.

Clark, C. (1940) *The conditions of economic progress*, London: Macmillan.

Cohen, M.J., March, J.G. and Olsen, J. (1972) 'A garbage can model of organisational choice', *Administrative Science Quarterly*, vol 17, pp 1-25.

Conservative Party (1978) 'Conservative Party Manifesto for 1978 General Election – 2nd draft' (www.margaretthatcher.org/record/displaydocument.asp?docid=110273), unpublished archive material.

Conservative Party (1979) *The Conservative Manifesto 1979*, London: Conservative Party.

CRD (Centre for Reviews and Dissemination) (2001) *Undertaking systematic reviews of research on effectiveness*, York: NHS CRD, University of York.

Crenson, M.A. (1971) *The unpolitics of air pollution: A study of non-decision making in the cities*, Baltimore: Johns Hopkins University Press.

Crick, B. (1962) *In defence of politics*, London: Weidenfeld & Nicolson.

Curthoys, N. (2003) *SmartGov: Renewing electronic government for improved service delivery*, London: iSociety/Work Foundation.

Cyert, R. and March, J. (1992) *A behavioral theory of the firm*, Oxford: Blackwell Publishers.

Dahl, R. (1961) *Who governs? Democracy and power in an American city*, New Haven, CT: Yale University Press.

Dahl, R. (1967) *Pluralist democracy in the United States*, Chicago, IL: Rand McNally.

David, M. (2002) 'Introduction: themed section on evidence-based policy as a concept for modernising governance and social science research', *Social Policy and Society*, vol 1, pp 213-14.

Davies, H., Nutley, S. and Smith, P. (1999) 'Editorial: what works? The role of evidence in public sector policy and practice', *Public Money and Management*, vol 18, pp 3-5.

Davies, H., Nutley, S. and Smith, P. (2000) *What works? Evidence-based policy and practice in public services*, Bristol: The Policy Press.

Davies, H., Nutley, S. and Smith, P. (2000) *What works? Evidence-based policy and practice in public services*, Bristol: The Policy Press.

Dawkins, R. (1976) *The selfish gene*, Oxford: Oxford University Press.

Deacon, A. (2000) 'Learning from the US? The influence of American ideas upon "new labour" thinking on welfare reform', *Policy & Politics*, vol 28, pp 5-18.

Deacon, B. (2001) 'International organizations, the EU and global social policy', in R. Sykes, B. Palier and P.M. Prior (eds) *Globalization and European welfare states*, Basingstoke: Palgrave, pp 59-76.

Delanty, G. (1999) *Social theory in a changing world*, Cambridge: Polity Press.

DiMaggio, P.J. and Powell, W.W. (1991) *The new institutionalism in organizational analysis*, Chicago, IL: University of Chicago Press.

Dolan, C. and Barrientos, S. (2003) 'Labour flexibility in African horticulture', *Insights: Development Research*, No 47, Institute of Development Studies, University of Sussex.

Dolowitz, D.P. (1997) 'British employment policy in the 1980s: learning from the American experience', *Governance-An International Journal of Policy and Administration*, vol 10, pp 23-42.

Dolowitz, D. (ed) (2000a) *Policy transfer and British social policy: Learning from the USA?*, Buckingham: Open University Press.

Dolowitz, D. (2000b) 'Policy transfer: a new framework for analysis', in D. Dolowitz (ed) *Policy transfer and British social policy: Learning from the USA?*, Buckingham: Open University Press, pp 9-37.

Dolowitz, D. (2000c) 'Welfare: the Child Support Agency', in D. Dolowitz (ed) *Policy transfer and British social policy: Learning from the USA?*, Buckingham: Open University Press, pp 38-58.

Dolowitz, D.P. (2001) 'The British Child Support Agency: did American origins bring failure?', *Environment and Planning C-Government and Policy*, vol 19, pp 373-89.

Dolowitz, D.P. and Marsh, D. (1996) 'Who learns what from whom: a review of the policy transfer literature', *Political Studies*, vol 44, pp 343-57.

Dolowitz, D.P. and Marsh, D. (2000) 'Learning from abroad: the role of policy transfer in contemporary policy-making', *Governance-An International Journal of Policy and Administration*, vol 13, pp 5-24.

Dolowitz, D.P., Greenwold, S. and Marsh, D. (1999) 'Policy transfer: something old, something new, something borrowed, but why red, white and blue?', *Parliamentary Affairs*, vol 52, pp 719-30.

Dorey, P. (2001) *Wage politics in Britain: The rise and fall of incomes policies since 1945*, Brighton: Sussex Academic Press.

Dowding, K. (1995) 'Model or metaphor? A critical review of the policy network approach', *Political Studies*, vol 43, pp 136-58.

Dowding, K. (2001) 'There must be an end to confusion: policy networks, intellectual fatigue, and the need for political science methods courses in British universities', *Political Studies*, vol 49, pp 89-105.

DTI (Department for Trade and Industry) (2000) *Closing the digital divide: Information and communication technologies in deprived areas*, London: DTI.

Duke, K. (2002) 'Getting beyond the "official line": reflections on dilemmas of access, knowledge and power in researching policy networks', *Journal of Social Policy*, vol 31, pp 39-59.

Dunleavy, P. (2003) 'Analysing political power', in P. Dunleavy, A. Gamble, R. Heffernan and G. Peele (eds) *Developments in British politics* 7, Basingstoke: Palgrave Macmillan, pp 338-59.

Dunsire, A. (1990) 'Implementation theory and bureaucracy', in T. Younis (ed) *Implementation in public policy*, Aldershot: Dartmouth.

Efficiency Unit (1988) *Improving management in government: The next steps*, The Ibbs Report, London: HMSO.

Elmore, R. (1978) 'Organizational models of social program implementation', *Public Policy*, no 26, pp 185-228.

Elmore, R. (1979) 'Backward mapping', *Political Science Quarterly*, vol 94, pp 601-16.

Elster, J. (1989) *The cement of society*, Cambridge: Cambridge University Press.

Esping-Andersen, G. (1990) *The three worlds of welfare capitalism*, Cambridge: Polity Press.

Esping-Andersen, G. (1996) *Welfare states in transition: National adaptations in global economies*, London: Sage Publications.

EU (1994) *Europe and the global information society*, Bangemann Report, Brussels: EU.

European Commission (1999) *Eurobarometer: Public opinion in the European Union: Report Number 52*, Brussels: EC.

European Commission (2001) *Eurobarometer: les Europeens, la Globalisation et la Liberalisation: Report 55.1*, Brussels: EC.

Evans, M. (1999a) *Policy networks: A British perspective*, Working Paper No 16, York: Department of Politics, University of York.

Evans, M. (1999b) 'Policy transfer networks and collaborative government: the case of social security fraud', *Public Policy and Administration*, vol 12, pp 30-48.

Evans, M. (2001) 'Understanding dialectics in policy networks', *Political Studies*, vol 49, pp 542-50.

Evans, M. and Cerny, P. (2003) 'Globalisation and social policy', in N. Ellison and C. Pierson (eds) *Developments in British social policy 2*, Basingstoke: Palgrave, pp 19-41.

Evans, M. and Davies, J. (1999) 'Understanding policy transfer: a multi-level, multi-disciplinary perspective', *Public Administration*, vol 77, pp 361-85.

Flora, P. (1986) *Growth to limits: The Western European welfare states since World War II*, Berlin: De Gruyter.

Foucault, M. (1977) *Discipline and punishment: The birth of the prison*, Harmondsworth: Penguin.

Foucault, M. (1988) *The history of sexuality*, London: Allen Lane.

Fraser, D. (2003) *The evolution of the British welfare state: A history of social policy since the Industrial Revolution*, Basingstoke: Palgrave.

George, V. and Wilding, P. (2002) *Globalisation and human welfare*, Basingstoke: Palgrave Macmillan.

Geva-May, I. and Pal, L. (1999) 'Good fences make good neighbours: policy evaluation and policy analysis – exploring the differences', *Evaluation*, vol 5, pp 259-77.

Giddens, A. (1976) *New rules of sociological method*, London: Hutchinson.

Giddens, A. (1979) *Central problems in social theory*, London: Macmillan.

Giddens, A. (1984) *The constitution of society: Outline of the theory of structuration*, Cambridge: Polity.

Giddens, A. (1990) *The consequences of modernity*, Cambridge: Polity Press.

Giddens, A. (1999) *Runaway world: How globalization is reshaping our lives*, London: Profile Books.

Giddens, A. (2000) *The Third Way and its critics*, Cambridge: Polity Press.

Giddens, A. (2001) *The global Third Way debate*, Cambridge: Polity Press.

Gladstone, D. (1995) *British social welfare: Past, present and future*, London: UCL Press.

Glennerster, H. (1995) *British social policy since 1945*, Oxford: Blackwell.

Goffman, I. (1959) *The presentation of the self in everyday life*, Harmondsworth: Penguin Books.

Golding, P. (2000) 'Forthcoming features: Information and communications technologies and the sociology of the future', *British Journal of Sociology*, vol 34, pp 156-84.

Gough, I. (1983) 'Thatcherism and the welfare state', in S. Hall and M. Jacques (eds) *The politics of Thatcherism*, London: Lawrence and Wishart, pp 148-68.

Gould, S.J. and Eldredge, N. (1977) 'Punctuated equilibria: the tempo and mode of evolution reconsidered', *Paleobiology*, vol 3, pp 115-51.

Graham, S. and Marvin, S. (2001) *Splintering urbanism: Networked infrastructures, technological mobilities and the urban condition*, London: Routledge.

Greener, I. (2002) 'Understanding NHS reform: the policy-transfer, social learning, and path-dependency perspectives', *Governance: An International Journal of Policy and Administration*, vol 15, pp 161-83.

Greenstein, F.I. (1969) *Personality and politics: Problems of evidence, inference and conceptualisation* (2nd edn), Chicago, IL/Princeton, NJ:, Markham/Princeton University Press.

Greenstein, F.I. (1992) 'Can personality and politics be studied systematically?', *Political Psychology*, vol 13, pp 105-28.

Gunn, L.A. (1978) 'Why is perfect implementation so difficult?', *Management Services in Government*, vol 33, pp 169-76.

Haas, E.B. (1990) *When knowledge is power: Three models of change in international organisations*, Berkley and Los Angeles, CA: California University Press.

Hall, P. (1992) 'The movement from Keynesianism to Monetarism: institutional analysis and economic policy in the 1970s', in S. Steinmo, K. Thelen and F. Longstreth (eds) *Structuring politics: Historical institutionalism in comparative analysis*, Cambridge: Cambridge University Press, pp 90-113.

Hall, P. (1993) 'Policy paradigms, social learning and the state: the case of economic policymaking in Britain', *Comparative Politics*, vol 25, pp 275-96.

Hall, P. and Taylor, R. (1996) 'Political science and the three new institutionalisms', *Political Studies*, vol 44, pp 936-57.

Ham, C. (1999) *Health policy in Britain: The politics and organisation of the National Health Service*, Basingstoke: Palgrave.

Hardey, M. (1999) 'Doctor in the house: the Internet as a source of lay health knowledge and the challenge to expertise', *Sociology of Health and Illness*, vol 21, pp 820-35.

Harvey, D. (1973) *Social justice and the city*, Oxford: Blackwell.

Hasluck, C. (2000) *Early lessons from the evaluation of New Deal Programmes*, London: Employment Service.

Haubrich, D. (2001) 'UK rail privatisation five years down the line: an evaluation of nine policy objectives', *Policy & Politics*, vol 29, pp 317-36.

Hay, C. (1999) *The political economy of New Labour: Labouring under false pretences*, Manchester: Manchester University Press.

Hayek, F. (1944) *The road to serfdom*, London: RKP.

Heclo, H. (1974) *Modern social politics in Britain and Sweden*, New Haven, CT: Yale University Press.

Heffernan, R. (2002) '"The possible as the art of politics": understanding consensus politics', *Political Studies*, vol 50, pp 742-60.

Held, D. and McGrew, A. (eds) (2000) *The global transformations reader*, Cambridge: Polity Press.

Held, D. and McGrew, A. (2001) 'Globalization', in J. Krieger (ed) *The Oxford companion to politics of the world* (2nd edn), Oxford: Oxford University Press.

Held, D., McGrew, A., Goldblatt, D. and Perraton, J. (1999) *Global transformations: Politics, economics and culture*, Cambridge: Polity Press.

Henkel, M. (1991) 'The new evaluative state', *Public Administration*, vol 69, pp 121-36.

Hill, M. (1993) *The welfare state in Britain: A political history since 1945*, Aldershot: Edward Elgar.

Hill, M. (1997) *The policy process in the modern state* (3rd edn), London: Prentice Hall/Harvester Wheatsheaf.

Hill, M. (2003) *Understanding social policy*, Blackwell: Oxford.

Hirst, P. and Thompson, G. (1999) *Globalization in question* (2nd edn), Cambridge: Polity Press.

HM Treasury (1998) *Modern public services for Britain: Investing in reform. Comprehensive Spending Review: New public spending plans 1999-2002*, London: The Stationery Office.

HM Treasury (2000) *Prudent for a purpose: Building opportunity and security for all. Comprehensive Spending Review 2000: New public spending plans 2001-2004*, London: The Stationery Office.

HM Treasury (2002a) *2002 Spending Review: Public service agreements*, London: The Stationery Office.

HM Treasury (2002b) *Opportunity and security for all: Investing in an enterprising, fairer Britain. Comprehensive Spending Review: New public spending plans 2003-2006*, London: The Stationery Office.

Hobbes, T. (1651) *Leviathan*, London: Andrew Crooke.

Hoggett, P. (1996) 'New modes of control in the public service', *Public Administration*, vol 74, no 1, pp 9-32.

Hogwood, B. and Gunn, L. (1983) *Policy analysis for the real world*, Oxford: Oxford University Press.

Holden, C. (2002) 'The internationalization of long term care provision: economics and provision', *Global Social Policy*, vol 2, pp 47-67.

Holliday, I. (2000) 'Is the British state hollowing out?', *The Political Quarterly*, pp 167-76.

Homans, G. (1961) *Social behaviour: Its elementary forms*, London: Routledge.

Hood, C. (1991) 'A public management for all seasons', *Public Administration*, vol 69, no 1, pp 3-19.

Hood, C. (1995) 'The New Public Management in the 1980s – variations on a theme', *Public Administration*, vol 20, no 2-3, pp 93-109.

Hooghe, D. and Marks, G. (2001) *Multi-level governance and European integration*, Lanham, MD: Rowan and Littlefield.

House of Commons Public Administration Committee (2003) *Fifth Report: On target? Government by measurement*, HC 62-I.

House of Lords Science and Technology Select Committee (1997) *Information society: 5th Report. Agenda for action in the UK*, HL Paper 77.

Hudson, B. and Hardy, B. (2001) 'Localization and partnership in the "New National Health Service": England and Scotland compared', *Public Administration*, vol 79, pp 315-35.

Hudson, J. (1999) 'Informatization and public administration: a political science perspective', *Information, Communication and Society*, vol 2, pp 318-39.

Hudson, J. (2002) 'Digitising the structures of government: the UK's information age government agenda', *Policy & Politics*, vol 30, pp 515-31.

Hudson, J. (2003) 'e-galitarianism? The information society and New Labour's repositioning of welfare', *Critical Social Policy*, vol 23, pp 268-90.

Hutton, W. (1995) *The state we're in: Why Britain is in crisis and how to overcome it*, London: Cape.

Huxham, M. and Sumner, D. (1999) 'Emotion, science and rationality: the case of the Brent Spar', *Environmental Values*, vol 8, pp 349-68.

Hwang, G.-J. (2002) 'The possibility of social policy: the political construction of state welfare in the Republic of Korea', Unpublished PhD thesis, University of York.

IBM (2002) *e-business utilisation in social security: 2001 update*, Basingstoke: IBM UK Limited.

Immergut, E. (1990) 'Institutions, veto points and policy results: a comparative analysis of health care', *Journal of Public Policy*, vol 10, pp 391-416.

Immergut, E. (1992a) *Health politics: Interests and institutions in Western Europe*, Cambridge: Cambridge University Press.

Immergut, E. (1992b) 'The rules of the game: the logic of health policy-making in France, Switzerland, and Sweden', in S. Steinmo, K. Thelen and F. Longstreth (eds) *Structuring politics: Historical institutionalism in comparative analysis*, Cambridge: Cambridge University Press.

IPPR (Institute for Public Policy Research) (1994) *Social justice: Strategies for national renewal*, London: Viking.

Jenkins, R. (2004: forthcoming) 'Globalisation and employment in Vietnam', *Journal of International Development*.

Jenkins, R. and Sen, A. (2003) 'Globalisation and manufacturing employment', *Insights: Development Research*, No 47, Institute of Development Studies, University of Sussex.

Jessop, B. (1994) 'The transition to post-Fordism and the Schumpeterian workfare state', in R. Burrows and B. Loader (eds) *Towards a post-Fordist welfare state?*, London: Routledge, pp 13-37.

Jessop, B. (1999) 'The changing governance of welfare: recent trends in its primary functions, scale, and modes of coordination', *Social Policy and Administration*, vol 33, pp 348-59.

Jessop, B. (2000) 'From the KWNS to the SWPR', in G. Lewis, S. Gewirtz and J. Clarke (eds) *Rethinking social policy*, London: Sage Publications.

Johnson, T. (1972) *Professions and power*, London: Macmillan.

Jones, K. (2000) *The making of social policy in Britain: From the Poor Law to New Labour*, London: Athlone.

Jordan, G. (1998) 'Indirect causes and effects in policy change: the Brent Spar case', *Public Administration*, vol 76, pp 713-40.

Julnes, G., Mark, M. and Henry, G. (1998) 'Promoting realism in evaluation: realistic evaluation and the broader context', *Evaluation*, vol 4, pp 483-504.

Kavanagh, D. (1990) *Thatcherism and British politics: The end of consensus?*, Oxford: Oxford University Press.

Kemeny, J. (1981) *The myth of home ownership: Public versus private choices in housing tenure*, London: Routledge.

Kemeny, J. (1995) *From public housing to the social market*, London: Routledge.

Kettl, D. (2000) *The global public management revolution: A report on the transformation of governance*, Washington, DC: Brookings Institute.

Keynes, J.M. (1936) *The general theory of employment, interest and money*, Cambridge: Cambridge University Press.

Kickert, W.J.M. and Koppenjan, J.F.M. (1997) 'Public management and network management: an overview', in W.J.M. Kickert, E.H. Klijn and J.F.M. Koppenjan (eds) *Managing complex networks: Strategies for the public sector*, London: Sage Publications, pp 35-61.

Kickert, W.J.M., Klijn, E.H. and Koppenjan, J.F.M. (1997) *Managing complex networks: Strategies for the public sector*, London: Sage Publications.

Kingdon, J.W. (1984) *Agendas, alternatives and public policies*, Boston, MA: Little Brown.

Klijn, E.-H. (1997) 'Policy networks', in W.J.M.Kickert, E.-H.Klijn and J.F.M.Koppenjan (eds) *Managing complex networks: Strategies for the public sector*, London: Sage Publications, pp 14-34.

Knill, C. and Lehmkuhl, D. (1999) 'How Europe matters: different mechanisms of europeanization', *European Integration Online Papers*, vol 3, no 7 (http://eiop.or.at/eiop/texte/1998-007a.htm).

Knoke, D. (1998) 'Who steals my purse steal trash: the structure of organizational influence reputation', *Journal of Theoretical Politics*, vol 10, pp 507-30.

Krasner, S. (1988) 'Sovereignty: an institutional perspective', *Comparative Political Studies*, vol 21, pp 66-94.

Kuhn, T. (1970) *The structure of scientific revolutions*, Chicago, IL: Chicago University Press.

Kühner, S. (2003) 'About the dream of perpetual expansion: welfare consolidation in comparative perspective', Unpublished MA thesis, University of York.

Lasswell, H.D. (1930) *Psychopathology and politics*, Chicago, IL: University of Chicago Press.

Lasswell, H.D. (1936) *Politics: Who gets what, when, how*, Cleveland, OH: Meridian Books.

Lasswell, H.D. (1948) *Power and personality*, New York, NY: W.W. Norton.

Latour, B. (1999) 'On recalling ANT', in J. Law and J. Hassard (eds) *Actor network and after*, Oxford: Blackwell, pp 15-25.

Leer, A. (1999) *Masters of the wired world: Cyberspace speaks out*, London: Pearson.

Leicester, G. (1999) 'The seven enemies of evidence-based policy', *Public Money and Management*, vol 19, pp 5-7.

Lewis, G., Gewirtz, S. and Clarke, J. (2000) *Rethinking social policy*, London: Sage Publications.

Liebfried, S. and Pierson, P. (2000) 'Social policy', in H. Wallace and W. Wallace (eds) *Policy-making in the European Union* (4th edn), Oxford: Oxford University Press, pp 267-92.

Lindblom, C.E. (1959) 'The science of muddling through', *Public Administration Review*, vol 19, pp 78-88.

Lindblom, C.E. (1977) *Politics and markets*, New York, NY: Basic Books.

Lindblom, C.E. (1979) 'Still muddling through', *Public Administration Review*, vol 39, no 6, pp 517-25.

Lindblom, C.E. (1988) *Democracy and market system*, Oslo: Norwegian University Press.

Lindblom, C. and Woodhouse, E. (1993) *The policy-making process*, Englewood Cliffs, NJ: Prentice Hall.

Lipsky, M. (1971) 'Street-level bureaucracy and the analysis of urban reform', *Urban Affairs Quarterly*, vol 6, pp 391-409.

Lipsky, M. (1979) *Street level bureaucracy*, New York, NY: Russell Sage Foundation.

Lowe, S. (1986) *Urban social movements: The city after Castells*, Houndmills: Macmillan.

Lowe, S. (2004) *Housing policy analysis: British housing policy and cultural and comparative context*, Houndmills, Basingstoke: Palgrave/Macmillan.

Lowe, S. and Tsenkova, S. (2003) *Housing change in East and Central Europe: Integration or fragmentation*, Abingdon: Ashgate.

Lowe, S., Keenan, P. and Spencer, S. (1999) 'Housing abandonment in inner cities: the politics of low demand for housing', *Housing Studies*, vol 14, no 5, pp 703-16.

Lowndes, V. (1997) 'Varieties of New Institutionalism: a critical appraisal', *Public Administration*, vol 74, no 2, pp 181-97.

Lukes, S. (1974) *Power: A radical view*, London: Macmillan.

Lush, L., Walt, G. and Ogden, J. (2003) 'Transferring policies for treating sexually transmitted infections: what's wrong with global guidelines?', *Health Policy and Planning*, vol 18, pp 18-30.

McGrew, A.G. and Lewis, P. (1992) *Global politics: Globalization and the nation state*, Cambridge: Polity Press.

MacKenzie, D. and Wajcman, J. (1999) *Social shaping of technology*, Buckingham: Open University Press.

Machlup, F. (1962) *The production and distribution of knowledge in the United States*, Princeton, NJ: Princeton University Press.

March, J.G. and Olsen, J.P. (eds) (1976) *Ambiguity and choice in organizations*, Oslo: Universitetsforlaget.

March, J.G. and Olsen, J.P. (1984) 'The new institutionalism: organizational factors in political life', *American Political Science Review*, vol 78, pp 734-49.

March, J.G. and Olsen, J.P. (1989) *Rediscovering institutions: The organizational basis of politics*, New York, NY: Free Press.

Marsh, D. (1998) *Comparing policy networks*, Buckingham: Open University Press.

Marsh, D. and Rhodes, R.A.W. (1992a) *Implementing Thatcherite policies: Audit of an era*, Buckingham: Open University Press.

Marsh, D. and Rhodes, R.A.W. (1992b) 'Policy communities and issue networks: beyond typology', in D. Marsh and R.A.W. Rhodes (eds) *Policy networks in British government*, Oxford: Clarendon Press, pp 249-68.

Marsh, D. and Rhodes, R.A.W. (1992c) *Policy networks in British government*, Oxford: Clarendon Press.

Marsh, D. and Rhodes, R.A.W. (1992d) 'Policy networks in British politics', in D. Marsh and R.A.W. Rhodes (eds) *Policy networks in British government*, Oxford: Clarendon Press, pp 1-26.

Marsh, D. and Smith, M.J. (2000) 'Understanding policy networks: towards a dialectical approach', *Political Studies*, vol 48, pp 4-21.

Marsh, D. and Smith, M.J. (2001) 'There is more than one way to do political science: on different ways to study policy networks', *Political Studies*, vol 49, pp 528-41.

Marsh, D., Richards, D. and Smith, M.J. (2000) 'Re-assessing the role of departmental cabinet ministers', *Public Administration*, vol 78, no 2, pp 305-26.

Marshall, T.H. (1950) 'Citizenship and social class', in T.H. Marshall (ed) *Citizenship and class and other essays*, Cambridge: Cambridge University Press, pp 3-51.

Masuda, Y. (1980) *The information society as post-industrial society*, Washington, DC: World Future Society.

May, C. (2001) *The information society: A skeptical view*, Cambridge: Polity Press.

Mead, G. (1934) *The mind, self and society*, Chicago, IL: Chicago University Press.

Melucci, A. (1996) *Challenging codes: Collective action in the information age*, Cambridge: Cambridge University Press.

Melucci, A. (1998) *The playing self*, Cambridge: Cambridge University Press.

Merton, R.K. (1957) *Social theory and social structure*, Glencoe, IL: Free Press.

Michels, R. (1911) *Political parties*, London: Constable (reprinted 1959).

Middlemass, K. (1979) *Politics in industrial society*, London: Andre Deutsch.

Middleton, S., Maguire, S., Ashworth, K., Legge, K., Allen, T., Perren, K., Battistin, E., Emmerson, C., Fitzsimmons, E. and Meghir, C. (2003) *The evaluation of Education Maintenance Allowance pilots: Three years evidence – a quantitative evaluation*, Department for Education and Skills Research Report RR499, London: DfES.

Mills, C.W. (1956) *The power elite: On the ruling groups in the United States*, New York, NY: Oxford University Press.

Morris, P., Bloom, D., Kemple, J. and Hendra, R. (2003) 'The effects of a time-limited welfare program on children: the moderating role of parents' risk of welfare dependency', *Child Development*, vol 74, pp 851-74.

Mossberger, K. and Wolman, H. (2003) 'Policy transfer as a form of prospective policy evaluation: challenges and recommendations', *Public Administration Review*, vol 63, pp 428-40.

Mullins, D. and Riseborough, M. (2000) *What are Housing Associations becoming*, Birmingham: Centre for Urban and Regional Studies, University of Birmingham.

Myles, J. and Pierson, P. (2001) 'The comparative political economy of pension reform', in P. Pierson (ed) *The new politics of the welfare state*, Oxford: Oxford University Press, pp 305-33.

Nadvi, K. and Thoburn, J. et al (2003) 'Vietnam in the global garment and textile chain: impacts on firms and workers', *Journal of International Development*, vol 16, no 1, pp 111-23.

National Statistics (2003) *Internet access: Individuals and households*, London: National Statistics.

Needham, C. (2003) *Citizen-consumers: New Labour's marketplace democracy*, London: Catalyst.

Negroponte, N. (1995) *Being digital*, New York, NY: Vintage Books.

Nora, S. and Minc, A. (1980) *The computerization of society*, Cambridge, MA: MIT Press.

Offe, C. (1985) 'New social movements: challenging the boundaries of institutional politics', *Social Research*, vol 52, no 4, pp 817-68.

Ohmae, K. (1990) *The borderless world*, London: Collins

O'Neil, F. (2000) 'Health: the internal market and the reform of the NHS', in D. Dolowitz (ed) *Policy transfer and British social policy: Learning from the US?*, Buckingham: Open University Press, pp 59-76.

Orwell, G. (1945) *Animal farm*, London: Secker and Warburg.

Orwell, G. (1949) *Nineteen Eighty-Four*, London: Secker and Warburg.

Osborne, D. and Gaebler, T. (1992) *Reinventing government*, Reading, MA: Addison-Wesley Publishing Company.

O'Toole, B. and Jordan, G. (1995) *Next steps: Improving management in government*, Aldershot: Dartmouth.

Packwood, A. (2001) 'Review article: Evidence-based policy: rhetoric and reality', *Social Policy and Society*, vol 1, pp 267-72.

Packwood, T., Keen, J. and Buxton, M. (1991) *Hospitals in transition: The resource management experiment*, Milton Keynes: Open University Press.

Palumbo, D. (1987) 'Politics and Evaluation', in D. Palumbo (ed) *The politics of program evaluation*, Newbury Park, CA: Sage Publications, pp 12-47.

Parry, R. (2003) 'Invest and reform: Spending Review 2002 and its control regime', in C. Bochel, N. Ellison and M. Powell (eds) *Social Policy Review 15*, Bristol: The Policy Press/SPA, pp 31-48.

Parsons, W. (1995) *Public policy: An introduction to the theory and practice of policy analysis*, London: Edward Elgar.

Pawson, R. (2002a) 'Evidence-based policy: in search of a method', *Evaluation*, vol 8, pp 157-81.

Pawson, R. (2002b) 'Evidence-based policy: the promise of "realist synthesis"', *Evaluation*, vol 8, pp 340-58.

Pawson, R. and Tilley, N. (1997) *Realistic evaluation*, London: Sage Publications.

Peck, J. and Theodore, N. (2001) 'Exporting workfare/importing welfare-to-work: exploring the politics of Third Way policy transfer', *Political Geography*, vol 20, pp 427-60.

Performance and Innovation Unit (2000a) *Adding it up: Improving analysis and modelling in central government*, London: Cabinet Office/Performance and Innovation Unit.

Performance and Innovation Unit (2000b) *e.gov: Electronic government services for the 21st century*, London: Cabinet Office.

Pierson, C. (2003) 'Learning from Labor? Welfare policy transfer between Australia and Britain', *Commonwealth & Comparative Politics*, vol 41, pp 77-100.

Pierson, C. and Castles, F.G. (2002) 'Australian antecedents of the third way', *Political Studies*, vol 50, pp 683-702.

Pierson, P. (1994) *Dismantling the welfare state? Reagan, Thatcher and the politics of retrenchment*, Cambridge: Cambridge University Press.

Pierson, P. (1995) 'Fragmented welfare states: federal institutions and the development of social policy', *Governance*, vol 8, pp 449-78.

Pierson, P. (2000) 'Path dependence, increasing returns and the study of politics', *American Political Science Review*, vol 94, pp 251-67.

Pierson, P. (ed) (2001) *The new politics of the welfare state*, Oxford: Oxford University Press.

Pollitt, C. (1993) *Managerialism and the public services*, Oxford: Blackwell.

Pollitt, C. (1994) 'The Citizens Charter: a preliminary analysis', *Public Money and Management*, vol 14, pp 9-14.

Pollitt, C. (1998) 'Evaluation in Europe: boom or bubble?', *Evaluation*, vol 4, pp 214-24.

Pollitt, C. (1999) 'Stunted by stakeholders? Limits to collaborative evaluation', *Public Policy and Administration*, vol 14, pp 77-90.

Pollitt, C. (2001) 'Convergence: the useful myth?', *Public Administration*, vol 79, pp 933-47.

Pollitt, C. and Bouckaert, G. (2000) *Public management reform: A comparative analysis*, Oxford: Oxford University Press.

Pollitt, C., Bathgate, K., Caulfield, J., Smullen, A. and Talbot, C. (2001) 'Agency fever? Analysis of an international policy fashion', *Journal of Comparative Policy Analysis*, vol 3, pp 271-90.

Power, A. and Mumford, K. (1999) *The slow death of great cities?*, York: Joseph Rowntree Foundation.

Pressman, J. and Wildavsky, A. (1973) *Implementation: How great expectations in Washington are dashed in Oakland; or Why it's amazing that federal programs work at all, this being a saga of the economic development administration as told by two sympathetic observers who seek to build morals on a foundation ruined by hopes* (2nd edn 1984), Berkeley, CA: University of California Press.

Quah, D. (1999) *The weightless economy in economic development,* CEP Discussion Papers 0417, London: Centre for Economic Performance, London School of Economics and Political Science.

Ravetz, A. with Turkington, R. (1995) *The place of home: English domestic environments, 1914-2000*, London: E & FN Spon.

Rhodes, R.A.W. (1988) *Beyond Westminster and Whitehall: The sub-central governments of Britain*, London: Unwin-Hyman.

Rhodes, R.A.W. (1990) 'Policy networks: a British perspective', *Journal of Theoretical Politics*, vol 2, pp 292-316.

Rhodes, R.A.W. (1994) 'The hollowing out of the state', *Political Quarterly*, vol 65, pp 138-51.

Rhodes, R.A.W. (1995) 'The institutional approach', in D. Marsh and G. Stoker (eds) *Theory and methods in political science*, London: Macmillan, pp 42-57.

Rhodes, R.A.W. (1996a) 'The new governance: governing without government', *Political Studies*, vol 44, pp 652-67.

Rhodes, R.A.W. (1996b) 'Governing without Governance: order and change in British politics', Newcastle University, Inaugural Lecture.

Rhodes, R.A.W. (1997a) 'Foreword', in W.J.M. Kickert, E.-H. Klijn and J.F.M. Koppenjan (eds) *Managing complex networks: Strategies for the public sector*, London: Sage Publications, pp xi-xv.

Rhodes, R.A.W. (1997b) *Understanding governance: Policy networks, governance, reflexivity and accountability*, Buckingham: Open University Press.

Richardson, J. (1999) 'Pressure groups and parties: a "haze of common knowledge" or the empirical advance of the discipline?', in J. Hayward, B. Barry and A. Brown (eds) *The British study of politics in the twentieth century*, Oxford: Oxford University Press. pp 181-222.

Rosamond, B. (2003) 'The Europeanization of British politics', in P. Dunleavy, A. Gamble, R. Heffernan and G. Peele (eds) *Development in British Politics 7*, Basingstoke: Palgrave/Macmillan, pp 39-59.

Rose, R. (1991) 'What is lesson drawing?', *Journal of Public Policy*, vol 11, pp 3-30.

Rose, R. (2003) 'When all other conditions are not equal: the context for drawing lessons', in C. Jones Finer, *Social policy reform in China*, Aldershot: Ashgate, pp 5-22.

Rothstein, B. (1998) *Just institutions matter: The moral and political logic of the universal welfare state*, Cambridge: Cambridge University Press.

Sabatier, P.A. (1986a) 'Top-down and bottom-up approaches to implementation research: a critical analysis and suggested synthesis', *Journal of Public Policy*, vol 6, pp 21-48.

Sabatier, P.A. (1986b) 'What can we learn from implementation research?', in F.-X. Kaufman, G. Majone and V. Ostrom (eds) *Guidance, control and evaluation in the public sector: The Bielfield Interdisciplinary Project*, New York, NY: Walter de Gruyter, pp 313-26.

Sabatier, P.A. (1988) 'An advocacy coalition framework of policy change and the role of policy-orientated learning therein', *Policy Sciences*, vol 21, pp 129-68.

Sabatier, P.A. and Mazmanian, P. (1979) 'The conditions of effect implementation: a guide to accomplishing policy objectives', *Policy Analysis*, vol 5, pp 481-504.

Sanderson, I. (2000) 'Evaluation in complex policy systems', *Evaluation*, vol 6, pp 433-54.

Sanderson, I. (2001) 'Performance management, evaluation and learning in "modern" local government', *Public Administration*, vol 79, pp 297-313.

Sanderson, I. (2002) 'Evaluation, policy learning and evidence-based policy making', *Public Administration*, vol 80, pp 1-22.

Saunders, P. and Williams, P. (1988) 'The constitution of home', *Housing Studies*, vol 3, no 2, pp 81-93.

Schattschneider, E.E. (1960) *The Semisovereign people*, New York, NY: Holt, Rinehart and Winston.

Scott, J. (1999) 'Rational choice theory', in G. Browning, A. Halcli, N. Hewlett and F. Webster (eds) *Theory and society: Understanding the present*, London: Sage Publications.

Seldon, A. (1994) 'Consensus: a debate too long', *Parliamentary Affairs*, vol 47, pp 501-14.

Simon, H. (1960) *The new science of management decision* (2nd edn), Englewood Cliffs, NJ: Prentice-Hall.

Simon, H. (1982) *Models of bounded rationality*, Cambridge, MA: MIT Press.

Skelcher, C., McCabe, A., Lowndes,V. and Nanton, P. (1997) *Community networks in urban regeneration*, Bristol/York: The Policy Press/Joseph Rowntree Foundation.

Skocpol, T. (1992) *Protecting soldiers and mothers: The political origins of social policy in the United States*, Cambridge, MA: Harvard University Press.

Skocpol, T. and Amenta, E. (1986) 'States and social policies', *Annual Review of Sociology*, vol 12, pp 131-57.

Smith, M.J. (1993) *Pressure, power and policy*, Hemel Hempstead: Harvester Wheatsheaf.

Smith, M.J. (1995) 'Pluralism', in D. Marsh and G. Stoker (eds) *Theory and methods in political science*, Houndmills: Macmillan, pp 209-27.

Smith, G., Noble, M. and Wright, G. (2001) 'Do we care about area effects?', *Environment and Planning A*, vol 33, p 1344.

Solesbury, W. (2001) *Evidence based policy: Whence it came and where it's going*, Working Paper 1, ESRC UK Centre for Evidence-based Policy and Practice.

Steinmo, S., Thelen, K. and Longstreth, F. (1992) *Structuring politics: Historical institutionalism in comparative perspective*, Cambridge: Cambridge University Press.

Stewart, L.H. (1992) *Changemakers: A Jungian perspective on sibling position and the family atmosphere*, London: Routledge.

Stone, D. (1999) 'Learning lessons and transferring policy across time, space and disciplines', *Politics*, vol 19, pp 51-9.

Stone, D. (2000) 'Non-governmental policy transfer: the strategies of independent policy institutes', *Governance: An International Journal of Policy and Administration*, vol 13, pp 45-70.

Stone, D. (2001) 'Think tanks, global lesson-drawing and networking social policy ideas', *Global Social Policy*, vol 1, pp 338-60.

Street, J. (1992) *Politics and technology*, London: Macmillan.

Struyk, R.J. (ed) (1996) *Economic restructuring of the former Soviet Bloc: The case of housing*, Washington, DC: Urban Institute Press.

Stubbs, P. (2002) 'Globalisation, memory and welfare regimes in transition: towards an anthropology of transnational policy', *International Journal of Social Welfare*, vol 11, pp 321-30.

Summers, R. and Heston, A. (1991) 'The Penn world table (Mark 5)', *Quarterly Journal of Economics*, vol 106, no 2, pp 327-68.

Swank, D. (2001) 'Political institutions and welfare state restructuring: the impact of institutions on social policy change in developed democracies', in P. Pierson (ed) *The new politics of the welfare state*, Oxford: Oxford University Press, pp 197-237.

Swank, D. (2002) *Global capital, political institutions and policy change in developed welfare states*, Cambridge: Cambridge University Press.

Tanzi, V. (2001) 'Taxation and the future of social protection', in A. Giddens (ed) *The global Third Way debate*, Cambridge: Polity Press, pp 189-99.

Tarrow, S. (1998) *Power in movement: Social movements and contentious politics*, Cambridge: Cambridge University Press.

Taylor, F.W. (1911) *Scientific management*, New York, NY: Harper and Row (reprinted in 1947).

Temple, M. (2000) 'New Labour's Third Way: pragmatism and governance', *British Journal of Politics and International Relations*, vol 2, pp 302-25.

Thelen, K. and Steinmo, S. (1992) 'Historical institutionalism in comparative politics', in S. Steinmo, K. Thelen and F. Longstreth (eds) *Structuring politics: Historical institutionalism in comparative perspective*, Cambridge: Cambridge University Press, pp 1-32.

Theodore, N. and Peck, J. (2001) 'Searching for best practice in welfare-to-work: the means, the method and the message', *Policy & Politics*, vol 29, pp 81-94.

Thompson, G., Frances, J., Levacic, R. and Mitchell, J. (1991) *Markets, hierarchies and networks: The co-ordination of social life*, Hemel Hempstead: Harvester Wheatsheaf.

Titmuss, R. (1970) *The gift relationship: From human blood to social policy*, London: Allen and Unwin.

Toffler, A. (1980) *The third wave*, London: Pan Books.

Touraine, A. (1995) *The critique of modernity*, Oxford: Blackwell.

Turok, I. and Edge, N. (1999) *The jobs gap in Britain's cities: Employment loss and labour market consequences*, Bristol/York: The Policy Press/Joseph Rowntree Foundation.

Uttley, S. (1991) *Technology and the welfare state: The development of health care in Britain and America*, London: Unwin Hyman.

Vickers, G. (1965) *The art of judgement: A study of policymaking* (2nd edn 1983), London: Chapman and Hall.

Virilio, P. (1999) *The information bomb*, London: Verso.

Ward, H. (2003) 'Rational choice', in D. Marsh and G. Stoker (eds) *Theory and methods in political science* (2nd edn), Basingstoke: Palgrave, pp 65-89.

Weber, M. (1949) *The theory of social and economic organization,* edited and translated by T. Parsons, New York, NY: Free Press.

Webster, D. (1998) 'Employment change, housing abandonment and sustainable development: structural processes and structural issues', in S. Lowe, P. Keenan and S. Spencer (eds) *Housing abandonment in Britain: Studies in the causes and effects of low demand housing*, York: Centre for Housing Policy, University of York.

Wellman, B. (1992) 'Social network research – substantive issues and methodological questions', *Contemporary Psychology*, vol 37, pp 1315-16.

Wendt, A. (1987) 'The agency-structure problem in international relations', *International Organization*, vol 41, pp 335-70.

Wetherly, R. and Lipsky, M. (1977) 'Street-level bureaucrats and institutional innovation: implementing special education reform', *Harvard Educational Review*, vol 47, no 2, pp 171-97.

Wildavsky,, A. (1979) *Speaking truth to power: The art and craft of policy analysis*, Boston, MA: Little, Brown.

Wilensky, H. (1975) *The welfare state and equality: Structural and ideological roots of public expenditure*, Berkeley, CA: University of California Press.

Williamson, O.E. (1985) *The economic institutions of capitalism: Firms, markets, relational contracting*, Basingstoke: Macmillan.

Wilson, B.M. (1998) *Costa Rica: Politics, economics and democracy*, Boulder, CO/London: Lynne Rienner Publishers.

Winner, L. (1977) *Autonomous technology: Technics-out-of-control as a theme in political thought*, Cambridge, MA: MIT Press.

Woods, N. (2000) 'The political economy of globalization', in N. Woods (ed) *The political economy of globalization*, Basingstoke: Macmillan, pp 1-19.

Young, K., Ashby, D., Boaz, A. and Grayson, L. (2001) 'Social science and the evidence-based policy movement', *Social Policy and Society*, vol 1, no 3, pp 215-24.

Index

Also available from The Policy Press

Discursive analytical strategies
Understanding Foucault, Koselleck, Laclau, Luhmann
Niels Åkerstrøm Andersen

Paperback £16.99 (US$29.95) ISBN 1 86134 439 2

Hardback £45.00 (US$59.95) ISBN 1 86134 440 6

240 x 172mm 160 pages January 2003

Health, well-being and older people
Jan Reed, David Stanley and Charlotte Clark

Paperback £19.99 (US$32.00) ISBN 1 86134 421 X

Hardback £50.00 (US$69.95) ISBN 1 86134 422 8

240 x 172mm 208 pages March 2004

The health and social care divide
The experiences of older people
Jon Glasby and Rosemary Littlechild

Paperback £18.99 (US$29.95) ISBN 1 86134 525 9

Hardback £50.00 (US$69.95) ISBN 1 86134 526 7

240 x 172mm 176 pages May 2004

Poverty, inequality and health in Britain: 1800-2000
A reader
Edited by George Davey Smith, Daniel Dorling and Mary Shaw

Paperback £17.99 (US$29.95) ISBN 1 86134 211 X

Hardback £50.00 (US$55.00) ISBN 1 86134 328 0

240 x 172mm 464 pages July 2001

Health inequalities
Lifecourse approaches
Edited by George Davey Smith

Paperback £25.00 (US$37.50) ISBN 1 86134 322 1

240 x 172mm 608 pages August 2003

Private complaints and public health
Richard Titmuss on the National Health Service
Edited by Ann Oakley and Jonathan Barker

Paperback £19.99 (US$32.50) ISBN 1 86134 560 7

Hardback £55.00 (US$69.95) ISBN 1 86134 561 5

240 x 172mm 256 pages tbc June 2004

Welfare and wellbeing
Richard Titmuss's contribution to social policy
**Edited by Pete Alcock, Howard Glennerster, Ann Oakley
and Adrian Sinfield**

Paperback £18.99 (US$29.95) ISBN 1 86134 299 3

240 x 172mm 256 pages October 2001

To order further copies of this publication or any other Policy Press titles please contact:

In the UK and Europe:
Marston Book Services, PO Box 269 Abingdon,
Oxon, OX14 4YN, UK
Tel: +44 (0)1235 465500
Fax: +44 (0)1235 465556,
Email: direct.orders@marston.co.uk

In the USA and Canada:
ISBS, 920 NE 58th Street, Suite 300, Portland,
OR 97213-3786, USA
Tel: +1 800 944 6190 (toll free)
Fax: +1 503 280 8832,
Email: info@isbs.com

In Australia and New Zealand:
DA Information Services, 648 Whitehorse Road
Mitcham, Victoria 3132, Australia
Tel: +61 (3) 9210 7777
Fax: +61 (3) 9210 7788,
E-mail: service@dadirect.com.au

Further information about all of our titles can
be found on our website:

www.policypress.org.uk